Mediating Environments is the first in the Next Cities publication series by UVa School of Architecture and its Next Cities Institute. The Next Cities series disseminates design research by faculty and students at UVa focused on the rapidly changing dynamics of global urban futures. The series expands on how design – in its theory and physical instantiation in the world – probes the questions and controversies of the day, continually writing new expressions of the city.

Published by Applied Research and Design Publishing, an imprint of ORO Editions.

Gordon Goff: Publisher
www.appliedresearchanddesign.com
info@appliedresearchanddesign.com

10 9 8 7 6 5 4 3 2 1 First Edition

ISBN: 978-1-940743-61-5

Color Separations and Printing: ORO Group Ltd.
Printed in China.

AR+D Publishing makes a continuous effort to minimize the overall carbon footprint of its publications. As part of this goal, AR+D, in association with Global ReLeaf, arranges to plant trees to replace those used in the manufacturing of the paper produced for its books. Global ReLeaf is an international campaign run by American Forests, one of the world's oldest nonprofit conservation organizations. Global ReLeaf is American Forests' education and action program that helps individuals, organizations, agencies, and corporations improve the local and global environment by planting and caring for trees.

Medi
ating
Envi
ron
ments

Arctic Design Group
Leena Cho & Matthew Jull

Down by the shore, stretching in front of us in the darkness was a solid ocean – quietly moving underneath enormous plates of earthly ice. It was an entirely new terrain, registering the relentless scouring from above and below. Flat, mountainous, broken, and deceptive, impossible to walk, let alone drag equipment without chopping trails, like one would do in a tropical jungle to move one small step forward.

The slowness of the day came from the asymptotic sunrise, at first curving upward and then downward, and obscured by the horizon. Sharp angles with big shadows, only to be levelled by deafening silence of white-outs. The air was thick. The cold was abrasive. How to walk in this place that seemed to at once be at the "end" but extend to infinity?

On the day of first arrival we had fifteen minutes of a faint orange ball in the distance, while the wind seemed to strengthen, sucking away any vestiges of warmth. Moving between inside and outside was a story of water vapor condensing, freezing, fogging, and misting. We donned our clothing as if it was scuba gear, checking for seams and cracks. Equipment locked in Ziploc bags to keep out this infiltrating menace to anything mechanical or optical.

The day never really began. It felt as if it was some kind of ethereal experience where you were never quite awake. The town huddled under a blanket of twilight, punctuated by riders circling the town for a few minutes and then falling quiet.

Contents

010 PREFACE
Next Arctic Cities ILA BERMAN

013 INTRODUCTION

018 ARRIVALS
20 Grounding the Arctic
22 Mediating Environments
28 Arctic Atlases
46 Shapes of Climate
52 Land-Water-Ice: Making Space for Architecture in the Arctic PHILIP STEINBERG
56 Out of This World GEOFF MANAUGH

062 FUNDAMENTALS
64 Re-thinking Extremes
68 Engineered North
78 Synthesized Intelligence
85 Methodologies for Environmental Recalibration
108 Conceptual Provocations
118 First Measures: Approaches and Pedagogies in the Far North DAVID GARCIA
122 Designing a Resilient Future JUDITH GRUNAU

130 PROPOSITIONS
132 Towards a New Cultural Project
139 Methodologies for Design Synthesis & Speculation
140 Alaskan Arctic
144 Key Design Challenges
154 Design Approaches and Propositions
200 Many Norths: The Making of an Arctic Vernacular LOLA SHEPPARD & MASON WHITE
207 Looking at Future Norths JANIKE KAMPEVOLD LARSEN
212 Polar Research Stations: Meeting the Challenge of Isolated Living HUGH BROUGHTON

226 Bibliography
228 Image List
230 Contributors
234 Credits

Next Arctic Cities

ILA BERMAN
Dean + Edward E. Elson Professor, University of Virginia School of Architecture

The Arctic is one of the most environmentally threatened regions on this earth and certainly one of the most extreme from the perspective of human and other life forms. It is so cold, remote, vast, and sparsely populated in terms of both vegetation and people, that it has become a territory that exists far more in our cultural imagination than in our lived reality. And yet, despite its distance from most of our everyday lives, it also provides quite conspicuous indications, with great clarity and in 'real time,' of the accelerating effects of global warming that are impacting this planet, underscoring its vulnerability and fragility in vivid ways, while also making evident the temporal, spatial, and material limitations of our traditional forms of individual inhabitation and collective civic infrastructure. As a number of the contributors to this volume have noted, those things we had determined to be fixed, constant, and immobile—such as territorial boundaries, urban settlements, and the ground upon which they are situated—are, within this zone, in continual flux, challenged by seasonal phase changes and unpredictable long-term geophysical modifications of the landscape brought about by the melting of polar ice. This latter condition has rendered the topographic domain of the Arctic far more fragmented, malleable, and fluid, which has led, not only to an upsurge in marine traffic due to the increased navigability of the area, but also to sea level rise, more intensified meteorological events around the globe, and locally, to amplifying the instability of existing northern urban communities.

As an enormously extended landscape overlaid with crisscrossing navigation channels and political boundaries circumscribing eight distinct nations, the Arctic is a wonderful exemplar of what Timothy Morton refers to as a *hyperobject*: a nonlocal entity that is "massively distributed in time and space relative to humans" and that involves "profoundly different temporalities than the human-scale ones we are used to."[1] The term is applicable not only because of the Arctic's immense size (which straddles continents and oceans), extreme atmospheric conditions, and intense glacial terrain, but also because these are the very conditions that have ensured its resistance to extensive human navigation, territorialization, and inhabitation, leading

1
Timothy Morton, *The Ecological Thought* (Cambridge, Mass.: Harvard University Press, 2010), 130–135.

to its relative invisibility in the cultural consciousness of architects, landscape architects, and urban planners and designers. Hyperobjects such as the Arctic are also difficult to classify as 'things,' because their phenomenal qualities or states of being, determined, for example, by frigid temperatures or bright white light (or conversely, darkness), lack the definition or clear contours seemingly necessary for our objectifying consciousness. The Arctic's 'nature' therefore demands to be encountered differently, not simply as an object of study through the metric lens of scientific investigation, a domain to be politically appropriated, or a resource to be exploited and instrumentalized, but rather as an immersive environment to be empirically experienced through an architecture that is responsive and adaptive to its immanent material and climatic conditions: its extreme thermal gradients, luminous intensities, and shifting mutable matters.

The lack of fit between our normative ideas of cities and the ways in which the architectural communities and constructed landscapes of the Arctic have evolved, makes us very conscious of the external forces—be they environmental, geological, and thermal, or cultural, political, economic, and technological—that have contributed to shaping our distinct modes of dwelling upon this earth, rendering evident the clear differences between highly orchestrated patterns of settlement and their designed infrastructures that have organized planned urban territories over time, and other more spatially distributed, scattered, informal, and nomadic forms of aggregated architectures that characterize many towns of the Far North. These autonomous and highly disconnected cities, towns, and terrestrial outposts also bring together unlikely bedfellows. Indigenous peoples, who have had a longstanding intrinsic relationship with the environment and have survived peacefully in these remote regions for millennia, now collide with the circulating goods, practices, and peoples imported from elsewhere, such as workers coming to instant company towns in order to harvest resources to fuel the industrial capitalist machine and its multinational economic interests. The authors, Leena Cho and Matthew Jull, founders of the Arctic Design Group, claim that it is precisely these collisions, dynamic environmental and socio-political conditions, and ad hoc urban characteristics that enable the Arctic to be a testing ground, experimental laboratory, and incubator for a new kind of adaptive urbanization. This book, *Mediating Environments*, the first volume in our Next Cities series, therefore acts as a vehicle to instigate discussion among designers and spatial researchers focused on these issues, while documenting the extensive work of those pioneers who are at the forefront of speculating on, and shaping the Next Arctic cities.

Introduction

The Arctic is a place where tension between the rendered and the experienced is arguably at its highest. Extreme cold climate conditions coupled with prospects and anxieties afforded by the impacts of climate change are often the dominating narratives shaping the discourse about the region. The loss of sea ice, the thawing of permafrost, the release of methane gas, and the displacement of species, peoples, and towns are only a handful of examples that are profoundly impacting the future of the Arctic. Simultaneously, the climatic shifts are helping to unlock the grips of a deep freeze and opening up new economic, political, and urbanistic opportunities. Nations are posturing for control of this territory. Global trade routes are bending north, and extractive industries and supporting infrastructures are gravitating towards the increasingly accessible and geopolitically strategic Arctic Ocean and adjacent lands. Caught in amidst these transformations is our capacity to soberly reflect, inflect, and steer the narratives of the region as a lived place that is both animated by and actively sculpting its physical and material landscapes.

Over the past decade there has been a veritable explosion of meetings, conferences, festivals, and symposia focused on the Arctic with stakeholders ranging from governments and private sectors to NGOs and universities. The eight Arctic nations–Canada, Finland, Greenland (Denmark), Iceland, Norway, Russia, Sweden, and United States–are enacting plans for their northern territories and developing strategic policy frameworks through the Arctic Council, for instance. Other countries are also getting involved by securing partnerships in research or economic development with the Arctic nations. Despite this growing interest in the region, there are only a handful of architects, landscape architects, and urban designers who are currently engaged in fundamental research on design and planning of Arctic communities, while the majority of the Arctic research is formulated from the perspectives of science, economics, and policy. As the global forces of change are becoming more pronounced in the Arctic, the future trajectories for living environments, city-making processes, and their adaptive capacities are brought into question and need to be addressed directly. Concurrently, the Arctic as a region of negotiation between the built and natural environments offers numerous lessons for design both within and beyond the polar territories. At the intersection of material, cultural, environmental, and technological dimensions, the Arctic is a catalyst for rethinking the mechanisms of built environment from the scale of building and infrastructural components to that of cities. It is also a prime testing ground to develop more culturally and environmentally attuned design approaches to address the impacts of climate change. At this critical moment, *Mediating Environments* delineates renewed design approaches and opportunities in the North. By actively foregrounding design in the contemporary Arctic discourse through research, practice and teaching, the book seeks productive modes of engagement with a wide range of disciplines and stakeholders to highlight and bring much needed attention to the Arctic inhabitants, their everyday living environments, and cultural practices. Our collective ability to not only respond to the Arctic's dynamic environment but also to envision alternative futures is critical for the long-term sustainability of the region.

Structure of the Book

The book is divided into three chapters: Arrivals, Fundamentals, and Propositions. The first chapter, Arrivals, presents the Arctic as a heterogeneous domain shaped by various environmental, political, economic, and cultural forces. Through a series of mappings, charts, photographs, and texts, this chapter offers glimpses of the pan-arctic, and positions the region as a dynamic and multivalent territory shaped by the intersecting flows of climates, materials, and people.

The second chapter, Fundamentals, critically engages environmental systems, morphologies, and processes within the high latitude – dynamic and cold climate of the Arctic. Climate organizes and sustains a broad range of activities in the Arctic, and we consider the various living, abiotic, and phenomenological agents catalyzed by the climate as the fundamental "building blocks" of design in this region. These elements are explored to understand how they manifest themselves physically, materially, and temporally and further, how they can be altered, adopted, and choreographed through a series of speculative prototypes at human scale.

The knowledge and speculation developed through the two previous chapters are then deployed and tested within the program-specific cultural contexts of Alaska. In the third chapter, Propositions, we identify four key design challenges many Alaskan Arctic communities face–legacies and practices surrounding house, ground, school, and land–and probe the underlying assumptions, overlooked opportunities, and misplaced priorities in design within a parallel framework of climate change and extreme environment. The sampled projects are not comprehensive surveys or solutions; rather they reveal existing issues many arctic communities face and call out the importance of human agency, autonomy, and adaptability in the making of resilient arctic communities.

In addition to the design-driven research, the book visually catalogs a range of activities the Arctic Design Group has organized and participated in the past five years, such as public exhibitions and a symposium. This series of small-step actions provide opportunities to share the work of the ADG with a broader audience but also to engage with the communities, our colleagues, and students to shape the ongoing and future discourses of the Arctic region.

Threaded throughout these chapters are Perspectives – transcribed and edited transcripts authored by eight designers and spatial researchers from around the world who are actively engaged with the design of the built environment in polar territories. Initially presented at the Arctic States symposium in 2015 at the University of Virginia, these colloquial essays provide an expanded context for the questions and issues raised in this book and are organized as such by chapter theme.

Through the lens of political geography and remote urbanism, the first grouping in Chapter 1, Arrivals, challenges the conventional modes of how we understand space and cities. Philip Steinberg takes us to the fascinating incident that took place in the Fletcher's Ice Island – an inhabited iceberg that drifted across political borders in the Arctic Ocean between 1958 and 1978. The fluid and non-binary material conditions of land, water, and ice in the Arctic, he argues, challenge the established norms for regulating and governing space, and further demand a conceptual reorientation of space that embraces the provisional, dynamic, and ambiguous physicality of the Arctic. Geoff Manaugh presents the Arctic as a distinct site of speculation for future forms of urbanism. He highlights that the prevalent urbanisms in the Arctic, e.g., company towns, extraction outposts, or quasi-cities, upend our comfortable definitions of what constitutes a city. While many of these cities such as Fermont, Canada lack coherent political structure or governance, they may be early indicators of a mutation of city form and even the de facto example of urbanism to establish life on "other worlds."

The second group of essays in Chapter 2, Fundamentals focuses on the environmental systems and processes unique to the Arctic and, as challenging as they may be, the novel integration of technologies, building science, and engineering in design. Likewise, the Arctic inspires bold initiatives and inventions, and David Garcia brings us to the domain of expeditions and prototypes in the extreme environment. This journey is inscribed in the methodology of engaging with the Arctic before engaging with architecture, he describes. The site-specific instruments of snow, seeds, fur, or light are critical reflections as well as speculations on a broader set of phenomenological and technological issues central to the Arctic such as shelter, growth, safety, energy, and warmth. From the scale of the detail to the house, Judith Grunau of the Cold Climate Housing Research Center (CCHRC) deep dives into examples of energy-efficient, durable, and cost-effective cold-climate building technologies in rural Alaska. Encompassing a full range of climatic conditions–from the windy, cool, and wet southeast to the frigid and snowy north–the Alaskan Arctic offers a prime testing ground for architectural systems in remote regions. Basic building components, assemblies, and logistics such as insulation, material resources, and construction season require attunement to both the Arctic's dynamic environment and the needs of residents in rural communities.

Finally, situating the Arctic in its complex and layered cultural histories, colonial legacies, transnational scientific and corporate enterprises, the third grouping in Chapter 3, Propositions highlights examples of design and design approaches that place people and communities, their well-being and agency at the forefront. Lola Sheppard and Mason White challenge the reductive and myth-driven abstractions of the Arctic, and instead present the region as a dynamic, present-day territory imbued with myriad cultural meanings and practices. Communities in the Canadian Far North are increasingly experiencing a cross-pollination of cultures, including between the traditional, indigenous spatial practices and the more recently arrived design, planning, and engineering disciplines. The emerging forms of hybridity–the "modern arctic vernaculars"–reflect profound adaptability and ingenuity of the arctic residents, and navigating this terrain necessitates changes in our "southern"-biased framework of reference in design. Janike Kampevold Larsen examines how landscape changes are met and dealt with by inhabitants of arctic communities. The impacts of climate change and the increasing extractive and tourism industries are significantly felt in the Norwegian Arctic, and are even more pronounced in small villages that have relied on local economy such as fishing. Through the work of her research group, Future North, in Vardø, she demonstrates the importance of practicing place-based landscape research and design as a vehicle to safeguard and, at times, rebuild the community resilience, its identity, and cultural heritage. Hugh Broughton navigates the extremes of environmental and logistical challenges for building an entirely self-sufficient and relocatable polar research station in Antarctica, and underscores the value of bringing design in what has traditionally been an engineering domain in this continent. The marriage between design and engineering generates innovations that answer the requirements of scientific research as well as social and psychological well-being of the crew members living in extreme isolation. Simultaneously, it connects wider disciplines behind the project, while reminding us of the unique expertise design brings – the coupling between the human and the environment.

Arrivals

GROUNDING THE ARCTIC

Concerns increasingly associated with the Arctic – melting sea ice, resource extraction, and territorial disputes – are overwhelmingly understood from the perspectives of the sciences or economics filtered through popular news media. While these efforts are critical for the formulation of national and international policies, they render the Arctic as a highly vulnerable and exploitable material territory. The apocalyptic view driven by the deterministic narrative of the warming planet further presupposes that the Arctic operates on principles of stability and permanence, and truncates its resilient and adaptive capacity in light of its transformation.

Such realities of the Arctic, also complicated by the long-held myths of the region as a pristine and empty place, are evidenced and reinforced in the ways in which the Arctic is often viewed, visualized, assessed, and managed. Intermittently discussed, however, are the cultural landscapes of northern communities that embody multifaceted spatial practices, environmental adaptations, and technological ingenuities.

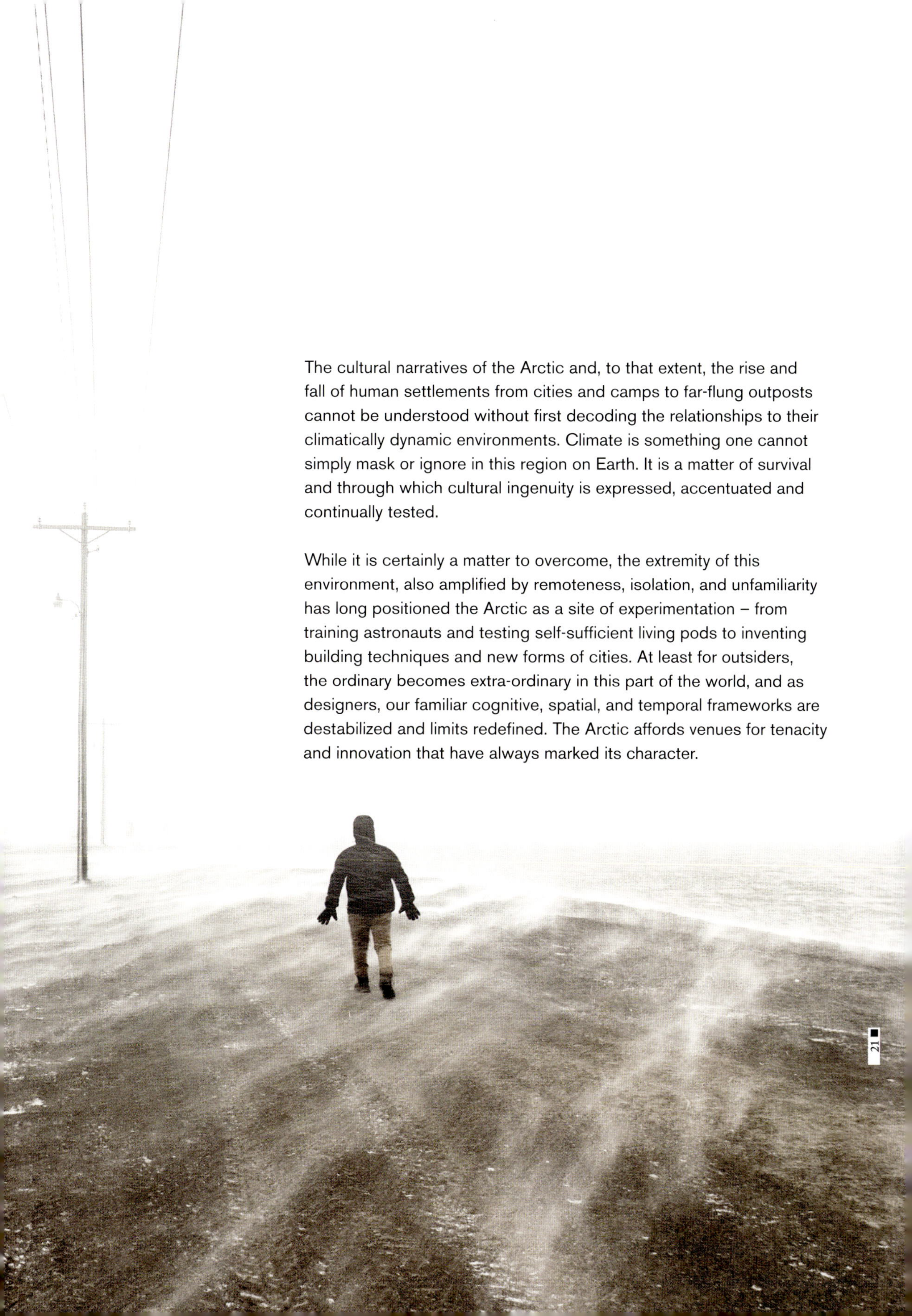

The cultural narratives of the Arctic and, to that extent, the rise and fall of human settlements from cities and camps to far-flung outposts cannot be understood without first decoding the relationships to their climatically dynamic environments. Climate is something one cannot simply mask or ignore in this region on Earth. It is a matter of survival and through which cultural ingenuity is expressed, accentuated and continually tested.

While it is certainly a matter to overcome, the extremity of this environment, also amplified by remoteness, isolation, and unfamiliarity has long positioned the Arctic as a site of experimentation – from training astronauts and testing self-sufficient living pods to inventing building techniques and new forms of cities. At least for outsiders, the ordinary becomes extra-ordinary in this part of the world, and as designers, our familiar cognitive, spatial, and temporal frameworks are destabilized and limits redefined. The Arctic affords venues for tenacity and innovation that have always marked its character.

Design, in its process and as product, has the capacity to act as an intervening agency and to reify the link between the living and the environment that envelops it. Its capacity to bring about a change, subtle or radical, can fundamentally restructure the relationships among things, and the modes by which our beliefs and ways of living are materialized. Likewise, the spatial practices of architecture, landscape architecture, and urbanism always seem to exist, and thrive, at the peripheries – between the disciplines, the membranes, the corporal and the conceptual, the past and the future, while foregrounding the present-day as a strategic operative domain.

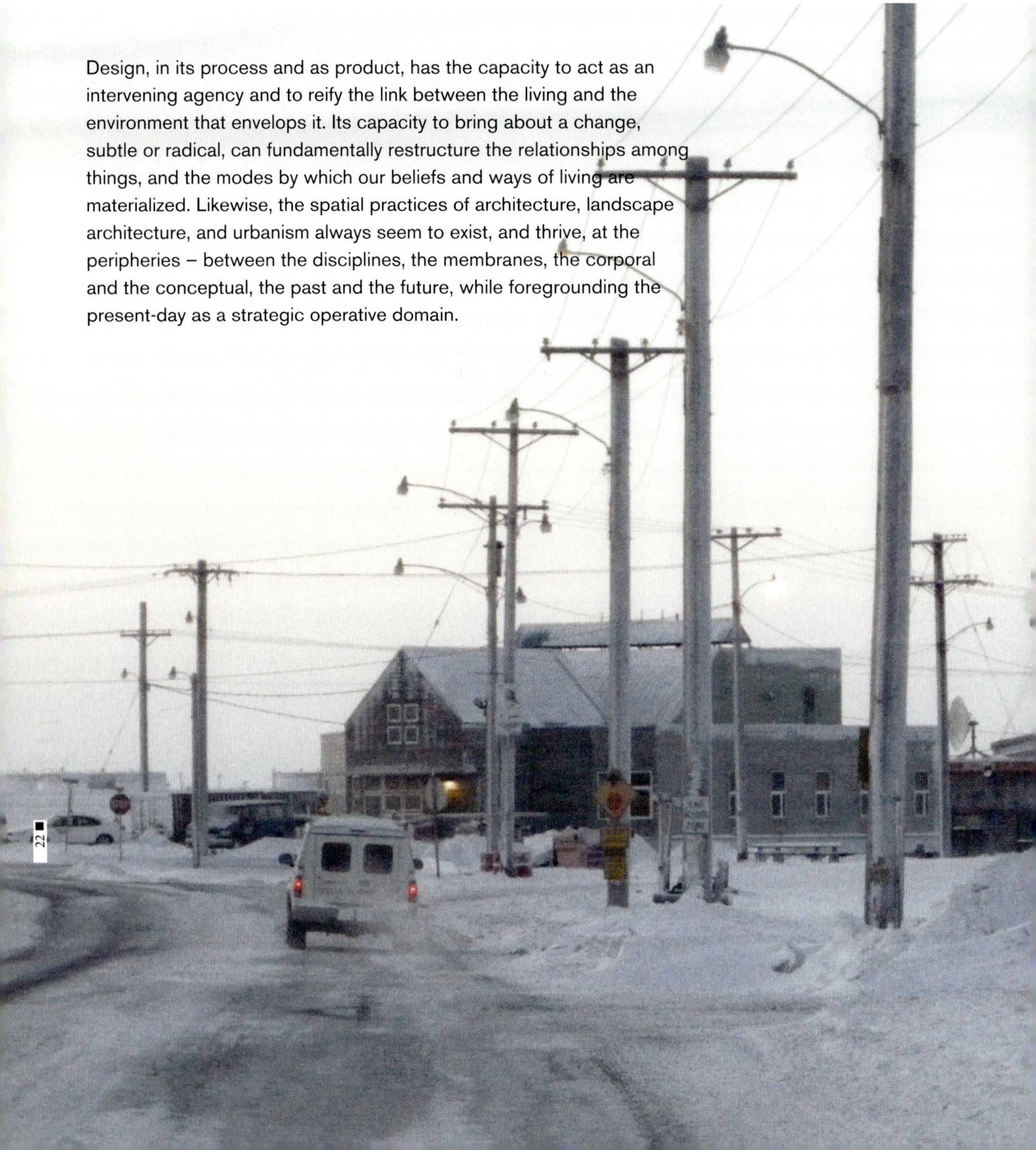

Design disrupts, negotiates, sutures, and unleashes. The act of mediating, as we see it, is, therefore, not merely about arriving at an agreement or solution but about creating prototypes for the future at the intersection of many, many peripheries.

The Arctic, a periphery of many kinds, is then a prime testing ground for re-examining our own conception of space and the many roles design plays in society. It is a forensic tool as much as it is a cultural geography. Likewise, the pleasure of certainty and definitive solutions are thrown off once we enter into the Arctic. The ocean becomes a walkable surface, the snow is a building, the walls ooze with mud and wind, and the life exists in the most improbable crannies like the underbelly of sea ice. Mediating environments—physical and cultural—requires deep understanding of their constituents and processes, not as an end to itself but as a means to transform them. The extremity of the Arctic then forces us to rethink the conventions of design principles, to re-evaluate the purposes and mechanisms of built structures, and to innovate cultural and material linkages. It challenges the habitual alphabet and the grammar of assembling cities, and calls for a new language. Ultimately, our understanding of these dynamics and our ability to not only respond to them but also to envision alternative futures are crucial for the long-term sustainability of the region, of people and communities, and the innumerable benefits that it conveys on the global Earth.

To this end, what we can learn from the Arctic extends beyond what defines it in the present moment. If the Arctic is a bellwether for extreme weather and environmental changes to come elsewhere, it is, and should be, a pioneering ground for adaptive urbanisms and new modes of living in the era of the Anthropocene. If it is a site where predominant ideologies of engineered systems and climate conditioning are accentuated, it is also then a platform to not only rethink but project new relationships with the environment. If it has been a laboratory for unlikely forms of urbanism—regardless of apparent challenges or impracticalities—such as entirely privatized, coerced, multinational, or autonomous cities, it is then an incubator for new paradigms of urbanization.

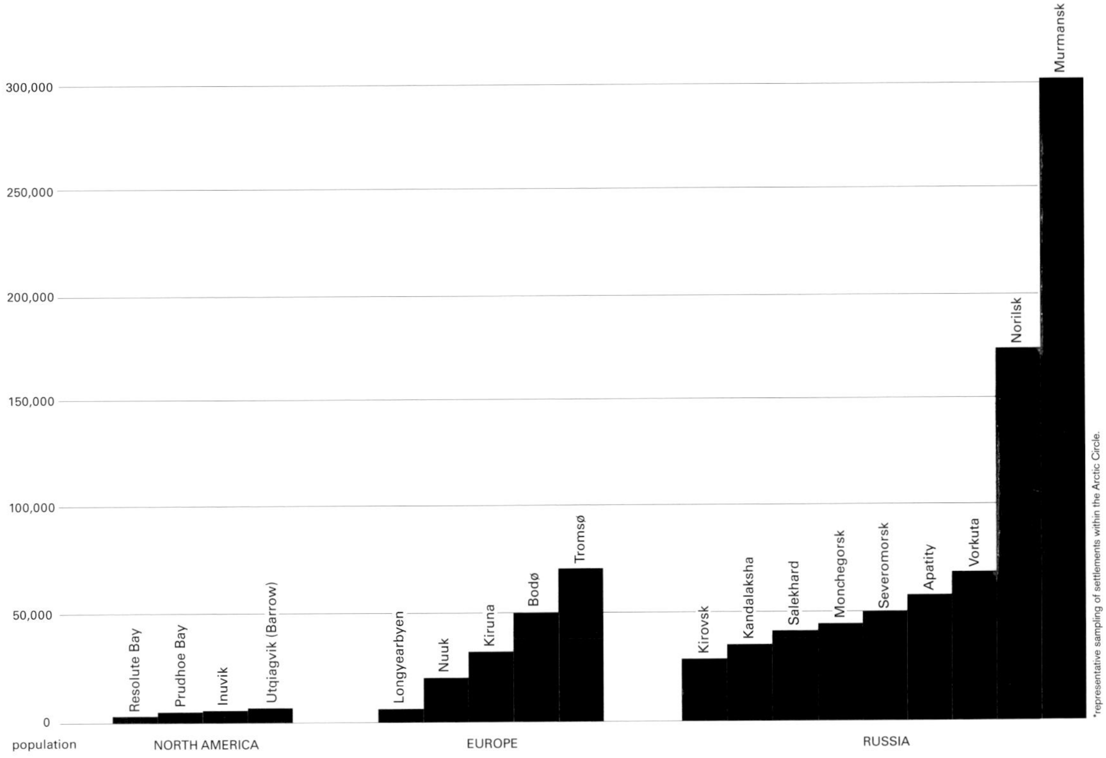

300,000
250,000
200,000
150,000
100,000
50,000
0
population
NORTH AMERICA
EUROPE
RUSSIA
Resolute Bay
Prudhoe Bay
Inuvik
Utqiagvik (Barrow)
Longyearbyen
Nuuk
Kiruna
Bodø
Tromsø
Kirovsk
Kandalaksha
Salekhard
Monchegorsk
Severomorsk
Apatity
Vorkuta
Norilsk
Murmansk
*representative sampling of settlements within the Arctic Circle.

Many of the imaginations these prompts inspire have been a way of life for people who have lived in the Arctic for millennia. From conceiving of this dynamic environment as "home" beyond the material confines that we typically understand to thinking holistically of the forces that shape the land and determine their survival and heritage, we have much to learn from Arctic communities at this nexus of shifting environmental, political, and economic contingencies.

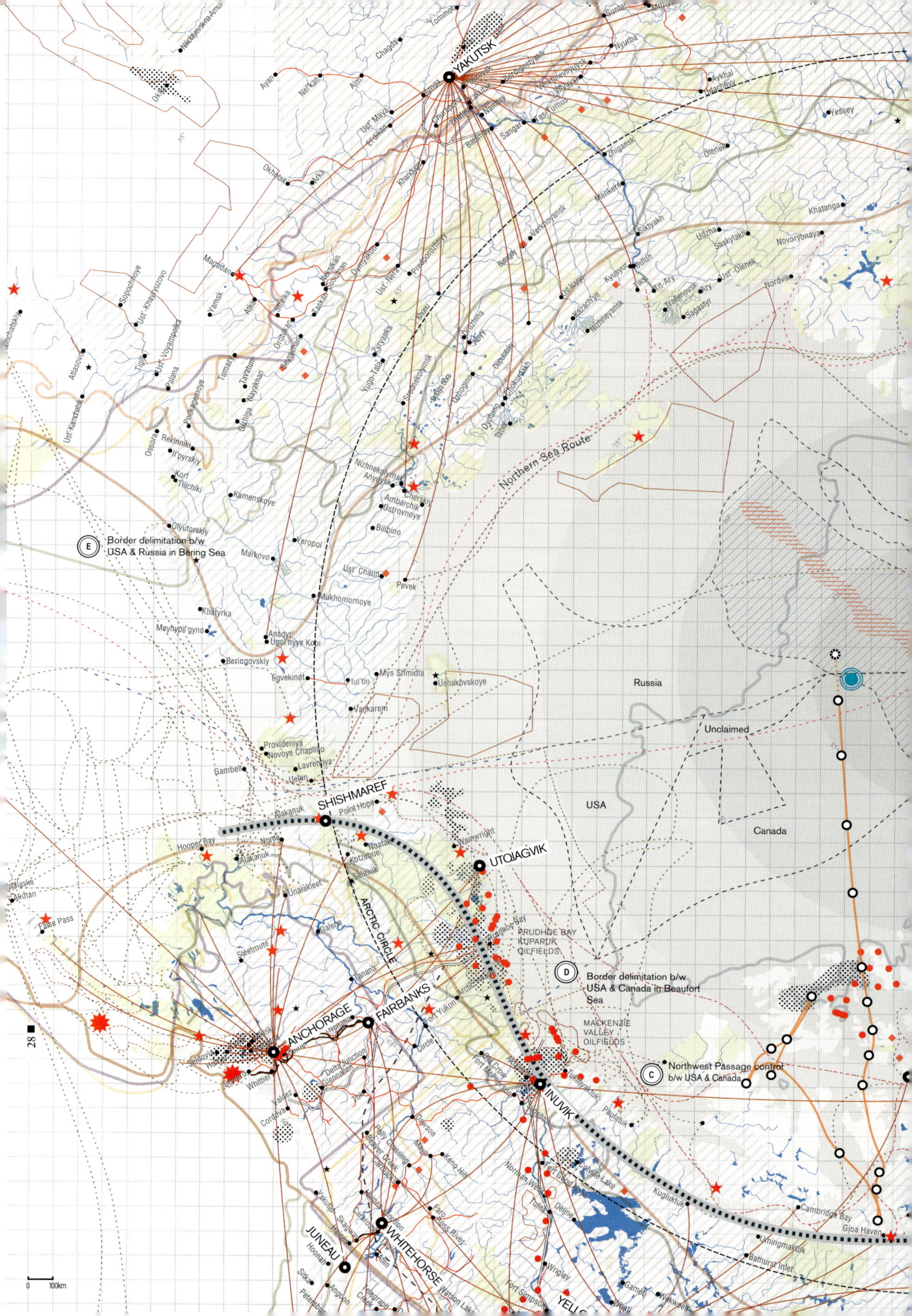
YAKUTSK
Northern Sea Route
Russia
Unclaimed
USA
Canada
SHISHMAREF
UTQIAGVIK
ARCTIC CIRCLE
PRUDHOE BAY
KUPARUK
OILFIELDS
D Border delimitation b/w USA & Canada in Beaufort Sea
E Border delimitation b/w USA & Russia in Bering Sea
FAIRBANKS
ANCHORAGE
MACKENZIE
VALLEY
OILFIELDS
C Northwest Passage control b/w USA & Canada
INUVIK
WHITEHORSE
JUNEAU
0 100km

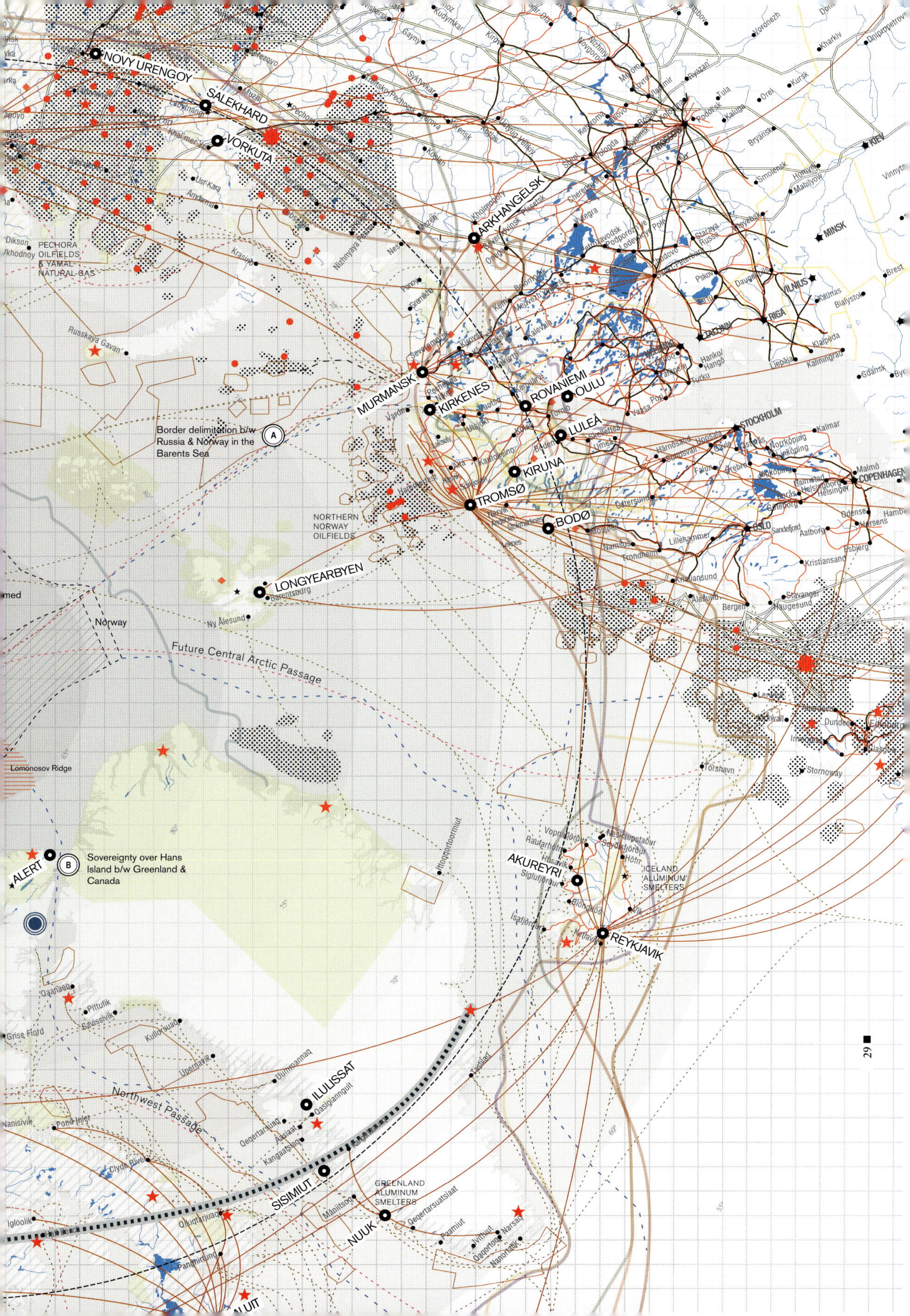
NOVY URENGOY
SALEKHARD
VORKUTA
PECHORA OILFIELDS & YAMAL NATURAL GAS
ARKHANGELSK
MURMANSK
KIRKENES
ROVANIEMI
OULU
LULEÅ
KIRUNA
TROMSØ
BODØ
STOCKHOLM
COPENHAGEN
OSLO
RIGA
VILNIUS
MINSK
KIEV
Border delimitation b/w Russia & Norway in the Barents Sea
A
NORTHERN NORWAY OILFIELDS
LONGYEARBYEN
Barentsburg
Ny Ålesund
Norway
Future Central Arctic Passage
Lomonosov Ridge
ALERT
B
Sovereignty over Hans Island b/w Greenland & Canada
AKUREYRI
ICELAND ALUMINUM SMELTERS
REYKJAVIK
Tórshavn
Stornoway
ILULISSAT
Northwest Passage
SISIMIUT
GREENLAND ALUMINUM SMELTERS
NUUK
IQALUIT

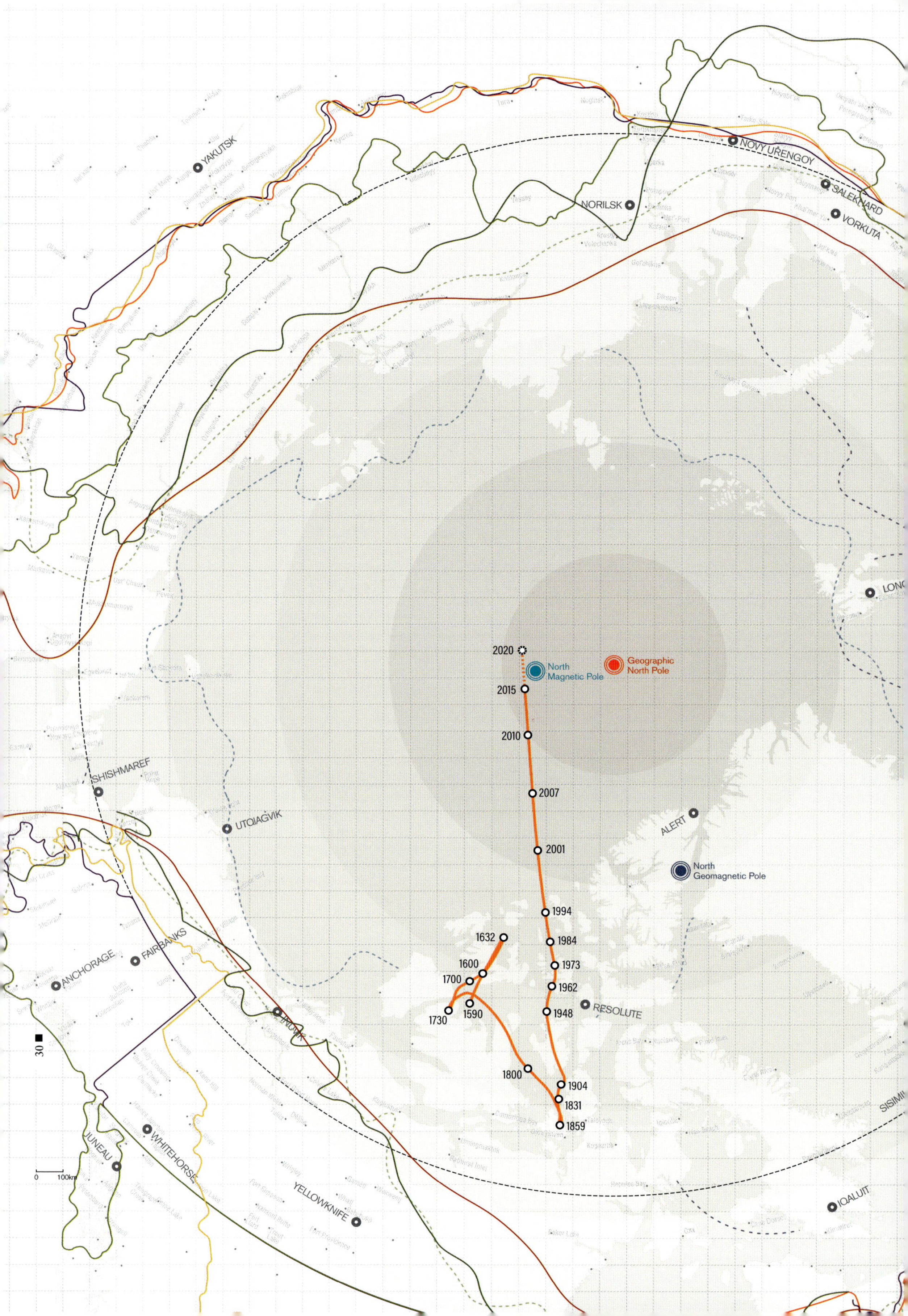
YAKUTSK
NOVY URENGOY
SALEKHARD
VORKUTA
NORILSK
2020
North Magnetic Pole
Geographic North Pole
2015
2010
2007
2001
1994
1984
1973
1962
1948
1904
1831
1859
1632
1600
1700
1730
1590
1800
ALERT
North Geomagnetic Pole
RESOLUTE
SHISHMAREF
UTQIAGVIK
FAIRBANKS
ANCHORAGE
INUVIK
WHITEHORSE
JUNEAU
YELLOWKNIFE
IQALUIT
SISIMIUT
0
100km

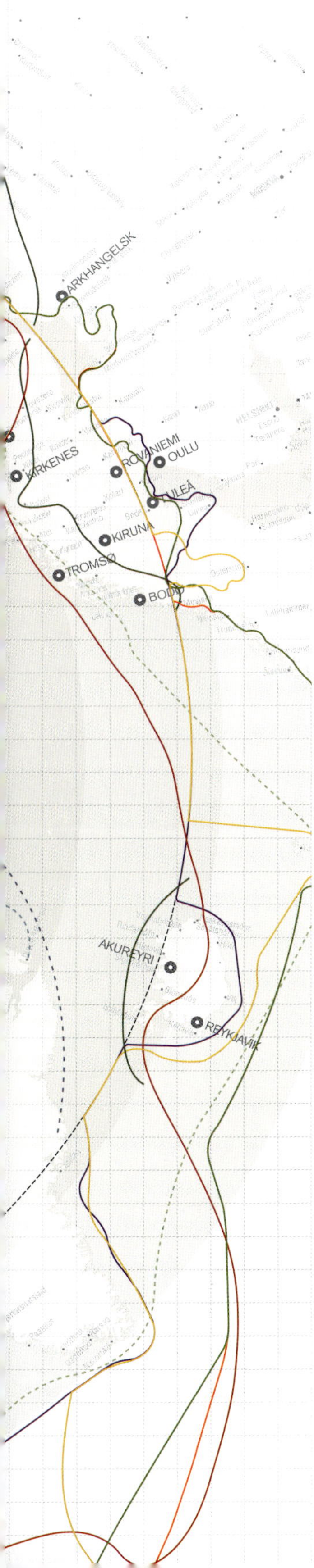

BOUNDARIES

Depending on the definition that is adopted, "Arctic" refers to a region that varies significantly in its boundary, ranging between 5.5 and 16 million square miles, extending from the north geographic pole to as far south as 50°N. Its most familiar definition is the area within the Arctic Circle (66°33'N), which is the latitude that marks the onset of annual periods of polar days and nights (24-hour sunlight in summer; 24-hour darkness in winter). But there are numerous other definitions adopted by governments or research organizations that include environmental and ecological factors such as the average position of the 10°C (50°F) isotherm in July, the northern extent of trees (the tree line), the southward maximum extent of permafrost, the southern edge of the subarctic climate zone, the northern extent of roads, living cost differentials, and geopolitical and national borders. Despite the common misconception of the Arctic as a pristine and snow-covered wilderness, it is in fact a highly heterogeneous region that includes areas with extremes of environment that are remote and isolated such as Alert, Canada and areas that are comparatively temperate and urbanized such as Reykjavik, Iceland, and is home to a large spectrum of diverse cultures.

- - - - - Arctic Circle (66° 33' 47.2" N)
—— 10°C (50°F) isotherm, July average
—— Tree Line
—— ARPA (Arctic Research and Policy Act; U.S. Govt)
—— AMAP (Arctic Monitoring and Assessment Program; Int. Arctic Council)
—— AHDR (Arctic Human Development Report; Int. Arctic Council)
—— EPPR (Emergency Prevention, Preparedness, and Response; Int. Arctic Council)
—— CAFF (Conservation of Arctic Flora and Fauna; Int. Arctic Council)
- - - - Phytographic Arctic Boundary (from CAFF; Int. Arctic Council)

OTHER MARKERS

- - - - - Average Extent of Sea Ice
—— North Magnetic Pole Movement

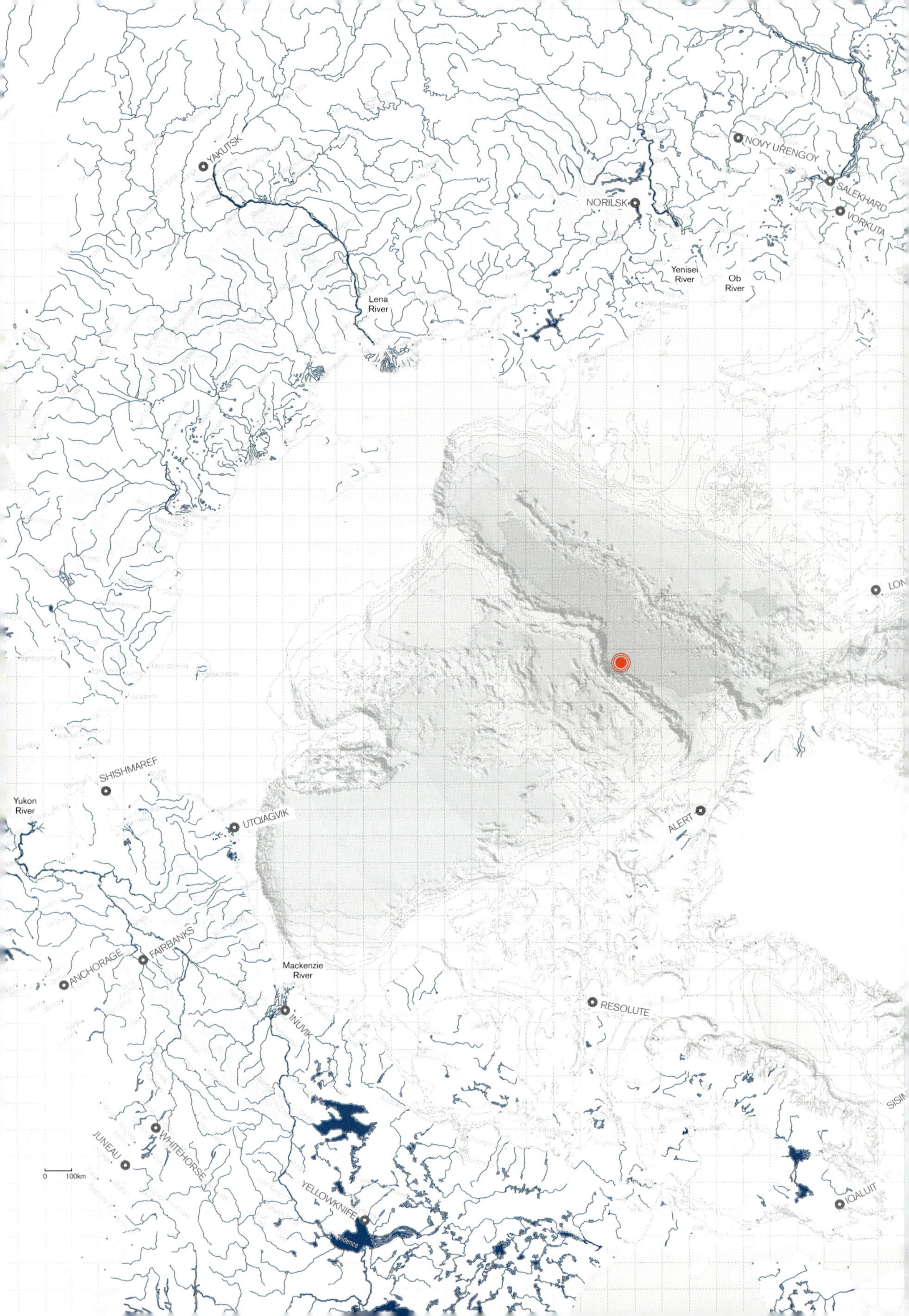
YAKUTSK
NORILSK
NOVY URENGOY
SALEKHARD
VORKUTA
Lena River
Yenisei River
Ob River
SHISHMAREF
Yukon River
UTQIAGVIK
ALERT
FAIRBANKS
ANCHORAGE
Mackenzie River
INUVIK
RESOLUTE
WHITEHORSE
JUNEAU
YELLOWKNIFE
IQALUIT
0 100km

OCEAN AND RIVERS

The Arctic Ocean covers an area of about 5.4 million square miles (14 million square kilometers), with a coastline of approximately 28,200 miles in length. It is the smallest and shallowest ocean and is covered in sea ice at least partially throughout the year; the extent of coverage reaches a maximum around in March and minimum in September. The transformation of the Arctic during these cycles of freezing and thawing are drastic, continually reshaping the boundary between solid and liquid, creating opportunities for mobility that are critical to life in the Arctic. Two of the largest threats from warming global temperatures is a reduction in sea ice coverage, leading to lowered albedo and increased solar heating of the ocean, as well as increased coastal erosion. The five major rivers that flow into the Arctic Ocean: the Mackenzie and Yukon Rivers in North America, and the Ob, Yenisei, and Lena Rivers in northern Russia, drain a total of about 9 million square miles (23 million square kilometers) of catchment area, and are some of the largest rivers on Earth. Their vast north to south extent leads to cycles of differential freeze and thaw over their length, creating ice jams and flooding in the adjacent low-lying land. Despite these complex cryo-hydrologic cycles, the rivers are key transportation routes, particularly for the major industrial cities in Russia such as Norilsk, Salekhard, Surgut, and Yakutsk.

Major Rivers
Inland Rivers & Lakes
Ocean & Sea

Bathymetric Depth (m)
-5000 -1500 0

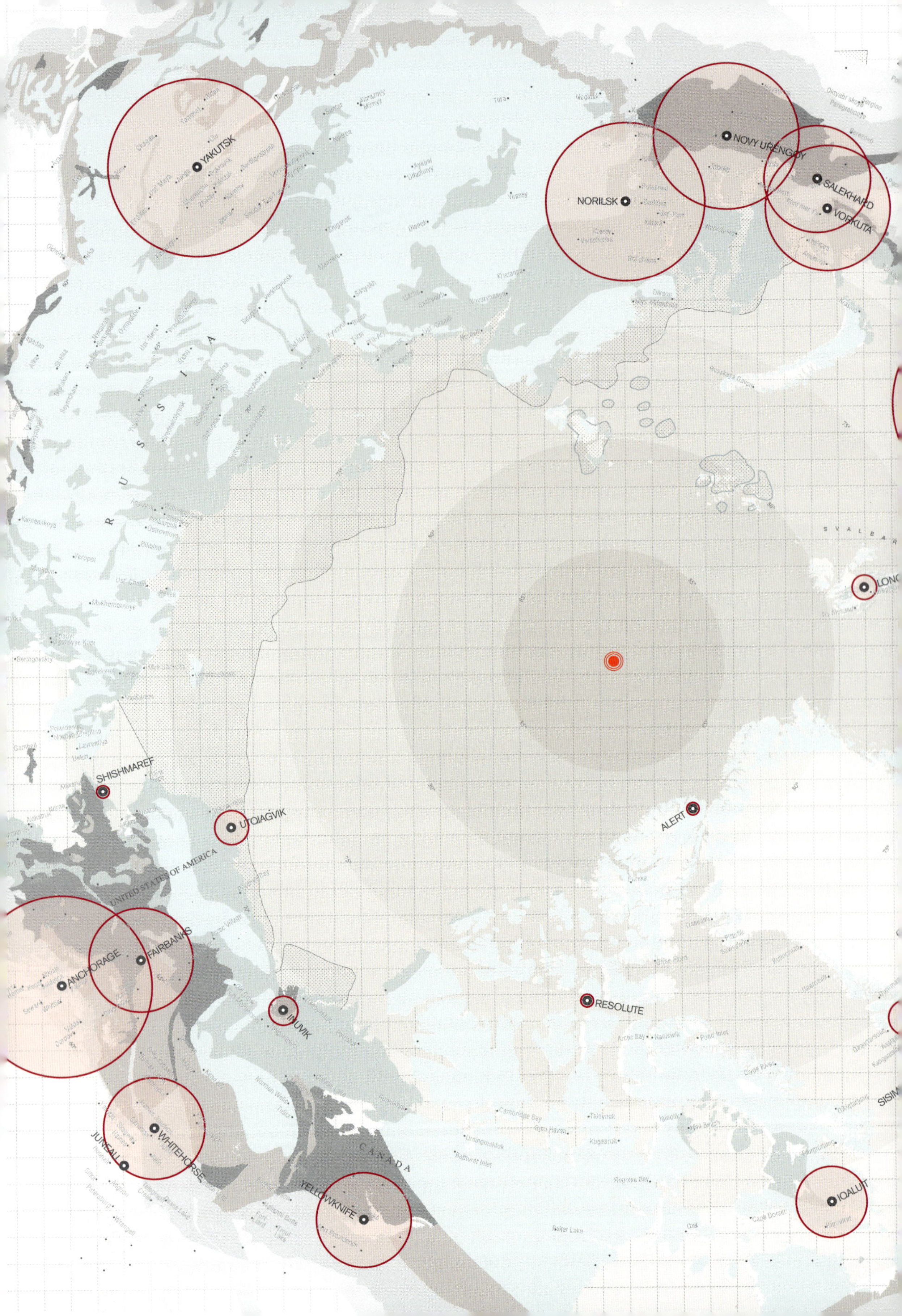
YAKUTSK
NOVY URENGOY
NORILSK
SALEKHARD
VORKUTA
R U S S I A
S V A L B A R
SHISHMAREF
UTQIAGVIK
ALERT
UNITED STATES OF AMERICA
FAIRBANKS
ANCHORAGE
INUVIK
RESOLUTE
WHITEHORSE
JUNEAU
YELLOWKNIFE
C A N A D A
IQALUIT

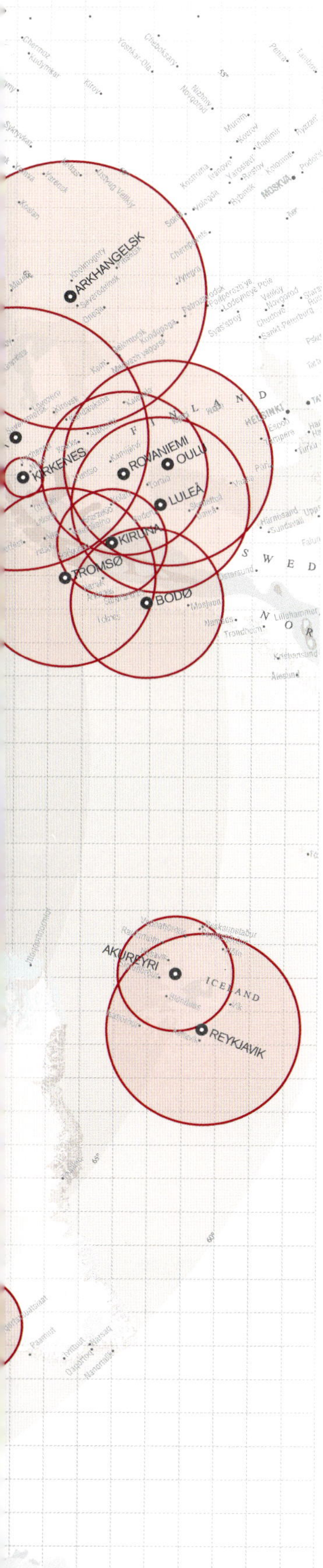

URBANIZATION

There are about 4 million people living in the Arctic as defined by the boundary adopted by the Arctic Council's Arctic Human Development Report (AHDR). About half of this population is located in Russia in (1.9 million), with the remainder split between Northern Europe (1.3 million) and North America (778,000). For the most part, cities in Arctic Russia surpass all other cities in the north in terms of the intensity of their degrees of urbanization – large populations, high density urban fabric, primarily in the form of prefabricated concrete multi-story buildings, well-developed infrastructure, and an abundance of heavy industry. These cities are located at high latitudes of in some of the most extreme and difficult environmental conditions on Earth. For comparison, one of the largest of these cities – Norilsk has a population of about 180,000, living in five, nine, and twelve story apartment complexes built on permafrost. In North America, the largest settlement at a similar latitude is Utqiagvik (Barrow) which has a population of around 4,200, is constructed mostly of wood frame, single story prefabricated houses, and is organized in a distributed manner similar to a suburban low density neighborhood. Within the AHDR region, Anchorage (population: 294,000) is the largest city in North America, and is the main population and economic center for Alaska. However, along with the cities in northern Europe with moderated climates and lack of permafrost such as Tromsø, Norway (population: 76,000) or Rovaniemi, Finland (population: 62,000), these population centers do not share many of the extreme conditions or characteristics of their more northerly neighbors.

EXTENT OF PERMAFROST, % OF AREA

Continuous (90-100%)

- Thick overburden cover (>5-10m)
- Thin overburden cover (<5-10m) and exposed bedrock

Discontinuous (50-90%)

- Thick overburden cover (>5-10 m)
- Thin overburden cover (<5-10m) and exposed bedrock
- Sporadic (10-50%)
- Isolated patches (0-10%)
- Subsea permafrost
- Arctic glaciers and ice sheets

POPULATION

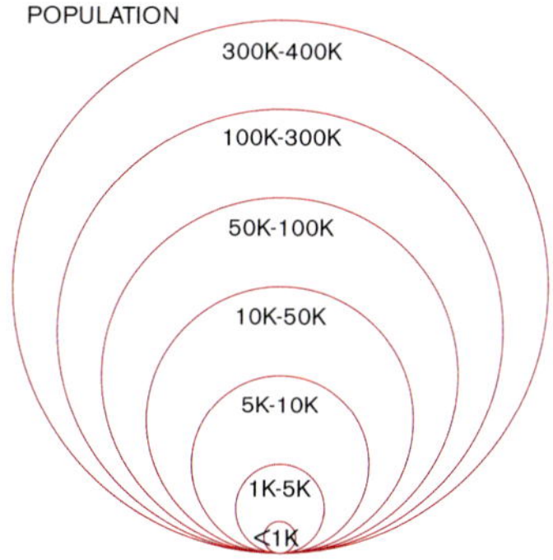

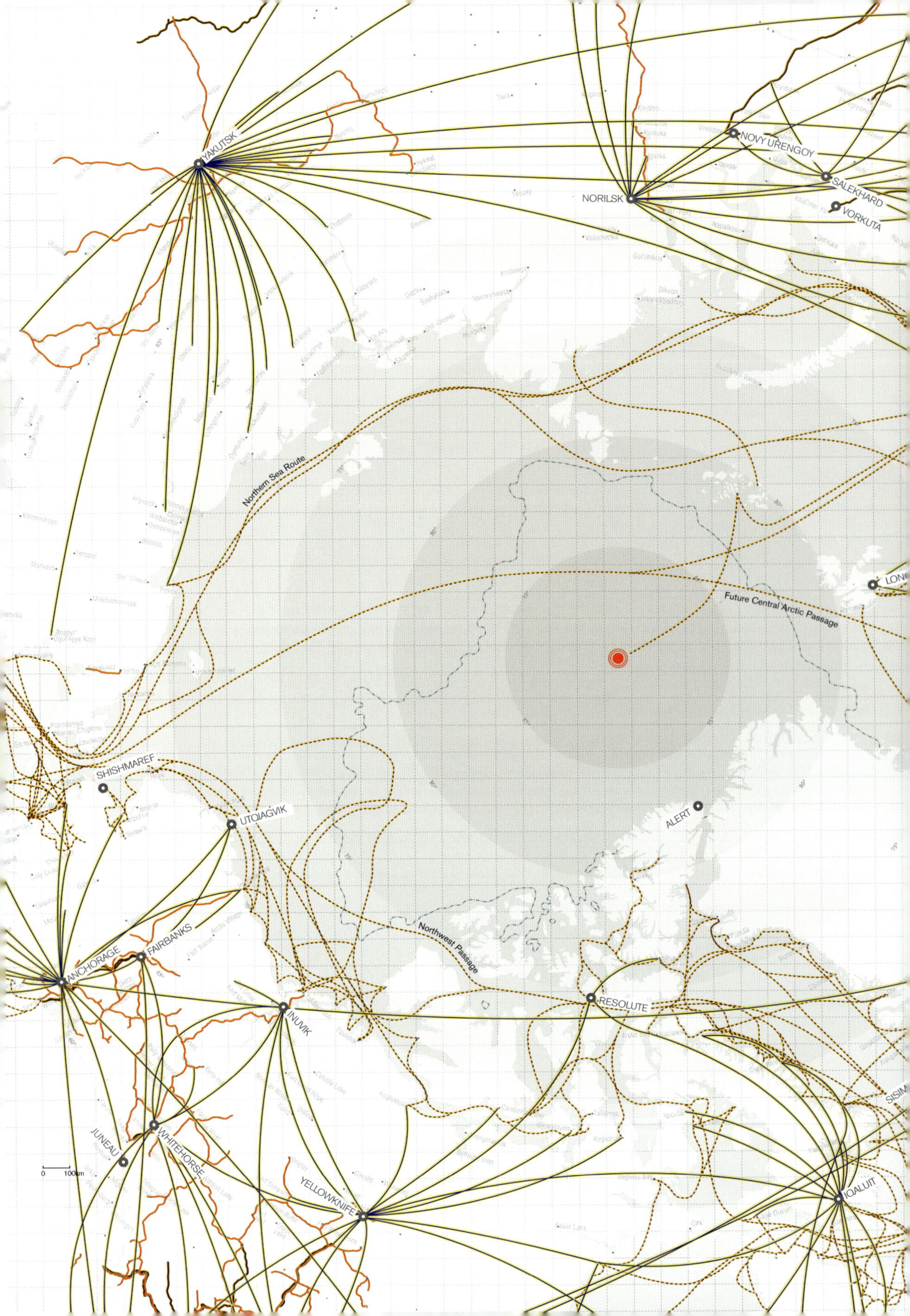
YAKUTSK
NORILSK
NOVY URENGOY
SALEKHARD
VORKUTA
Northern Sea Route
Future Central Arctic Passage
SHISHMAREF
UTQIAĠVIK
ALERT
Northwest Passage
ANCHORAGE
FAIRBANKS
INUVIK
RESOLUTE
JUNEAU
WHITEHORSE
YELLOWKNIFE
IQALUIT
0
100km

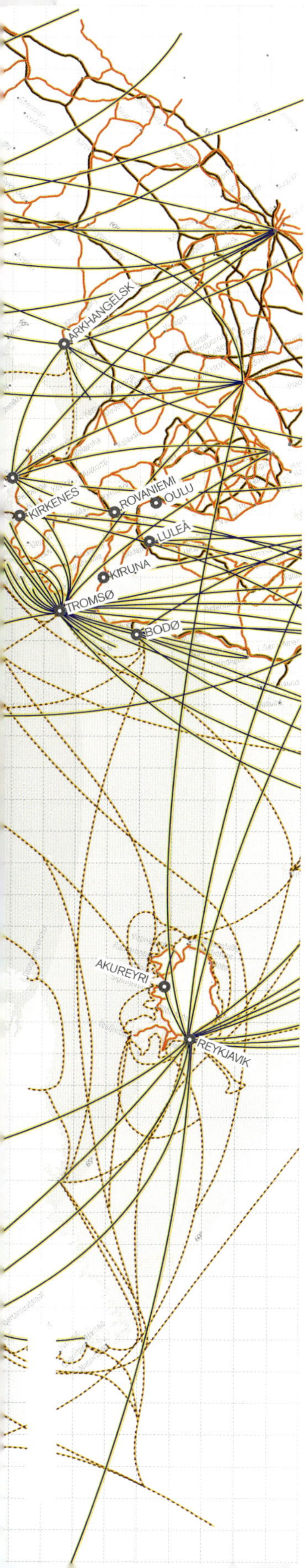

MOBILITY INFRASTRUCTURE

A defining feature for much of the Arctic is geographic remoteness and isolation. Historically, and for centuries, the extreme environmental conditions made the region completely inaccessible except only to the indigenous peoples who lived there. With the introduction of new navigation technologies as well as development of modern air, sea, and land travel in the 20th century, the Arctic slowly developed a network of mobility infrastructure primarily in the form of airstrips, but also roads and ice-hardened ships that led to the development of small communities and large industrial cities. Two of the main economic and technological drivers for this development were an abundance of natural resources such as oil and gas, and national security interests during the Cold War that led to the construction of mining cities and military outposts in some of the most remote locations on Earth. Because the eight Arctic nations each have varying priorities toward their northern frontiers, as well as vastly different scales of territory, the state of mobility infrastructure and service differs significantly throughout the Arctic. The three forms of transportation can be characterized as follows: 1) Air transport - the most common, effective yet costly form of transport of people and perishable goods in the Arctic from commercial airliners to small single engine bush planes. 2) Maritime transport - a seasonally dependent but economical and efficient form of moving large volumes of cargo into the remote Arctic settlements and for mining. In the winter, much of the Arctic Ocean is frozen and impassable except by ice breaker. 3) Land transport - possibly the least effective means of getting into or out of the Arctic except for transport of mining camp equipment on winter roads through frozen tundra and lakes. Roads are few, being restricted to populated areas, which generally serve local rather than inter-regional needs.

Water Transport
Sea Ice Limit
Land Transport (Highway)
Land Transport (Railway)
Air Transport

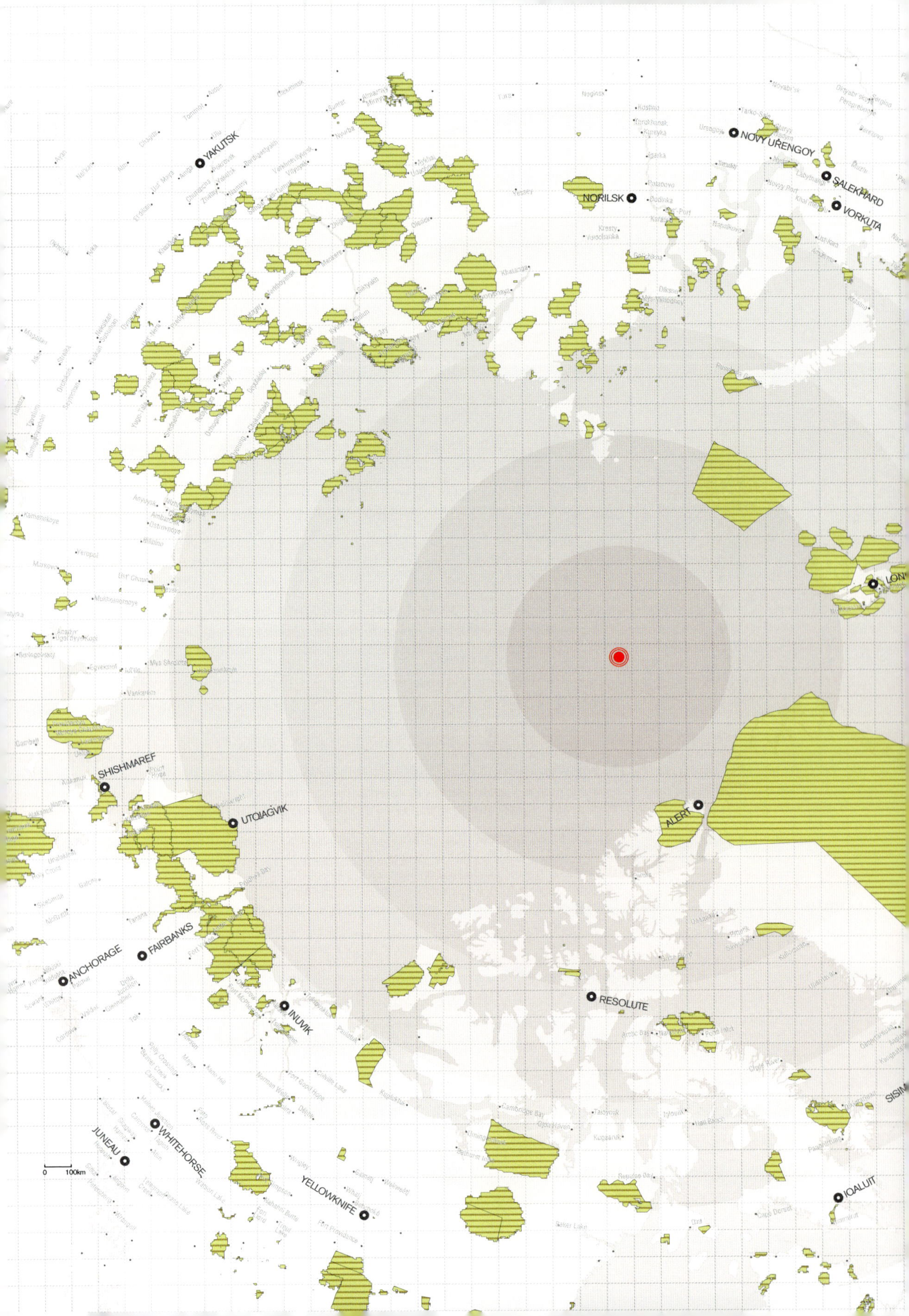

YAKUTSK
NORILSK
NOVY URENGOY
SALEKHARD
VORKUTA
SHISHMAREF
UTQIAGVIK
ALERT
FAIRBANKS
ANCHORAGE
INUVIK
RESOLUTE
WHITEHORSE
JUNEAU
YELLOWKNIFE
IQALUIT
0
100km

PROTECTED AREAS

Designated by the Conservation of Arctic Flora and Fauna (CAFF), the Arctic Council's biodiversity working group representing all eight Arctic nations, there are currently 1,127 protected areas in the Arctic region covering an area of about 1.4 million square miles. With the goal of preserving biodiversity, these areas have been established in strategically important areas, helping to maintain crucial ecological features, such as caribou migration and calving areas, shorebird and waterfowl staging and nesting sites, seabird colonies, and critical components of marine mammal habitats. The extent of protected areas within the CAFF boundary has almost doubled since 1980, and most recently, about 20% of the Arctic's terrestrial area and 5% of the Arctic's marine areas are protected. Within the CAFF boundary, there are ninety-two areas recognized under global international conventions, including twelve World Heritage sites and eighty Ramsar sites. Designation and monitoring in Europe and North America takes different approaches. For example, protected areas in the EU's Natura 2000 network are established on a mix of privately owned lands and state-owned lands, although in some Scandinavian countries most protected areas are on state-owned land. In North America, the protected areas are largely located on federal or state-owned land, are formally designated, and are very large in size. While they represent relatively undisturbed landscapes, the protected areas often come into conflict with economic activities and environmental contamination, degrading the biodiversity, subsistence-based cultural practices of indigenous peoples and their values, deeply connected to the environment. Together, these protected areas are important for research and monitoring, recreation, and education.

Protected Areas

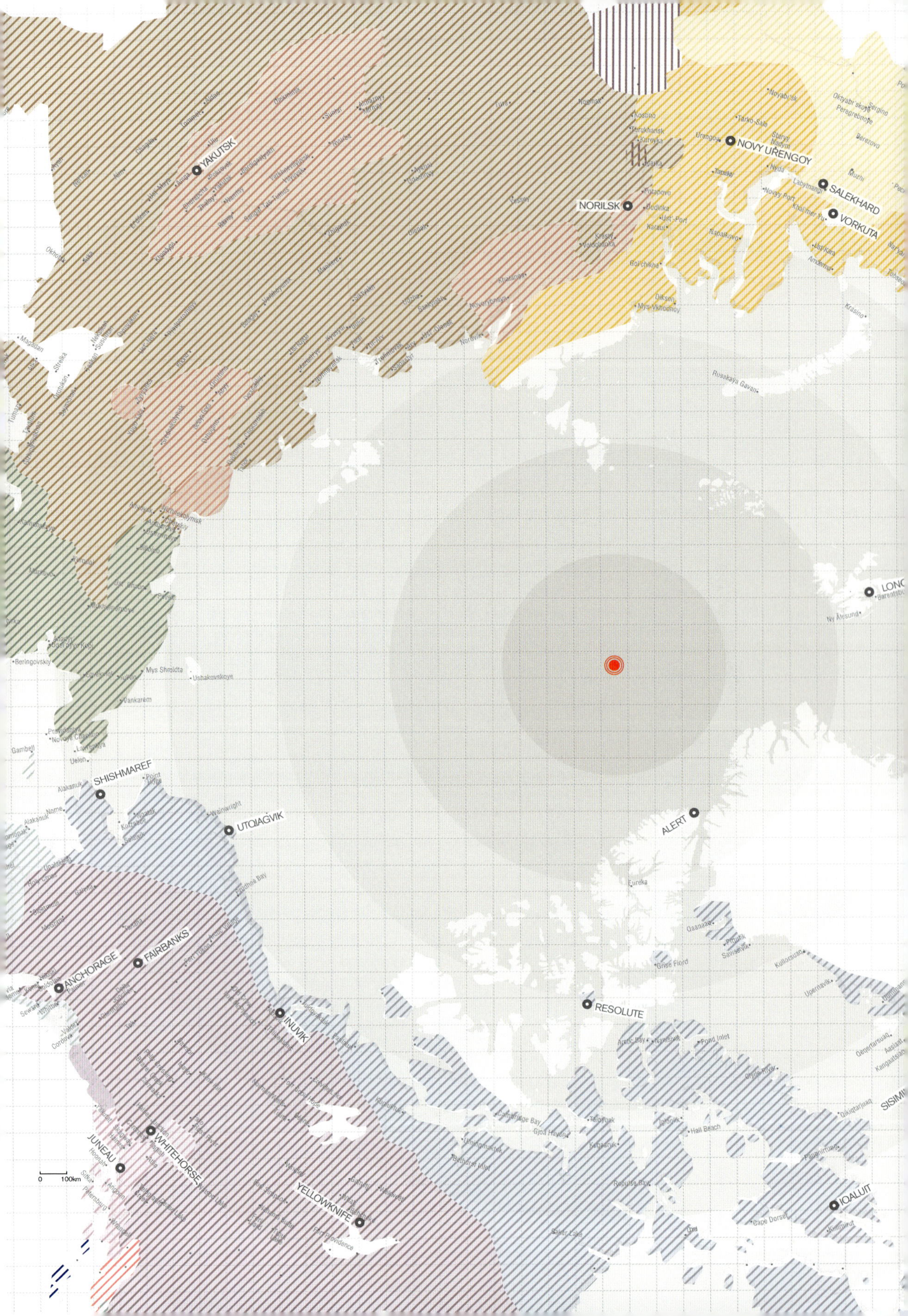
YAKUTSK
NORILSK
NOVY URENGOY
SALEKHARD
VORKUTA
SHISHMAREF
UTQIAGVIK
ALERT
ANCHORAGE
FAIRBANKS
INUVIK
RESOLUTE
WHITEHORSE
JUNEAU
YELLOWKNIFE
IQALUIT
0 100km

INDIGENOUS PEOPLES

The Arctic is a homeland for many indigenous peoples who constitute the core of the region's permanent human population. About forty different indigenous groups live within the Arctic but they comprise about 10% of the total northern population due to a large influx of new residents working in extractive industries. While cultural heritage as well as political and economic legacy they have experienced vary widely, what many indigenous groups share in common is an undeniably strong connection to land and environment, with traditional forms of livelihood and hunting now interwoven with modern technology, healthcare, and infrastructure. Over the past one hundred years, many of the indigenous groups in the Arctic particularly in North America, who were largely nomadic and had subsistence-based lifestyle, experienced a drastic shock and cultural destabilization due to government-sanctioned policies which aimed to introduce western values and development to the north. As a result of forced sedentarization, many of these groups have struggled to maintain their cultures and traditional ways of life. Although there have been efforts to introduce autonomy and self-governance, extreme poverty and unhealthy living conditions are common. Coupled with increasing impacts of climate change, these communities are facing further disruption of subsistence ways of life and food security, damage to buildings and infrastructure, increased coastal erosion and flooding events, and direct physical harm through rapid changes in environmental conditions and weather events.

- Chukotko-Kamchatkan
- Tunguso-Manchurian
- Yukagiran
- Nivkh
- Samodic
- Finno-Ugric
- Inuit
- Yupik
- Aleut
- Eyak

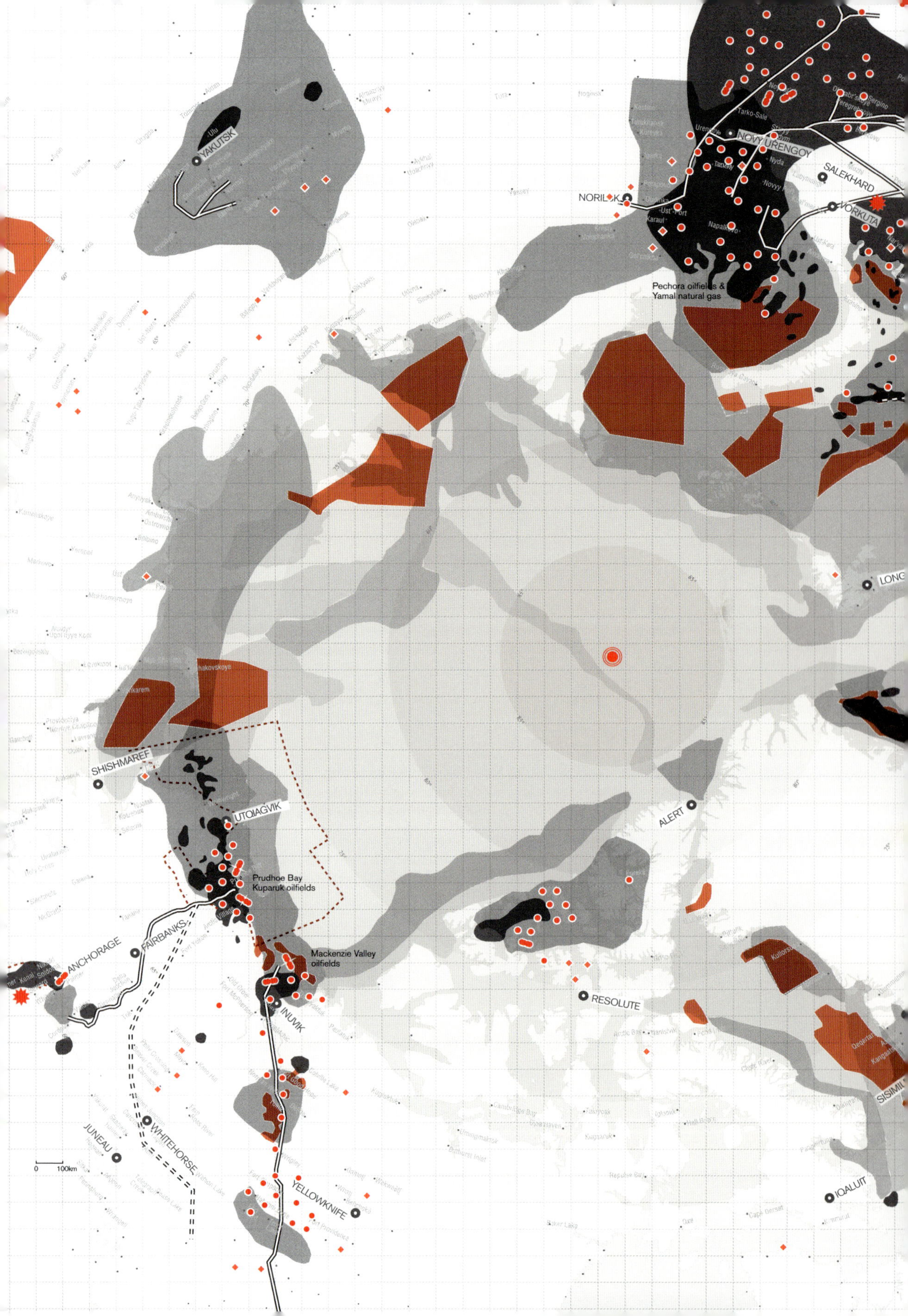

YAKUTSK
NORILSK
NOVY URENGOY
SALEKHARD
VORKUTA
Pechora oilfields &
Yamal natural gas
LONG
SHISHMAREF
UTQIAGVIK
ALERT
Prudhoe Bay
Kuparuk oilfields
ANCHORAGE
FAIRBANKS
Mackenzie Valley
oilfields
RESOLUTE
INUVIK
SISIMIUT
JUNEAU
WHITEHORSE
YELLOWKNIFE
IQALUIT
0
100km

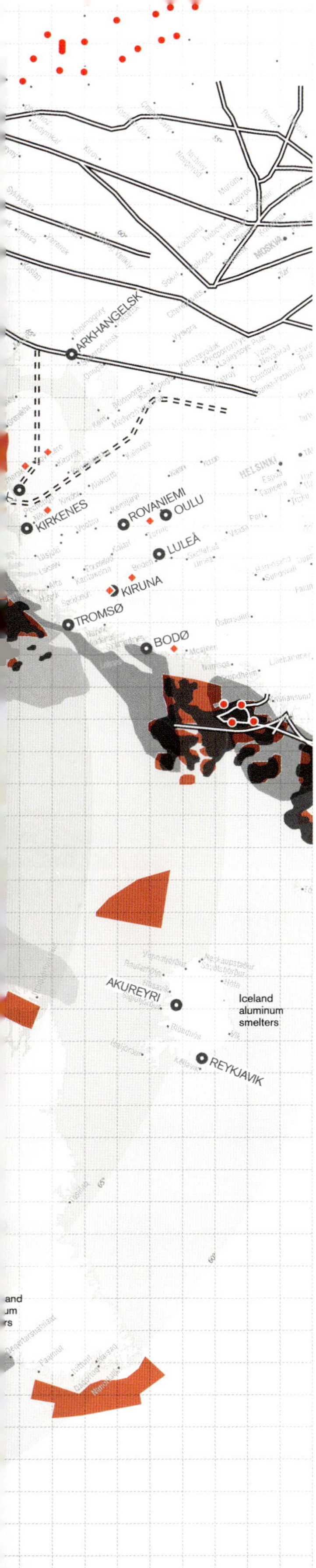

NATURAL RESOURCES

The U.S. Geological Survey estimates that the Arctic holds 13% of the remaining undiscovered petroleum, 30% of undiscovered gas, and includes large mineral deposits such as nickel, copper, gold, zinc, and uranium, as well as rare earth elements. Diamonds and nickel are plentiful, the waters are rich with fish, and the region is bordered by the vast boreal forest belt, which holds one-third of global forests and perhaps 40% of economic forest resources. Currently about 25% of the world's natural gas and 10% of its oil comes from onshore development on the North Slope of Alaska (Prudhoe Bay and Kuparuk fields) and Russia (Yamal Peninsula). Offshore exploration is becoming increasingly viable due to changes in climate, improvements in extraction technologies, as well as increasing oil prices. Such enterprises backed by scientific research and international policies are one of the most potent catalytic forces for Arctic urbanization and are at the forefront of the major global energy industry. To this end, the modern history of the Arctic, one could argue, is a history of interactions between advanced industrial metropolises located in the South and resource-rich hinterlands located to the North. The resource exploitation in the Arctic has generated numerous conflicts with competing environmental, cultural, and political interests. For instance, drilling or mining operations have produced physical disturbances in areas of tundra underlain with permafrost while oil and gas operations continue to cause severe air and water pollution.

Oil & Gas Extraction
Mineral Extraction
Oil Spill / Pipeline Breach (>50,000T)
Existing Pipelines (Oil & Gas)
Future Pipelines
Production Areas
Current Licenses
Future Licenses

Probability of Oil & Gas presence (> 50M barrels)
100% 30-49%
50-99% 10-29%

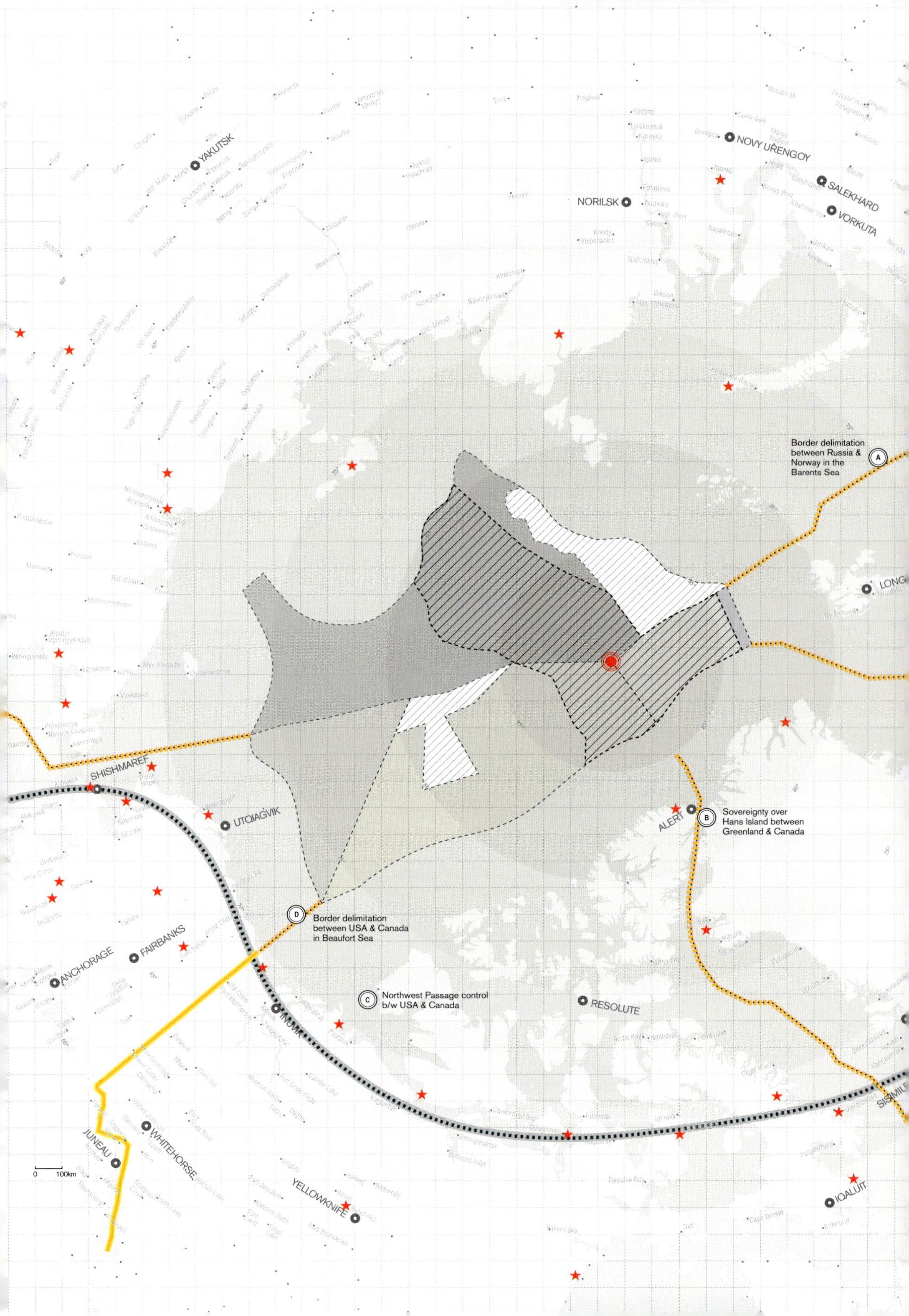
YAKUTSK
NOVY UŘENGOY
SALEKHARD
VORKUTA
NORILSK
Border delimitation between Russia & Norway in the Barents Sea
A
LONG
SHISHMAREF
UTQIAGVIK
ALERT
B
Sovereignty over Hans Island between Greenland & Canada
D
Border delimitation between USA & Canada in Beaufort Sea
FAIRBANKS
ANCHORAGE
C
Northwest Passage control b/w USA & Canada
RESOLUTE
INUVIK
SISIMIU
JUNEAU
WHITEHORSE
YELLOWKNIFE
IQALUIT
0 100km

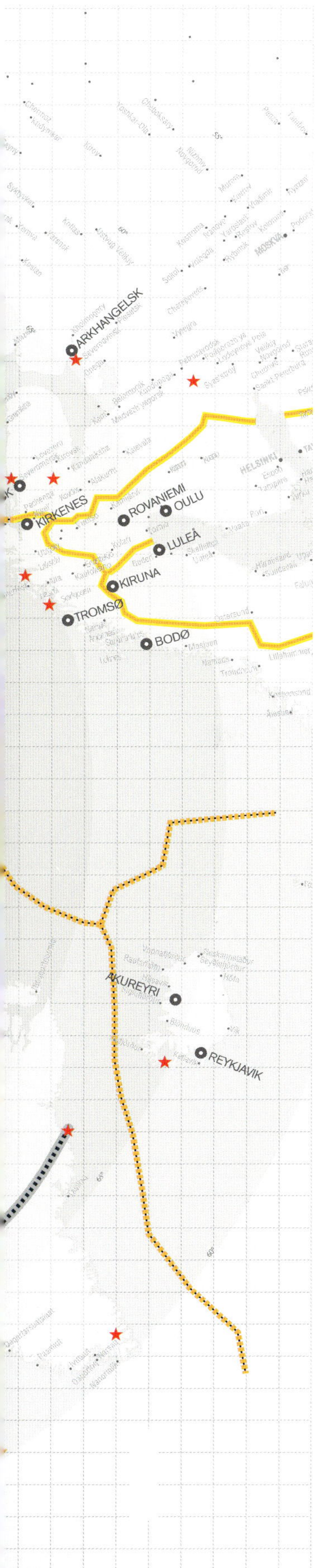

GEOPOLITICS

The eight Arctic nations – Canada, Finland, Greenland (Denmark), Iceland, Norway, Russia, Sweden and United States – are enacting plans for their northern territories and developing strategic policy frameworks through the Arctic Council. But unlike the south polar region, where the Antarctic Treaty System has effectively frozen existing jurisdictional claims and restrained the growth of new claims, the Arctic is an area where any effort to solve regional problems and regulate development, militarization, and environmental protection must come to terms with the undeniable reality of multiple, and in some instances, expanding jurisdictions. Currently, the eight Arctic nations are involved in territorial disputes due in large part to uncertainty over who owns the seabed beyond the 200 nautical miles of Exclusive Economic Zone off their northern coasts. With an estimated 22% of the world's recoverable energy resources, and potential economic benefits of control of new global shipping routes, asserting Arctic territorial claims is of major concern as the extent of sea ice retreats and accessibility increases. By far, Russia is leading this effort, with fleets of ice breakers and development of oil and gas along its northern border. Other countries are also getting involved by securing partnerships in research or economic development with the Arctic nations. Policing these waterways and resources within national borders is also promoting military build-up and infrastructure in the region.

Political Boundaries
200 Nautical-mile Limit
DEW Line
★ Presence of Military Base

Territorial Claims

Russia
USA
Canada
Norway
Unclaimed
Denmark

○ Territorial disputes

SHAPES OF CLIMATE

Alert, Canada
(82.5018°N, 62.3481°W)

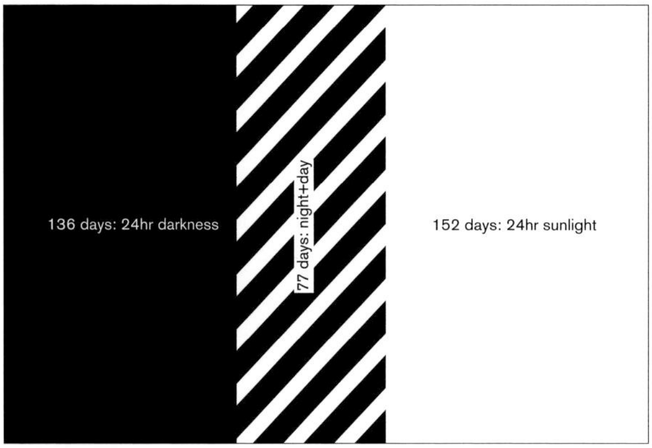

Number of polar days & polar nights / yr

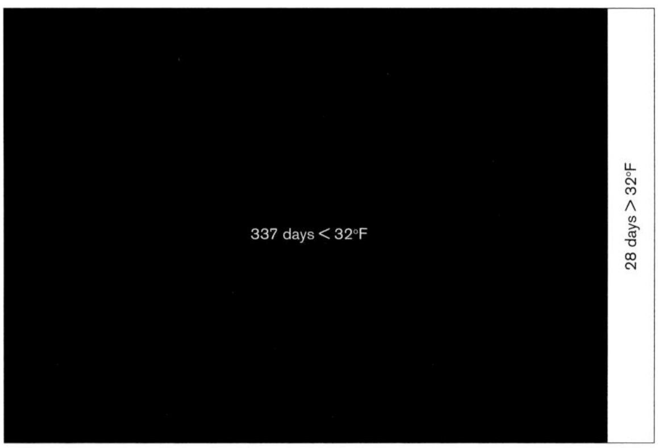

Average number of days / yr below 32°F (0°C)

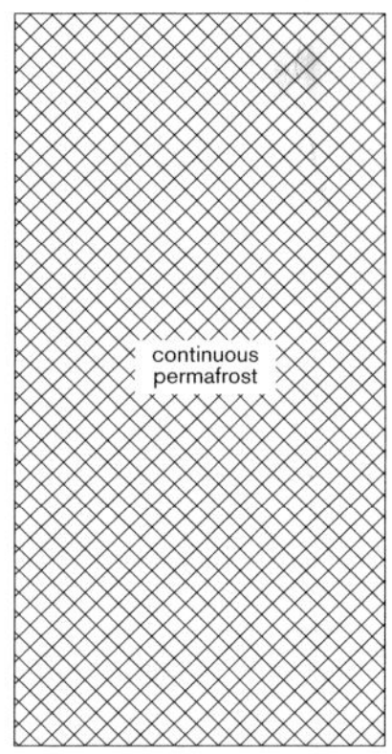

Ground type

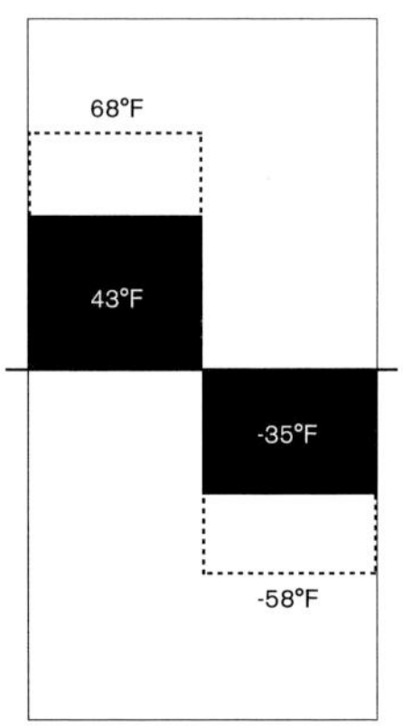

Temp Max
Temp avg high
(F°)

Temp Min
Temp avg low
(F°)

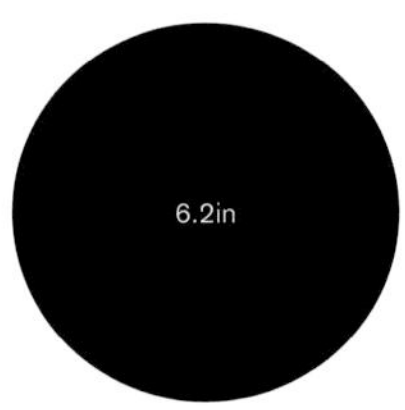

Average rainfall / yr (in)

Tromsø, Norway
(69.6492°N, 18.9553°E)

Number of polar days & polar nights / yr

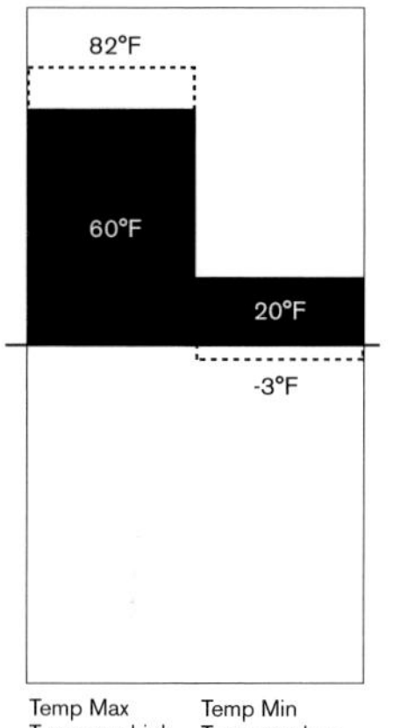

Temp Max
Temp avg high
(F°)

Temp Min
Temp avg low
(F°)

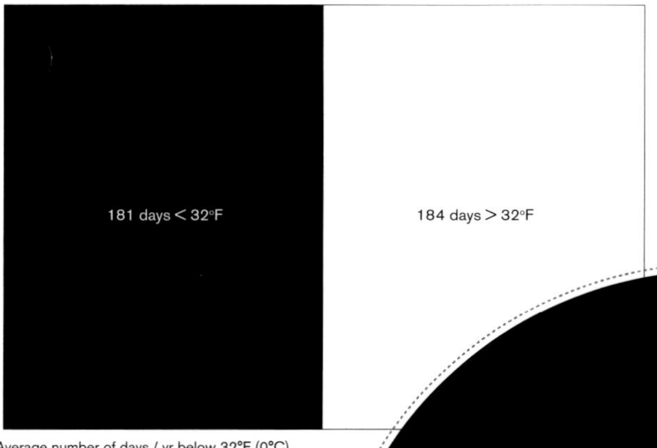

Average number of days / yr below 32°F (0°C)

Ground type

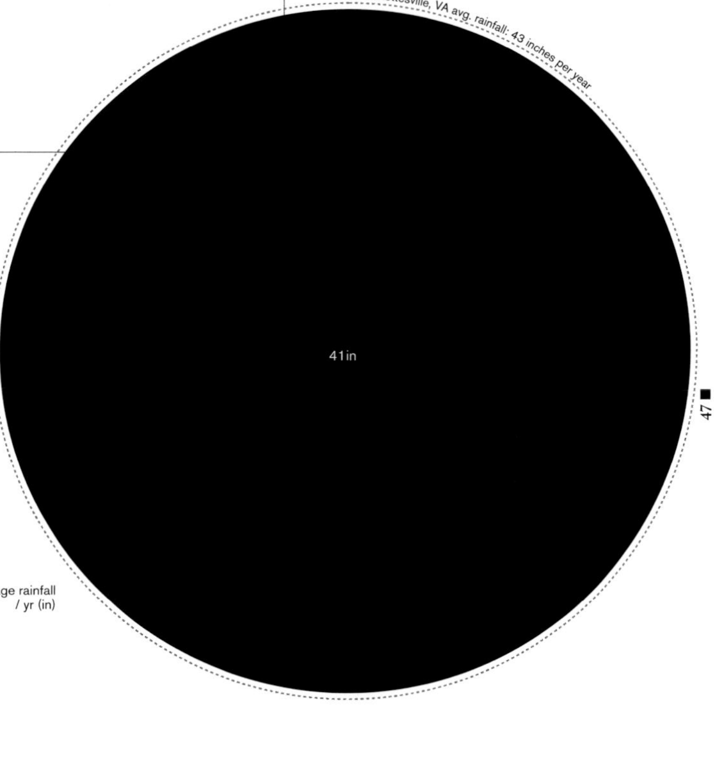

Average rainfall
/ yr (in)

Utqiagvik, USA
(71.2906°N, 156.7886°W)

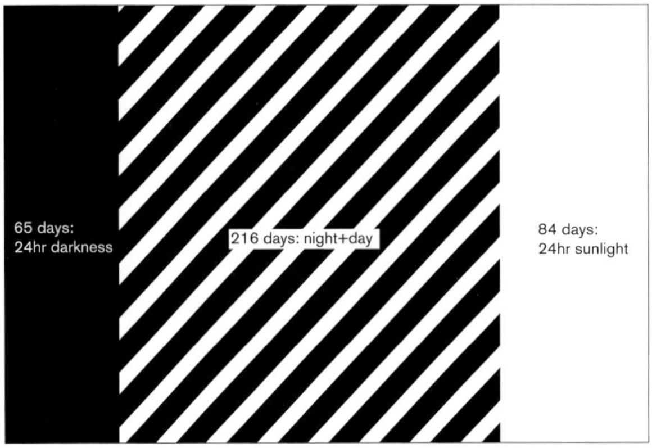

Number of polar days & polar nights / yr

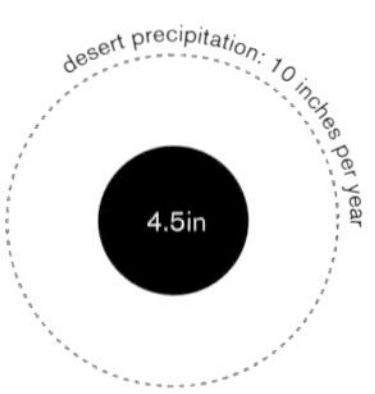

Average rainfall / yr (in)

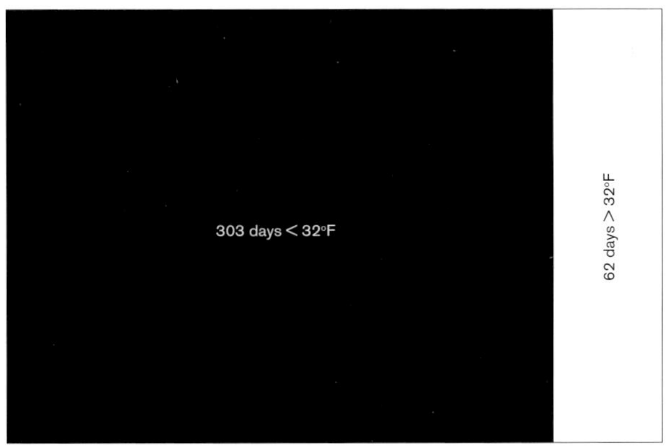

Average number of days / yr below 32°F (0°C)

Ground type

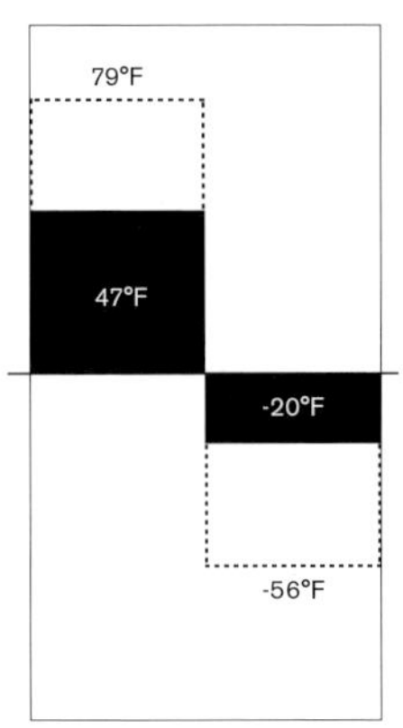

Temp Max
Temp avg high
(F°)

Temp Min
Temp avg low
(F°)

Yakutsk, Russia
(62.0355°N, 129.6755°E)

Number of polar days & polar nights / yr

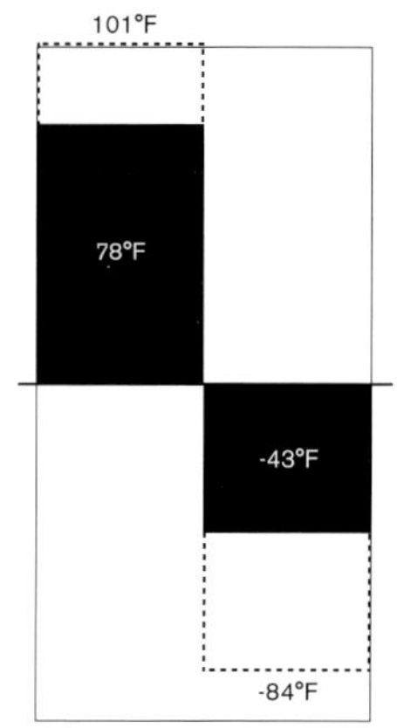

Temp Max
Temp avg high
(F°)

Temp Min
Temp avg low
(F°)

Ground type

Average rainfall / yr (in)

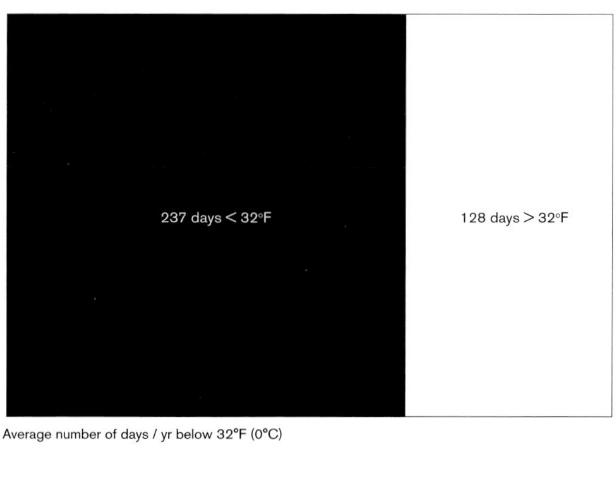

Average number of days / yr below 32°F (0°C)

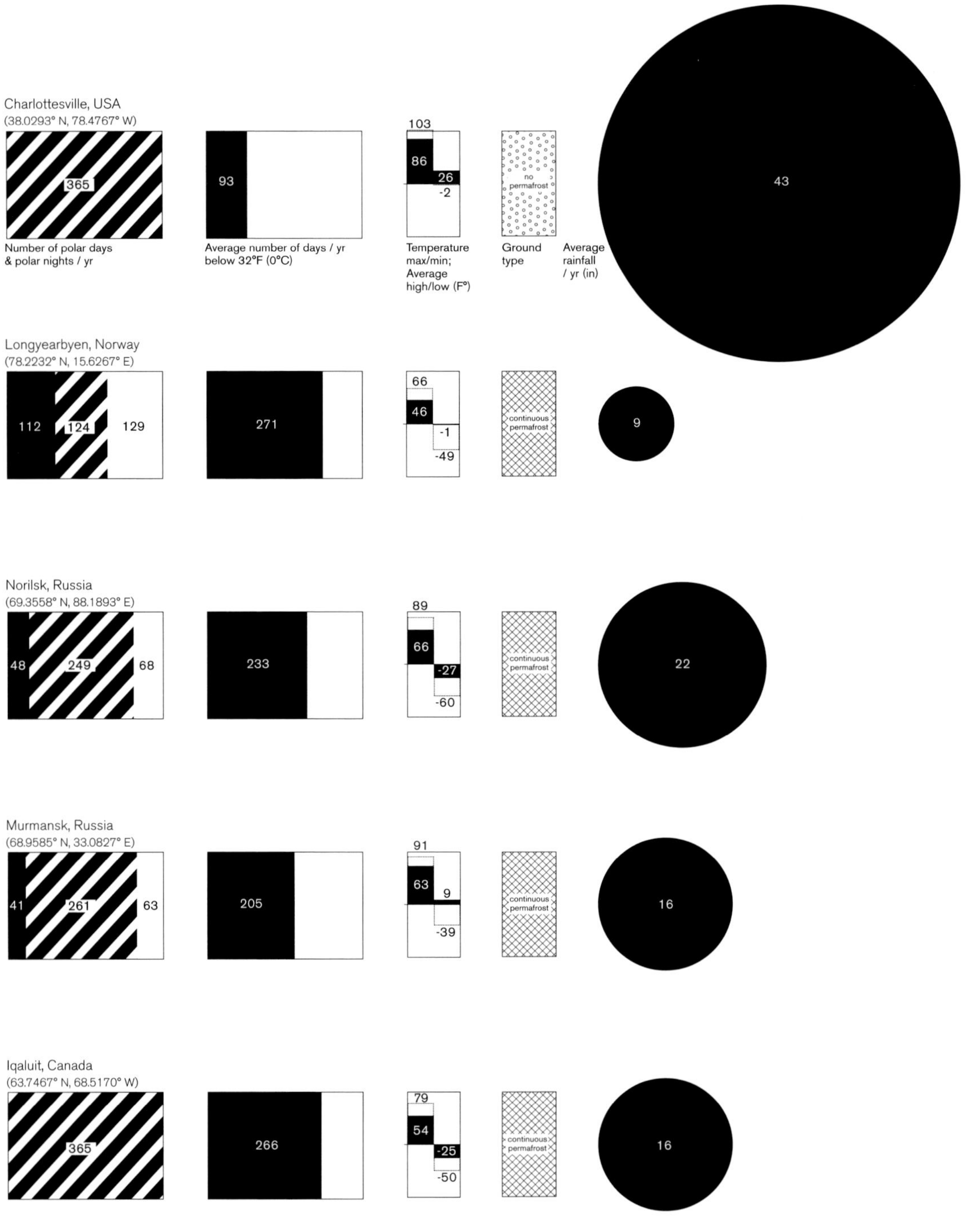
Charlottesville, USA
(38.0293° N, 78.4767° W)
365
Number of polar days & polar nights / yr
93
Average number of days / yr below 32°F (0°C)
103
86
26
-2
Temperature max/min; Average high/low (F°)
no permafrost
Ground type
Average rainfall / yr (in)
43
Longyearbyen, Norway
(78.2232° N, 15.6267° E)
112
124
129
271
66
46
-1
-49
continuous permafrost
9
Norilsk, Russia
(69.3558° N, 88.1893° E)
48
249
68
233
89
66
-27
-60
continuous permafrost
22
Murmansk, Russia
(68.9585° N, 33.0827° E)
41
261
63
205
91
63
9
-39
continuous permafrost
16
Iqaluit, Canada
(63.7467° N, 68.5170° W)
365
266
79
54
-25
-50
continuous permafrost
16

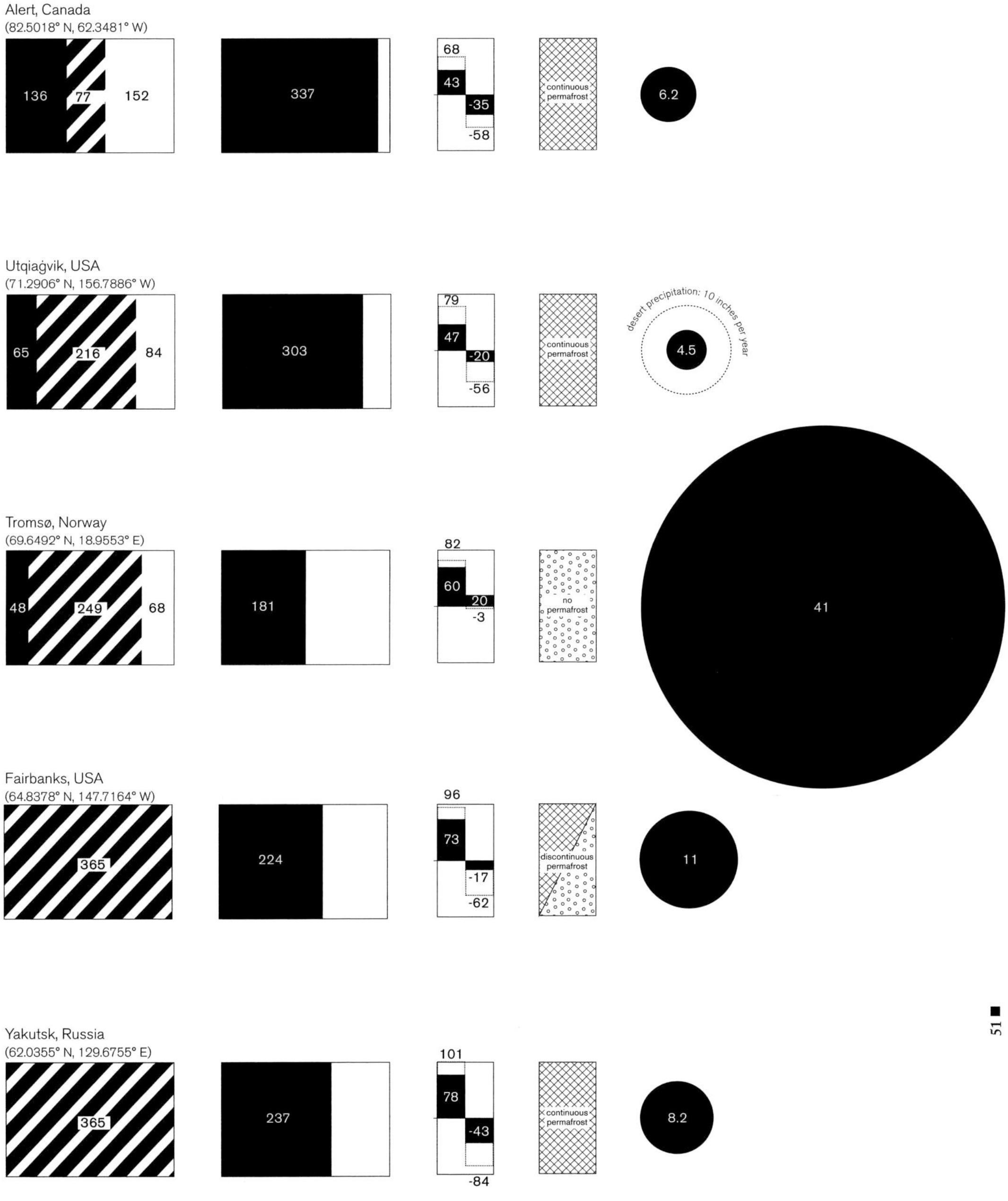
Alert, Canada
(82.5018° N, 62.3481° W)
136
77
152
337
68
43
-35
-58
continuous permafrost
6.2
Utqiaġvik, USA
(71.2906° N, 156.7886° W)
65
216
84
303
79
47
-20
-56
continuous permafrost
desert precipitation: 10 inches per year
4.5
Tromsø, Norway
(69.6492° N, 18.9553° E)
48
249
68
181
82
60
20
-3
no permafrost
41
Fairbanks, USA
(64.8378° N, 147.7164° W)
365
224
96
73
-17
-62
discontinuous permafrost
11
Yakutsk, Russia
(62.0355° N, 129.6755° E)
365
237
101
78
-43
-84
continuous permafrost
8.2

Land-Water-Ice: Making Space for Architecture in the Arctic

PHILIP STEINBERG

Professor of Political Geography, Durham University, UK

I want to begin by taking you back to July 16, 1970. On that day, a gentleman named Mario Escamilla, realized that a 15-gallon barrel of homemade raisin wine was missing from his home. He was pretty sure that he knew who had taken the wine: his neighbor, "Porky" Leavitt. Mario and Porky had had issues with alcohol before. In fact, just a few weeks earlier, there was an incident where Porky came after Mario with a meat cleaver as part of an altercation. Mario went over to Porky's place, and sure enough there was Porky drinking the wine mixed with 190-proof grain alcohol and grape juice. Together with Porky was Bennie Lightsy who was the boss of both Mario and Porky. They got into a fight, they yelled at each other. Mario went back to his home. A few minutes later, there was a knock on the door. Mario went to answer it and, remembering the whole meat cleaver incident, first grabbed a loaded rifle. It turned out not to be Porky, but Bennie Lightsy. Mario and Bennie continued their argument and got into a scuffle. Eventually, the rifle accidentally discharged and, next thing you knew, Bennie Lightsy was dead on the floor.

This all might sound like the opening to a Western or, maybe closer to home, a southern morality tale about the evils of drink. But, actually it's a Northern story, from a place called T-3 [Figure 1] or Fletcher's Ice Island. T-3 was a 30-square-mile, 200-foot thick slab of glacial ice that was occupied by the U.S. military as a research station, from 1952 to 1978, as it floated around the Arctic Ocean. Typically, there were twenty to thirty civilian employees on T-3. Most were doing research on a range of topics concerning the properties of ice.[1]

Figure 1: The settlement on T-3 where Escamilla, Lightsy, and Leavitt lived and worked.

Bennie Lightsy was the chief meteorologist and the station chief. Escamilla was an electronics technician, and Porky Leavitt was a local Inuk who performed general maintenance tasks. A drift track of T-3 from 1962 to 1974, part of the time that was a U.S. Navy Research Station, shows where T-3 was around the time of the shooting [Figure 2]. It is about 200 miles off the coast of Ellesmere Island, the northernmost island of Canada. At the time of the shooting, T-3 was in international waters. This fact raises an interesting question: who had jurisdiction to try the case?

In one sense, it seems simple because there was an American flag flying over the research station. However, from the U.S. perspective, this American flag meant pretty much nothing. U.S. Naval Policy since the early 19th century prioritized preserving the freedom of navigation; meaning, the last thing the U.S. wanted was to create a precedent allowing countries around the world to claim chunks of ice saying, "this is our territory." That could lead to the divvying up of the ocean, which would interfere with the free movement of both military and commercial vessels. Indeed, from the U.S. perspective and that of international law, including the U.N. Convention on the Law of the Sea, frozen ocean is about the same as liquid ocean. Only one of the 320 articles in the Law of the Sea notes that parts of the ocean are frozen; otherwise, it assumes the ocean is liquid. From this perspective, T-3 was

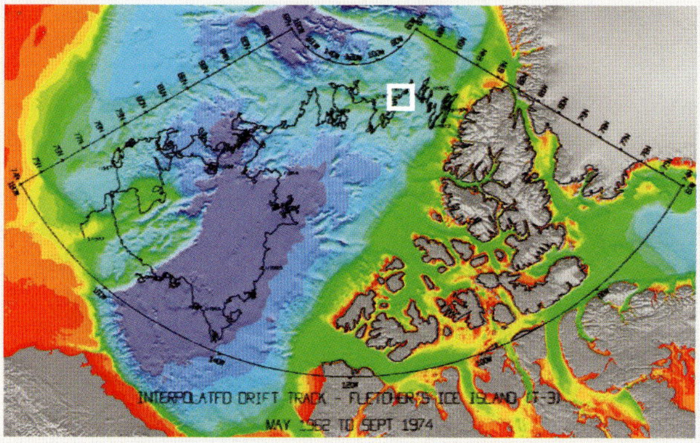

Figure 2: Interpolated drift track, May 1962 to September 1974. A white square indicates the location of T-3 around the time of Mario and Bennie's altercation.

a frozen piece of High Seas floating on top of liquid High Seas. Legally, it was undifferentiated ocean.

There are two problems with this construction. The first is that T-3 actually consisted of glacial ice that calved off Ellesmere Island. The second problem is that if a crime is committed on the High Seas, jurisdiction reverts to the flag state of the ship on which the crime occurs, but of course T-3 was not a ship.

Canada sent a memo to the U.S. saying, "Well, why don't you just call it a ship? You could claim sovereignty but you wouldn't be making any territorial claims, setting a precedent and all those things." The problem there is that under international maritime law the flag state of a vessel is responsible for ensuring that its vessel does not cause a hindrance to navigation. And of course, you can't steer an iceberg. So the U.S. envisioned all sorts of liability problems down the road if T-3 were considered an American ship.

In the end, Escamilla was removed by helicopter to Thule Air Force Base in Greenland. This led some to suggest that perhaps he should be tried under Danish law because Greenland was a dependency of Denmark and the first state land on which he landed. Eventually, from Thule he was flown to Dulles Airport. In the end, Escamilla was tried in the Second District Court of Virginia where he was found guilty of involuntary manslaughter. However, the District Court judge never explained his basis for claiming jurisdiction. One possibility is that the judge was thinking that all the parties involved were U.S. nationals and that the crime occurred in the ocean which is a sort of juridical vacuum, a super-territorial space, a space beyond territory. Alternately, he may have considered T-3 to be a vessel, an extra-territorial space and thereby an extension of U.S. territory. Or, he may have considered T-3 to be an uninhabited, unclaimed island in which case, under the 1856 Guano Islands Act, the U.S. could claim temporary authority over T-3 as a, proto-territorial space. Indeed, today it is still not clear whether a space like T-3 is an ocean, a ship, or an island.

I begin with the story of T-3 because it tells us a lot about how the complex shifting world of land, water, and ice that is the Arctic, and it complicates established norms for regulating, governing, settling, and transforming space.[1] And those kinds of questions have important implications as we design futures for the region.

I want to go a bit further into what makes the Arctic interesting and what makes T-3 interesting as a complex dynamic space. For this purpose, it is useful to contrast the Arctic with the world as we are used to thinking of it. This is what some of my colleagues and I call the "modern territorial imaginary." The "modern territorial imaginary" is a way of thinking of space that pairs binaries. On the one hand there is a geopolitical, or social, binary that divides space into points of fixity, points on the surface with differentiated natures. As people over time transform these points and their natures, societies develop and social divisions of labor emerge. Eventually states and boundaries form. These are the inside spaces, the territories. There are also the outside spaces. Spaces seen as fundamentally beyond society because they have none of what are deemed to be society's essential social processes: production in place, social development, state institutions, etc. In fact, these non-territories are seen as uncontrolled, unbounded, undeveloped and effectively asocial; and really the only reasons to go into them are either to cross through them to get to another space that matters or perhaps to go into them to extract resources that can be used to develop inside spaces.

The power of this binary is that it is fused with an equally idealized geophysical binary that divides space into land and ocean. The real force of this occurs when these two binaries are paired and naturalized through objects like a standard political map of the world. On such maps, the ocean is typically depicted as a background without boundaries or other signs of social activity. Against this background is a foreground of land, states, bounded places of society, named territories where things can happen. Frequently colors are added to naturalize this binary division. The ocean is depicted as blue, evoking the materiality of water, while land is depicted as brown evoking the materiality of a fundamentally different space.

Returning to the case from T-3, the legal debate revolved around how to place T-3 within the geopolitical binary. Was it an inside space? Was it an outside space? Was it something in between? I think it was difficult to place T-3 within the geopolitical binary because it was so difficult to place it within the geophysical binary. Was it land? Was it water? Was it something in between? In other words, the idealized pairing of the two binaries to create categories of "blue" and "brown" space don't work well in the Arctic.

I should point out that there are problems with the binaries and their pairing everywhere. The geopolitical binary certainly is contestable. Most political, social, and cultural theorists would have real problems with the idea of there being a simple binary division of inside and outside spaces. Societies are not fixed in space or time, cultures move across borders, and state power is not solely restricted to the inside of state territories. Likewise, probably most geoscientists would have problems with the notion of a strict and stable distinction between land and sea. Spaces like wetlands, swamps, and barrier islands create a lot of juridical confusion.

Even if one accepts these binaries, they don't always pair up well. For instance, in the 17th century when the modern territorial imaginary was coming to the fore, cartographers had real problems representing the Grand Banks, the rich fishing grounds off the coast of Newfoundland. This was certainly–geophysically—water, ocean. It's wet. But geopolitically the region was thought of as a distinct place with distinct value. The Grand Banks couldn't be represented as land because it wasn't land, but it didn't really have all the social and political properties of water. Cartographers chose an intermediate representation: stippling.

The modern territorial imaginary doesn't apply that well anywhere, and it is particularly problematic in the Arctic, for a number of reasons. First of all, Arctic land doesn't have all of the "land like" functional properties. If what makes brown space "brown" is that it can be improved through agriculture and controlled and developed in all these ways that we have come to think of in the temperate zones, that's all much more problematic in the Arctic. Arctic water doesn't have all those "water like" properties. It's almost too simple to say, but when water is frozen instead of liquid the difference between water and land just is not as dramatic. The boundary is often not that well communicated in the Arctic; if it is all frozen and covered with snow, you often don't actually know if you are on land or water at a given time. The physical conditions are dynamic in both time and space, dynamic in time through seasonal cycles and also through climate change. Seasonal cycles of course happen but again they are particularly extreme in various ways in the Arctic, as is climate change. Also—and this is a strange one conceptually—but Arctic space is exceptionally dynamic space, because the Arctic itself is constantly moving around not just in geologic time, as exists in the rest of the world, but in the very experienced time of, say, shifting ice floes. So, as an example of this dynamism, both in time and space, T-3 no longer exists. Shortly after it was abandoned by the U.S. military, it floated around the north side of Greenland, came down the Davis Strait on the east coast of Greenland and dissipated into the Atlantic Ocean.

Finally, I want to finish up by reminding us that not only is the Arctic different because of its geophysical characteristics, but also because of its location. Indeed, it was the Arctic's location that ultimately led to the Escamilla case being thrown out on appeal. When Escamilla was found guilty he challenged it on several grounds, one of them being jurisdiction. The appeal said this shouldn't have been tried in a U.S. court. The appellate panel split three to three on the jurisdictional issue and they never issued a statement. So, it is still not known whether under U.S. Law an ice island is a ship, an island, a chunk of ocean or something else. One of the other grounds had to do with the instructions given to the jury. In the original trial, the jury was instructed by the judge that "the law of United States was applicable to this case in the same manner as it would be applicable to the crime committed in Northern Virginia, so you can just forget about T-3 other than for background." Well, the appellate panel commented that this instruction was in error. The appellate decision noted, "It would seem plain that what is negligent or grossly negligent conduct in the Eastern district of Virginia may not be negligent or grossly negligent on T-3 when it is remembered that T-3 has no governing authority, no police force, is relatively inaccessible from the rest of the world, lacks medical facilities and the dwellings lack locks. In short, absent self-restraint on the part of those stationed on T-3 and an effective group leader, T-3 is a place where no recognized means of law enforcement exist and each man must look to himself for immediate enforcement of his rights. Certainly all these factors are ones which must be considered by the jury given the problem of determining whether the defendant was grossly negligent."

To conclude, the Arctic changes our notion of the world in many ways. We think of the world as being divided into meta-continents that are separated by oceans. That vision changes when you look at things from a polar perspective. We see that the Arctic is a space that's provisional, ambiguous, indeterminate, dynamic, mobile, and at least from the perspective of southern capitals, remote. These are all characteristics that challenge the application of law and the assertion of sovereignty which are the sort of things that I tend to research, but I think they also present specific challenges for architecture and design because architecture, much like the state, has typically assumed backgrounds that are solid, stable, and static. And the Arctic is anything but.

NOTE:

1. For more on U.S. military activities on T-3, as well as the murder of Bennie Lightsy and the subsequent trial of Mario Escamilla, see Johanne Bruun and Phillip Steinberg, "Placing territory on ice: militarisation, measurement, and murder in the High Arctic," in *Territory Beyond Terra*, eds. Kimberley Peters, Phillip Steinberg, and Elaine Stratford, 147-164 (London: Rowman & Littlefield International, 2018).

Out of This World

GEOFF MANAUGH
Journalist, Curator, and Author of BLDGBLOG, USA

I want to start with the overall notion of urbanism and discuss what constitutes a city in the first place. Several years ago, before the global financial crisis hit, there was widespread talk that we were living through a "building boom." This was at the height of various super projects such as buildings in Dubai or OMA's CCTV headquarters in Beijing. Nearly every news cycle brought more stories about some new super city in the middle of nowhere. I mention all this because that same period was very conspicuously not referred to as an "architecture boom." But what would it mean to see an *architecture* boom? How would an architecture boom differ from a building boom, in any case, and is there a real difference?

One comment really struck me from an interview I recorded a number of years ago with architectural historian, Ole Bouman. Bouman is the former head of the Netherlands Architecture Institute and a writer and curator. He had written a paper arguing that it was a critical mistake to confuse what he called "large congregations of architecture" for actual cities. When I asked what he meant by this, he said something to the effect of, if you don't distinguish between real cities and large congregations of architecture—if you think that applying urban form is the same as building a city—then you have fundamentally misunderstood what cities are in the first place. To repeat that: you can have large congregations of architecture and still not have a city. It might look like a city, walk like a city, even smell like a city, but, in Bouman's terms, it's just bunch of buildings. There is no real "there," and certainly no city.

This reminds me of the new cliché: more than 50% of the human species now live in cities. You can't go to any architecture conference and not have at least one person mention this statistic. But that statistic is, in a sense, wrong. Those people are not living in "cities." In other words, the 51% of human beings who are now described as city dwellers or as urbanists are actually dwelling amongst "large congregations of architecture" and not inside cities at all. There are buildings everywhere but no cities to be seen. This brings us back to the central question of, "What is a city?" If we want to talk about Arctic urbanism for example, or Arctic cities, are we absolutely certain that we are talking about cities? Are we talking about urbanism or are we just talking about congregations of architecture, whether those congregations are large or small?

There is a very similar take on this same question in a great book by Paul Hirst, called *Space and Power*. In effect, Hirst asks the exact same question that Bouman did. Can we really say we are talking about cities when these places are, in Hirst's words, just "a dense concentration of built environment"? You could ask the question of basically anything from a refugee camp like Zaatari in Jordan to the instant cities of Chinese industrial urbanization, or even about peripheral "boomburbs" on the outer edge of Silicon Valley, Los Angeles, Washington, DC, or Houston.

More relevant to our conversation, you can ask the same question about Arctic extraction outposts, company towns in the far north that are built to service nearby mines and hydroelectric projects. Are these cities? Can we really talk about them in terms of urbanism? If not, what is actually happening out there? Hirst makes one important distinction worth highlighting here. For Hirst, a city is not just a certain minimum number of buildings or a certain quantity of architectural material. Rather, he writes, a "city can only be fully understood as a political institution," one "defined by its role in governance."[1] Hirst specifically notes that this does not include the large conglomerations that have grown up around highway intersections in the United States or the vast shantytowns attached to cities in developing countries. For Hirst, these latter examples lack what he calls coherent government. So, what is a city? What is governance? What is coherent government versus incoherent government? Can you have large congregations of architecture and not have a city, in the same way that perhaps you can have a city—a place of coherent government—without large congregations of architecture?

I now want to shift gears a bit and talk briefly about the research of Alessandra Ponte. Ponte is an architectural historian and a designer based at the University of Montréal. I had the pleasure of meeting her in 2015 in Tromsø, Norway, at a conference discussing Arctic urbanism.[2] I want to piggyback on Ponte's research, in a sense. Ponte presented some fascinating findings from studios she taught at the University of Montréal, including student field trips that they took to the pop up corporate towns and instant cities of the Canadian far north. These are places that are not literally Arctic, in the sense that they are actually physically south of the Arctic Circle, but Ponte's analysis even includes the idea of something being 'northern enough' to satisfy this same analysis. In any case, these are towns, villages, settlements, outposts, and cities built and run entirely by corporate entities. They are often then taken apart—physically dismantled—and effectively closed down whenever the nearby mine, dam, or other project is complete. We might say that these cities are erased.

There are a few details from Ponte's research that I want to highlight here. First of all, the towns are almost entirely privately run and operated. This means they do not have mayors. They do not have Canadian police. They have their own private security forces. They do not offer municipal amenities in the sense we might think of, such as libraries and museums. Although, Ponte pointed out, that this being Canada, most of them do have ice hockey rinks.

Figure 1: Known locally as the "wind screen," a residential superstructure blocks constant northern wind in the far northern Canadian town of Fermont.

Even more fascinating, though, was a small town called Fermont, which is owned and operated by ArcelorMittal, the international mining conglomerate. Fermont features a residential megastructure that Ponte described as being designed specifically to help block the constant northern wind [Figure 1]. The wall actually redirects the wind around the center of town and acts as a kind of weather-altering wall. It's known locally as the "wind screen" and it puts architecture to work by creating a local microclimate and thus making the site more hospitable for the residents.

But what is actually happening here? Is this urbanism? Is Fermont a city? Indeed, are any of these outposts cities in any recognizable sense? For someone like Paul Hirst, of course, the answer is obviously no: there is no coherent government involved, especially in a place like this, that is run by spreadsheet and funded almost entirely by commodity extraction, international investment, and venture capital. With that being the case, urbanism is therefore not the right discourse when discussing a place like this.

However, I want to suggest that these Arctic and sub-Arctic outposts are early indicators of a mutation in city form that is becoming more— not less—common. It's worth noting that, recently, there has also been a rapid rise of interest, mostly from financial publications and business magazines, in entirely privatized urban settlements. These quasi-cities go under a variety of names, including "charter cities". Other researchers—in particular, Keller Easterling—have been doing great work exploring the discourse of "the zone" – that is, the free trade zone or special economic zone that now serves as a kind of discursive portal through which various new types of urban and quasi-urban forms can be built and administered.[3] So, channeling our own inner Ole Bouman or Paul Hirst, we might say that these charter cities, corporate towns, extraction outposts, and special economic zones are experimental congregations of architecture, but that they are also forcing us to change what we call a city. While Hirst and Bouman might say those are not cities in any governmental or cultural sense, we might add that they are not cities yet. They are cities to come.

Figure 2: Cities are central to Elon Musk's vision for Mars settlement, something he seems to consider an existential imperative.

Finally, I want to suggest that these experimental cities, quasi-cities, and new popup corporate towns might have genuinely historic effects in the near future. Libertarian billionaire Elon Musk, who is one of the cofounders of PayPal and is now the CEO of both Tesla and SpaceX, recently gave an interview to *Aeon* magazine where he basically exhorted all of us to channel our energies and resources toward building cities on Mars. For Musk, it's a kind of an existential imperative for human survival that we expand beyond the Earth and start settling other planets [Figure 2]. Crucially, it's worth noting that Musk refers again and again to cities: cities are central to Musk's vision for Mars settlement and exploration. It is through cities that we will gain a foothold on the Red Planet and it is cities that will protect us or offer shelter from the alien environment.

Now, recall the example of Fermont. Fermont is a privately-owned extraction industry outpost in the remote northern wild of Canada and it is protected by its own weather-altering super wall. If you picture Fermont then you perhaps get a sense of what Musk really means when he uses the word "city." Cities on Mars will not be a new Paris or a second Manhattan or even a pop-up Chicago. A city on Mars means Fermont: it means a privately-run cluster of architecture without coherent government in sight.

What does it mean that the most marginal examples of urban or quasi-urban settlements here on Earth—these remote corporate outposts, pop-up villages, and company towns—might, in fact, become the de facto example of urbanism on other worlds? What are the political implications of the fact that the very types of settlements that seem to fall outside of Paul Hirst's and Ole Bouman's definitions of the city are precisely what is most likely to be built as a city in these extreme environments, again whether that is northern Canada, the Arctic, or Mars? Finally, if cities are, as Musk suggests, necessary tools for settling in hostile and remote environments, does this mean that urbanism is becoming an expeditionary tool? How does this change the most basic sense of what cities are meant to offer?

My overall point here is that we think we know what cities are today. We have a political definition for how to recognize urbanism when we see it and we think we are capable of differentiating places like San Francisco from a refugee camp or from an Arctic mining outpost. However, the new types of settlements in the far north, as we saw in Alessandra Ponte's work, let alone the speculative settlements on other worlds discussed by Elon Musk will eventually—and, I would say, quite fundamentally—upend our comfortable definitions of what constitutes a city. In fact, I will go further to say, it might someday be the case that only this new breed of pop-up expeditionary outposts and privately run instant cities will assume the mantle and the nomenclature of urbanism. If so, will any of us even recognize cities in the decades to come?

NOTES:

1. Paul Hirst, *Space and Power: Politics, War, and Architecture* (Cambridge; Malden, MA: Polity, 2005), 9.

2. This refers to the Arctic Frontiers conference held in January 2015 in Tromsø, Norway. Arctic Frontiers was an interdisciplinary event that sought "to explore the potential and converging powers of change in settlements, cities, and territories of the North." For more information, visit http://www.oculs.no/events/future-north-session-arctic-frontiers/ (Accessed 12 July 2018).

3. For more on the rise of the invisible rules that control the infrastructural and everyday spaces in cities, see Keller Easterling, *Extrastatecraft: The Power of Infrastructure Space* (London; New York: Verso, 2014).

Fundamentals

RE-THINKING EXTREMES

The environmental conditions in the Arctic create an enormous challenge for designing and constructing viable buildings and cities. As a region of geographic extremity, the Arctic exhibits radical cycles of transformation, where seasonal changes blur the distinction between solid and liquid, the conventional concept of biosphere is challenged, and the difference between day and night is erased or distorted. Although people have lived in the Arctic for millennia in nomadic or semi-nomadic groups that developed highly sophisticated adaptable systems for living, modern efforts to develop buildings and cities are short-lived, having begun only in the early part of the 20th century. These attempts have had varying degrees of success, from the creation of large industrial cities that foregrounded development through "trial by error" in the former Soviet Union, to scattered settlements and hub communities in North America that resemble a kind of Arctic suburbia, with detached single-family homes. Often, what these developments share in common is a brute force approach, whereby priorities placed on solving the logistical and technical challenges of development are based on models imported from the south, and augmented by engineered strategies and mechanical systems of climate control to overcome the extreme conditions.[2] In this chapter, we begin our search for an expanded design vocabulary for the Arctic by exploring fundamental properties and processes of the physical environment and use this knowledge to develop alternative design strategies. We seek an integrated approach that reasserts the importance of design—vis-à-vis architecture, landscape architecture, and urban design—to foreground social, cultural, and environmental priorities while simultaneously seeking functional and pragmatic designs. The goal is to develop new typologies of buildings, landscape interfaces and cities that are far more strongly integrated with Arctic context, reduce the over-reliance on mechanical systems, and to develop new spatial potentials for people who call the Arctic home. Can a new intelligence for the design of the built environment emerge that can more fully serve the needs of the inhabitants?

1
Walter Gropius, *Scope of Total Architecture* (London: Collier Books, 1962), 87.

2
Eb F. Rice, *Building in the North* (Fairbanks: Geophysical Inst. Of the University of Alaska, 1975), 10, 26, 34. There are some exceptions to this with design being foregrounded in the more moderate climates in Tromsø, Norway and the relatively affluent own of Longyearbyen in Svalbard, which was a former coal mining town.

"If you take, for instance, the basic difference imposed on … design by the climatic conditions, you will realize that diversity of expression can result from this fact alone if the architect will use the utterly contrasting indoor-outdoor relations of these two regions as focus for [their] design conception."[1]

A

2B
2C
2E
2F
2H
2I

Series 3

LOW CLEARANCE
MAXIMUM CLEARANCE

The ideas that were developed for the design of traditional homes in the Arctic by indigenous people are unmatched. With simple materials that were readily available, complex structural and material systems were developed that utilized sophisticated thermodynamic principles, allowing them to thrive for thousands of years in an extreme and dynamic environment. Their ideas for igloos and sod houses were deeply connected to the land and provided the means to mediate the extreme environmental conditions with little to no external energy input. Today, the built environment in the Arctic is best characterized by fixed settlements based on European ideas, often with poorly designed buildings imported from the south, heated with energy intensive mechanical systems, and completely decoupled from the context. These modern comforts have their roots in the transformation of the built environment after the advent of environmental control technologies and arrival of modernism in the early 20th century.

Prior to the invention of mechanical building systems after the industrial revolution, considerably more importance was placed on the design of buildings, which could "ameliorate those extreme conditions that are beyond the body's ability for adaptation."[3] Through consideration of siting, orientation, massing, structure, and material properties, the built environment could serve to mediate the climate by redirecting, transforming, storing, attenuating, and amplifying exterior material and energy flows. After the introduction of mechanical environmental control systems, architecture began to change and the potential of design to serve as an environmental mediator was replaced, providing an opportunity to completely decouple the architecture from its context; regional vernacular became increasingly irrelevant. "The more it conditioned, the more independent it became from exterior conditions. It became a manufactured rather than a mediated environment."[4]

In his seminal book, *Architecture of the Well-tempered Environment*, published in 1969, Reyner Banham embraced this new engineered reality, and critiqued the inertia of architecture to incorporate or

3
Michelle Addington, "Contingent Behaviours," *Architectural Design* 79, no. 3 (May/June 2009): 13. James Marston Fitch and William Bobenhausen, *American Building: The Environmental Forces That Shape It* (New York: Oxford University Press, 1999), 1.

4
Addington, "Contingent Behaviours," 13.

5
Reyner Banham, *Architecture of the Well-tempered Environment*, 2nd ed. (Chicago: University of Chicago Press, 1984)

6
Banham, *Architecture of the Well-tempered Environment*, 239.

7
Addington, "Contingent Behaviours," 14.

8
Inaki Abalos and Juan Herreros, *Tower and office: from modernist theory to contemporary practice* (Cambridge, MA; London: MIT Press, 2003); Kiel Moe, *Insulating modernism: isolated and non-isolated thermodynamics in architecture* (Basel; Boston: Birkhäuser, 2014), 12.

acknowledge its importance.[5] On the one hand, modernism, with its free façade and emphasis on glass and reinforced concrete, was largely enabled by the new technologies but was too preoccupied by the aesthetics of the new structural advances at the time.[6] On the other, "environmental management" and the delivery of conditions that would not be noticed became a new prerogative for the vast majority of buildings being constructed, and architecture was relegated to an afterthought in the mass production of "habitable volumes."[7] Within hermetically sealed environments, the principal requirement was to optimize the level of comfort until it became unnoticeable and constant. The energy crisis of the early 1970s and realization of the environmental consequences of CO_2 marked a shift away from the use of energy intensive mechanical systems in buildings. Efficiency metrics such as LEED were introduced to hold architects and engineers accountable. However, critique centered on the inability of architects to understand the full implications of energy and thermodynamics in the constructed environment, and lack of interest to develop a design agenda that went beyond simply increasing energy efficiency via higher performance insulation.[8]

Increasingly, the potential of buildings to mediate the environment has been re-introduced to augment mechanical systems and hybridized environmental control, leading to a reconfiguration of binary interior-exterior relationships and development of permeable gradients and buffers. Efforts to develop dynamic and responsive buildings have gained widespread attention with the increasingly available and affordable digital technologies and new material experiments.[9] An ability to modify the transfer of energy across the building envelope, based on diurnal or seasonal changes, is increasingly becoming a reality.[10] Flexibility of building massing in terms of adaptation, transformation, movability, and real-time interaction to adjust thermal mass, permeability, ventilation, and interior spatial configurations are also being explored.[11] Even further, ideas about modifying the microclimate surrounding buildings are increasingly becoming the new design norm.

9
Achim Menges, "Performative Wood: Integral Computational Design for Timber Constructions," in *reForm( ) – Building a Better Tomorrow: Proceedings of the 29th Annual Conference of the Association for Computer Aided Design in Architecture (ACADIA)*, eds. Tristan de Estree Sterk, Russell Loveridge, and Douglas Pancoast, 66-74 (Chicago: The School of the Art Institute of Chicago, 2009), 68-73.

10
R.C.G.M. Loonen, M. Trčka, D. Cóstola, and J.L.M. Hensen, "Climate adaptive building shells: State-of-the-art and future challenges," *Renewable and Sustainable Energy Reviews 25* (Sept. 2013): 485. Also see Marta Barozzi, Julian Lienhard, Alessandra Zanelli, and Carol Monticelli, "The sustainability of adaptive envelopes: developments of kinetic architecture," *Procedia Engineering 155* (2016): 275-284.

11
Branko Kolarevic, "Towards architecture of change," in *Building Dynamics: Exploring Architecture of Change*, ed. Branko Kolarevic, and Vera Parlac (London; New York: Routledge, 2015), 9,11. Also see Robert Kronenburg, *Flexible: Architecture that Responds to Change* (London: Laurence King, 2007).

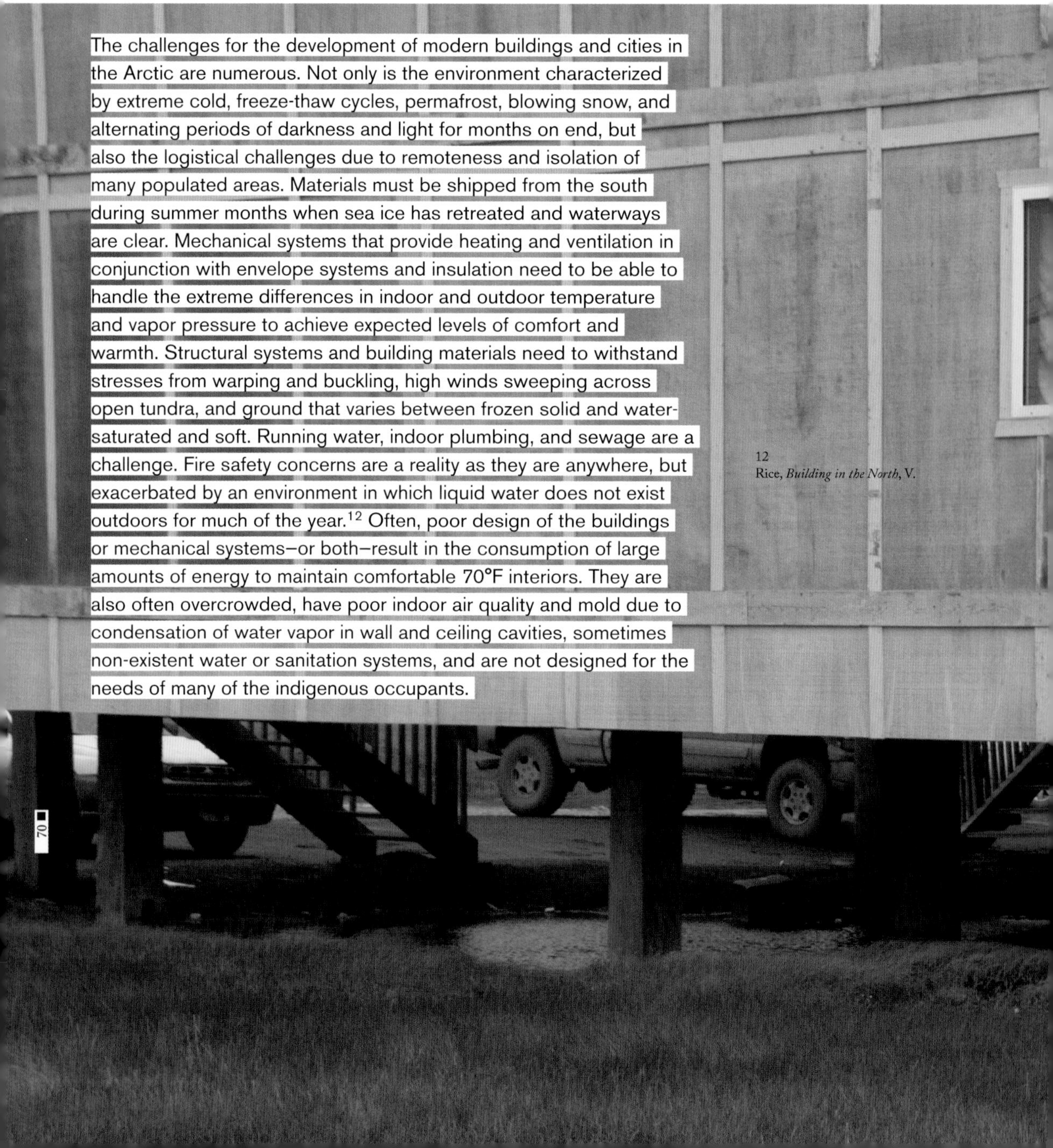

The challenges for the development of modern buildings and cities in the Arctic are numerous. Not only is the environment characterized by extreme cold, freeze-thaw cycles, permafrost, blowing snow, and alternating periods of darkness and light for months on end, but also the logistical challenges due to remoteness and isolation of many populated areas. Materials must be shipped from the south during summer months when sea ice has retreated and waterways are clear. Mechanical systems that provide heating and ventilation in conjunction with envelope systems and insulation need to be able to handle the extreme differences in indoor and outdoor temperature and vapor pressure to achieve expected levels of comfort and warmth. Structural systems and building materials need to withstand stresses from warping and buckling, high winds sweeping across open tundra, and ground that varies between frozen solid and water-saturated and soft. Running water, indoor plumbing, and sewage are a challenge. Fire safety concerns are a reality as they are anywhere, but exacerbated by an environment in which liquid water does not exist outdoors for much of the year.[12] Often, poor design of the buildings or mechanical systems—or both—result in the consumption of large amounts of energy to maintain comfortable 70°F interiors. They are also often overcrowded, have poor indoor air quality and mold due to condensation of water vapor in wall and ceiling cavities, sometimes non-existent water or sanitation systems, and are not designed for the needs of many of the indigenous occupants.

12
Rice, *Building in the North*, V.

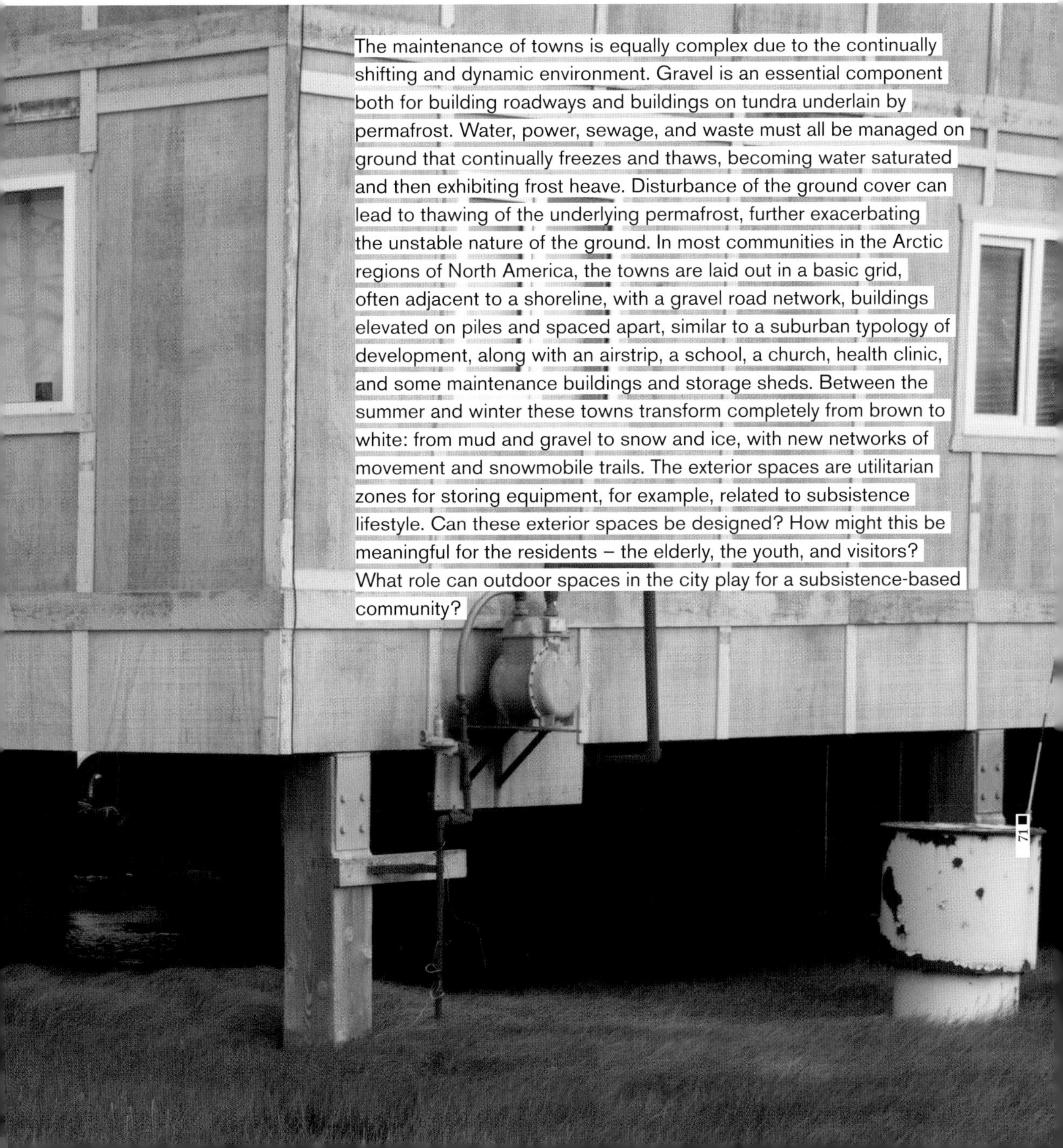

The maintenance of towns is equally complex due to the continually shifting and dynamic environment. Gravel is an essential component both for building roadways and buildings on tundra underlain by permafrost. Water, power, sewage, and waste must all be managed on ground that continually freezes and thaws, becoming water saturated and then exhibiting frost heave. Disturbance of the ground cover can lead to thawing of the underlying permafrost, further exacerbating the unstable nature of the ground. In most communities in the Arctic regions of North America, the towns are laid out in a basic grid, often adjacent to a shoreline, with a gravel road network, buildings elevated on piles and spaced apart, similar to a suburban typology of development, along with an airstrip, a school, a church, health clinic, and some maintenance buildings and storage sheds. Between the summer and winter these towns transform completely from brown to white: from mud and gravel to snow and ice, with new networks of movement and snowmobile trails. The exterior spaces are utilitarian zones for storing equipment, for example, related to subsistence lifestyle. Can these exterior spaces be designed? How might this be meaningful for the residents – the elderly, the youth, and visitors? What role can outdoor spaces in the city play for a subsistence-based community?

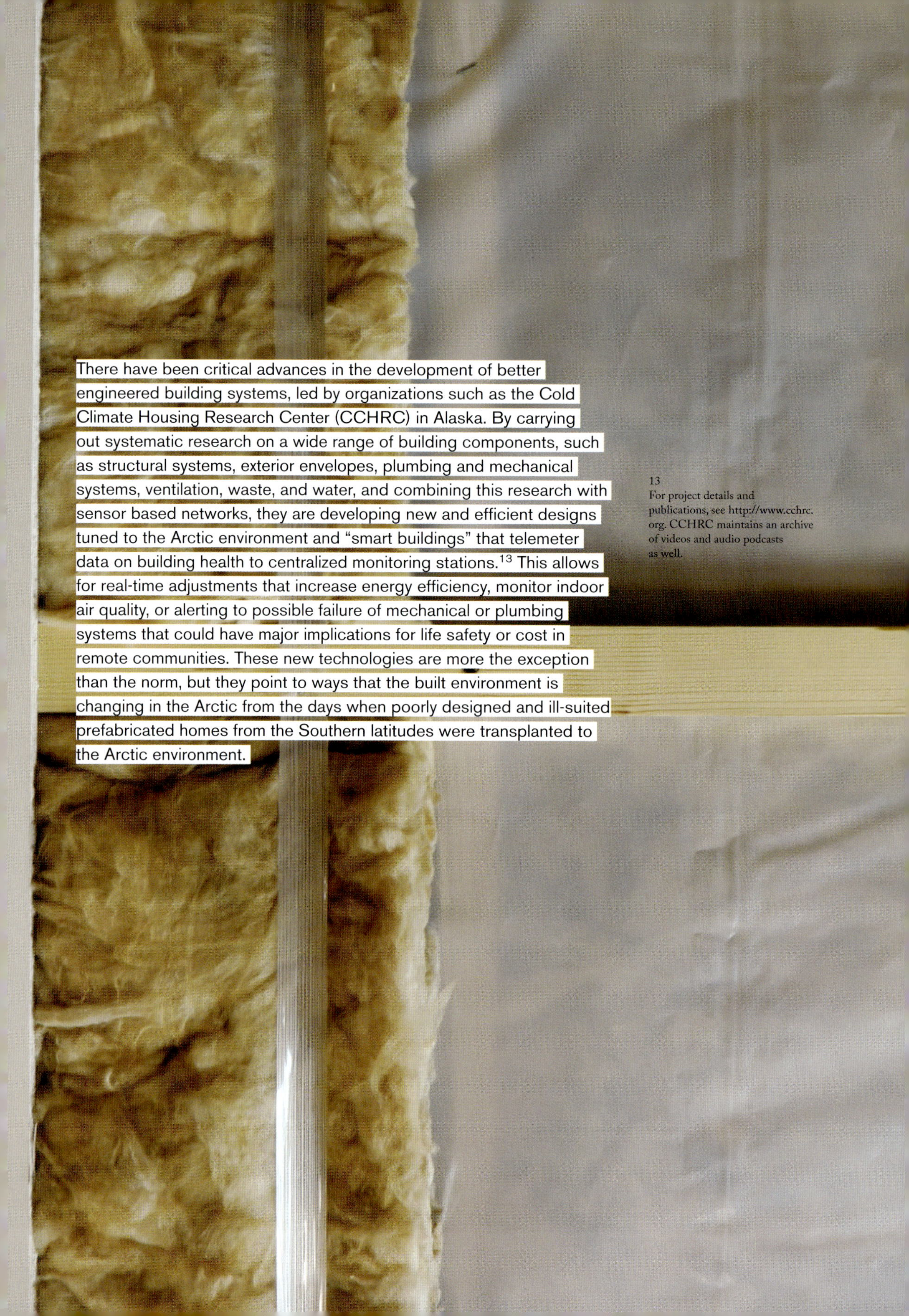

There have been critical advances in the development of better engineered building systems, led by organizations such as the Cold Climate Housing Research Center (CCHRC) in Alaska. By carrying out systematic research on a wide range of building components, such as structural systems, exterior envelopes, plumbing and mechanical systems, ventilation, waste, and water, and combining this research with sensor based networks, they are developing new and efficient designs tuned to the Arctic environment and "smart buildings" that telemeter data on building health to centralized monitoring stations.[13] This allows for real-time adjustments that increase energy efficiency, monitor indoor air quality, or alerting to possible failure of mechanical or plumbing systems that could have major implications for life safety or cost in remote communities. These new technologies are more the exception than the norm, but they point to ways that the built environment is changing in the Arctic from the days when poorly designed and ill-suited prefabricated homes from the Southern latitudes were transplanted to the Arctic environment.

13
For project details and publications, see http://www.cchrc.org. CCHRC maintains an archive of videos and audio podcasts as well.

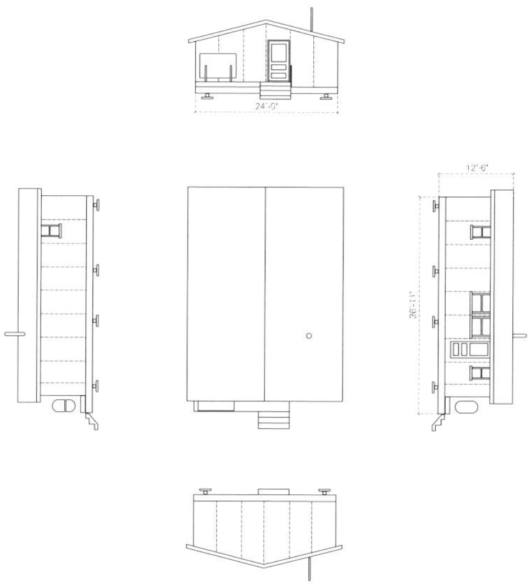
24'-5"
12'-6"
36'-11"

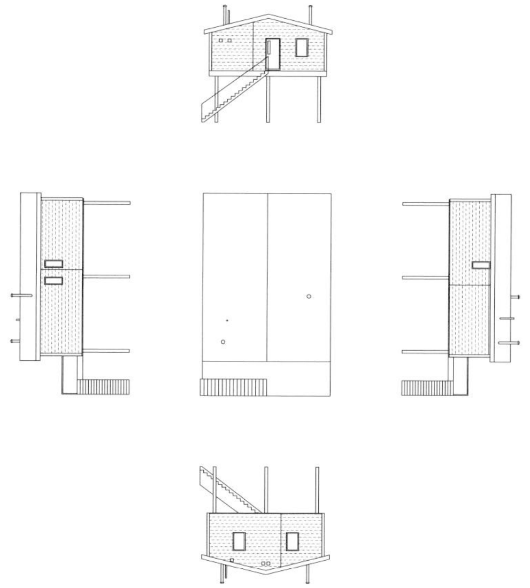

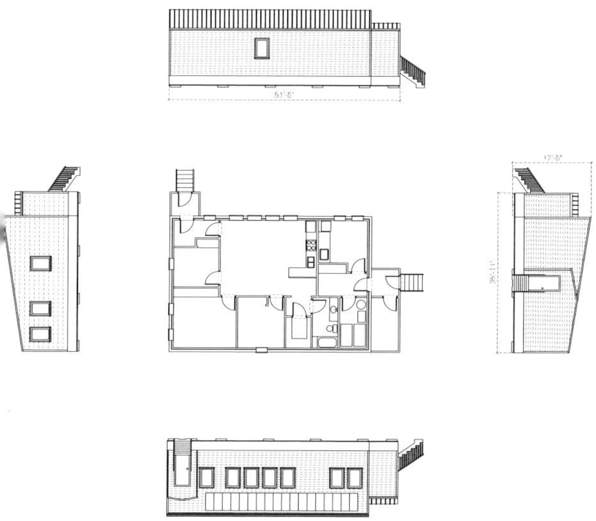
51'-5"
17'-5"
35'-11"

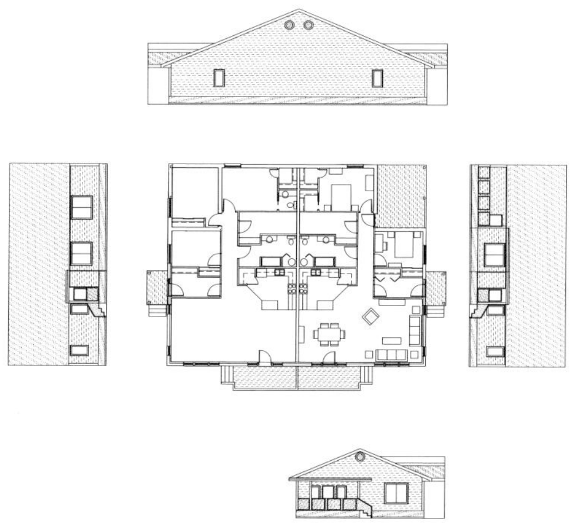

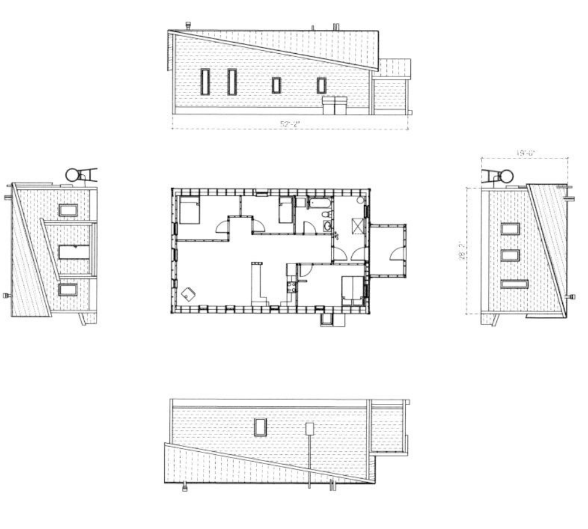
52'-2"
15'-6"
26'-2"

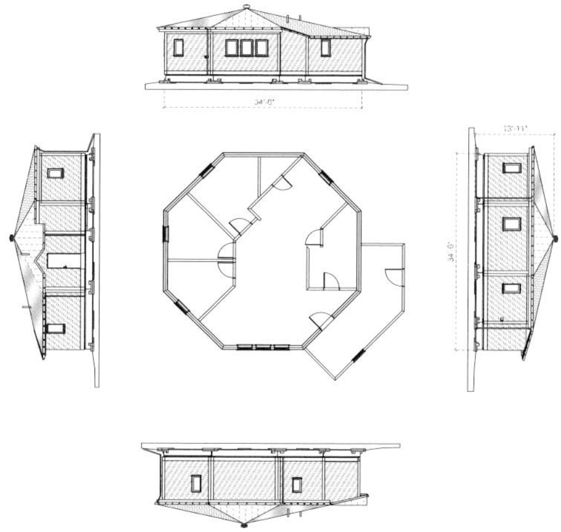
34'-0"
13'-11"
34'-0"

The resulting outcome of engineering and logistical challenges in the Arctic is a diminished role for architecture, landscape architecture, and urban design. Design innovation resides largely in MEP and structural systems, which are hidden from view, and are often based on taking conventional building typologies and either embedding new technologies to make them more efficient and cost-effective, or adopting a strictly formal approach that is still heavily reliant on engineered systems that perpetuates binary indoor-outdoor relationships. The approach adopted by the Arctic Design Group is not one against engineering but towards a greater synthesis between engineering and design, as well as science and design. What if the level of sophistication that has been developed for insulated wall sections was also directed toward the phenomenological aspects of an entire building or community? What if the goal was not to only design for energy efficiency, but to strengthen the cultural or social interactions of inhabitants? Can the design of the built environment become more integral to the Arctic and people who live there? The challenge is beyond technical problem-solving, it is the creation of new paradigms that merge modern building systems with the needs and identity of people, and the potential of design to mediate the climate by redirecting, transforming, storing, attenuating, and amplifying exterior material and energy flows.

Such an approach was most successfully developed by architect Ralph Erskine, who is arguably the best known northern architect. His careful analysis and study of the relationship between buildings and climate in northern Sweden led to a series of important projects that merged environmental and social concerns. A central feature of his work was to reconnect and strengthen the relationship between people and the environment by considering simple design elements such as building-ground interface, outdoor seating, windows, and exterior cladding,

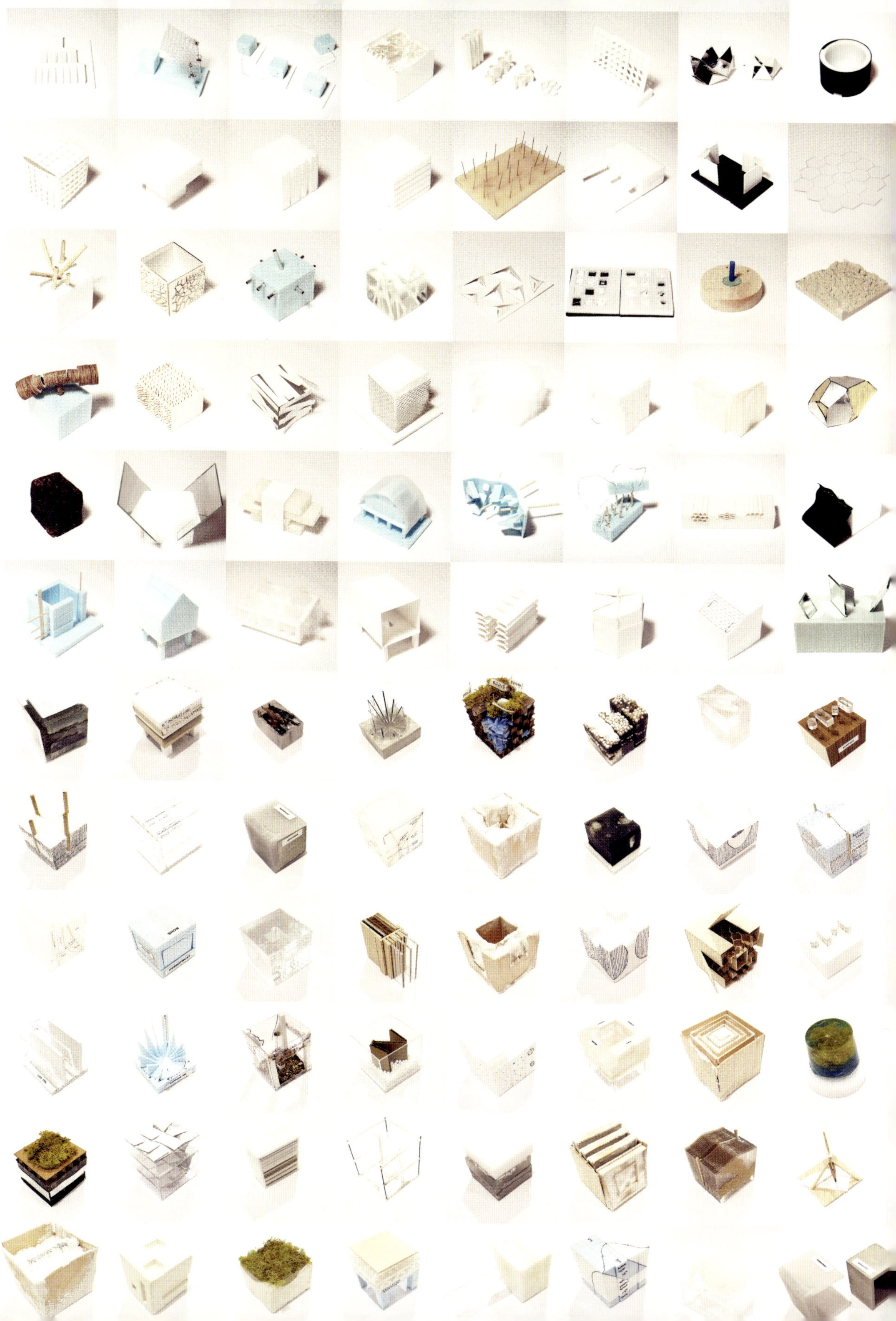

THERMAL WRAP

and microclimates. For Erskine, architecture and town planning was a means to live symbiotically with the natural environment, to create new efficiencies, and to use the formal and spatial language that resulted as a *cultural catalyst.*[14] Starting with simple designs for a compact house he built for himself, Erskine explored the potentials of compact building massing, heat storage, and siting to develop an efficient and adaptable design for cold climates. Later projects began to take on the role as climate modifiers at an urban scale, such as in Arctic Canada, as they amplified or attenuated the cold climate conditions where needed for the residents. Despite the criticism he received for the design for a "culturally integrated" new town for Resolute (74°N), apart from early Soviet planners, Erskine's efforts to merge environmental and cultural considerations in town planning and to search for new urban forms in the Arctic still remain a worthy example.

14
Matthew Jull, "Toward a Northern Architecture: The Microrayon as Arctic Urban Prototype," *Journal of Architectural Education 70*, no. 2 (Sep. 2016): 218. Also see Matthew Jull, "South Camp Inn," *The Site Magazine*, November 2017, 48.

A comprehensive summary of design principles and concerns for the built environment in the Arctic was developed by Harold Strub in his book *Bare Poles.*[15] Based on experience working as an architect in northern Canada, Strub provides an overview of information about town planning and the design of building components–vapor barriers, roofs, floors, window frames, and doorways–and explains the effects of sunlight, temperature, wind, rain, snow, and humidity on these components as well as on construction materials. Strub also identifies three key design deficiencies in Arctic settlements: the programming of the built environment; the shape, location, and orientation of buildings within communities; and the construction and maintenance of the building envelope, which contains and regulates a comfortable environment for the user. Together, this work forms an important starting point for the development of ideas about expanding the capacity of design in the Arctic environment.

15
Harold Strub, *Bare Poles: Building Design for High Latitudes* (Ottawa: Carleton University Press, 1996). The cultural narratives and design principles described in *Bare Poles* are adapted into drawings in the following pages.

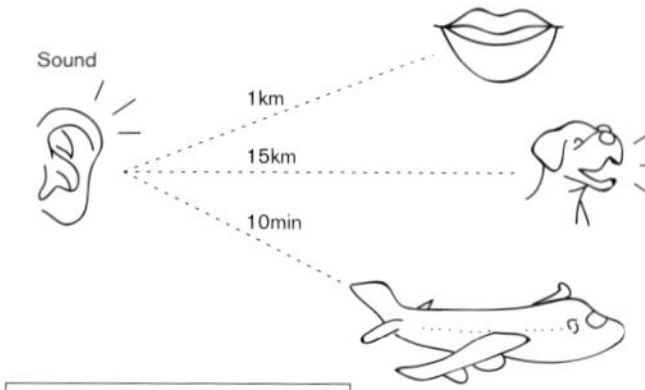

In cold temperatures, sound travels far. The hum of an airplane can be heard 10 min before seeing it.

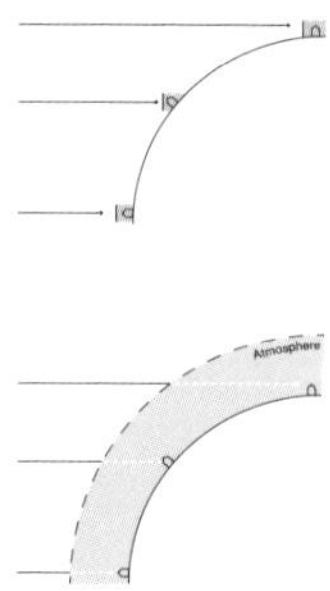

The closer to the equator, sunlight is focused on horizontal surfaces. The closer to the poles, sunlight is focused on vertical surfaces.

At higher latitudes, the atmosphere absorbs more energy from sunlight.

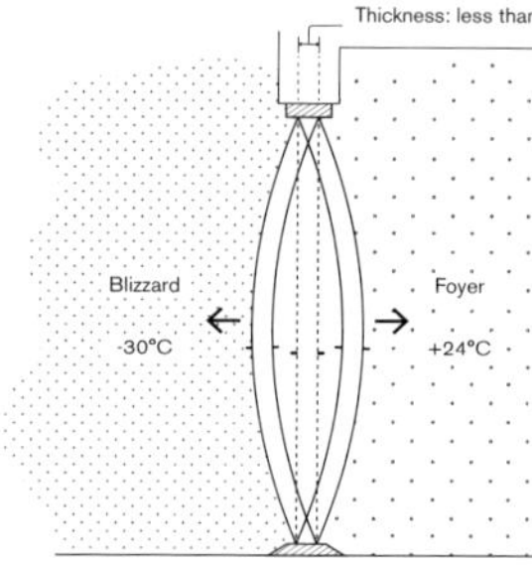

Building materials must be properly packaged to survive the harsh winter.

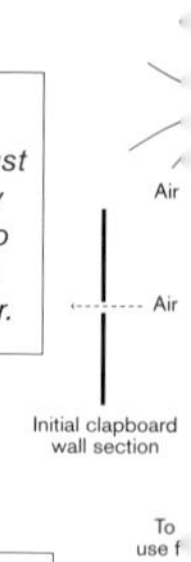

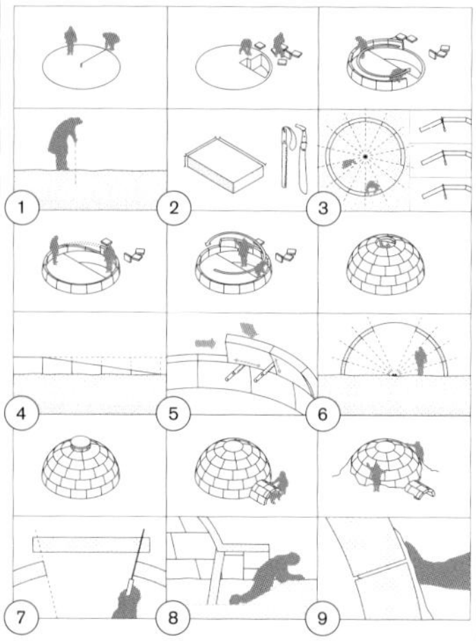

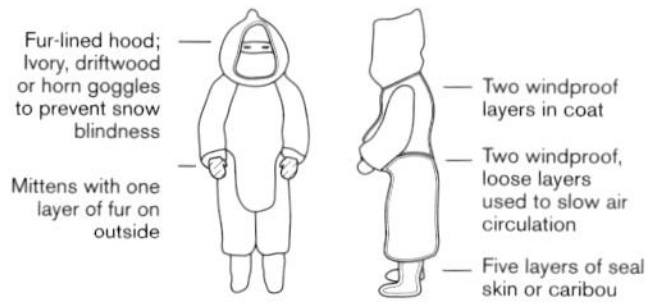

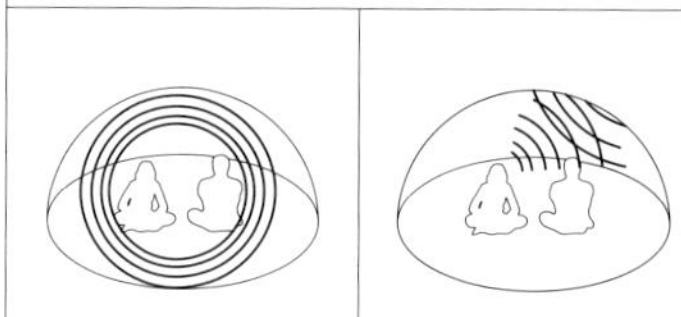

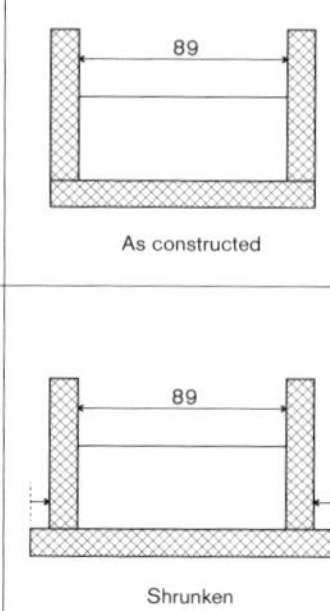

At least one edge of the settlement must reach the sea, river, or lake.

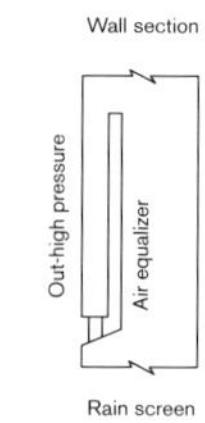

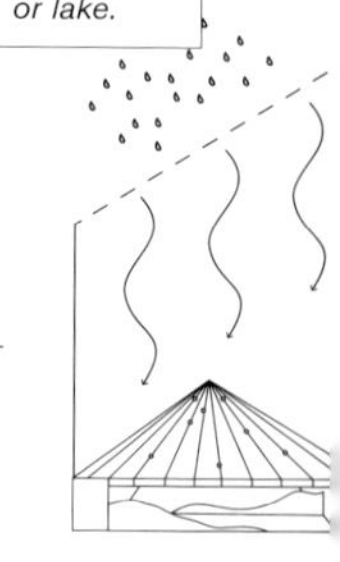

Rain barrier prevents the building assembly and structure from ge

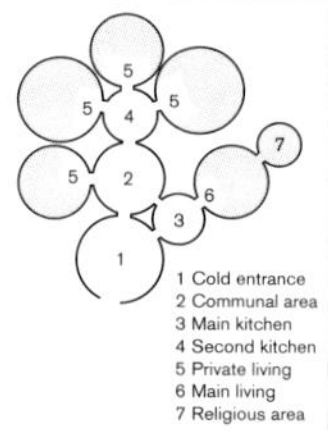

Families cluster in a semicircle, each home about 5m apart. Entrances are parallel to the wind so that air currents clear away snowdrifts.

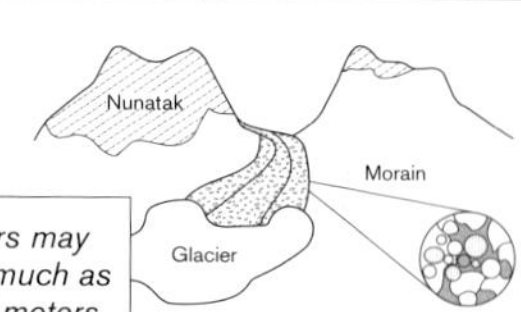

Glaciers may shift as much as several meters a week, leaving behind a trail of moraine.

The igloo can come in several sizes but the average Eskimo igloo is said to be about 3 to 4 meters and can comfortably house 5 adults.

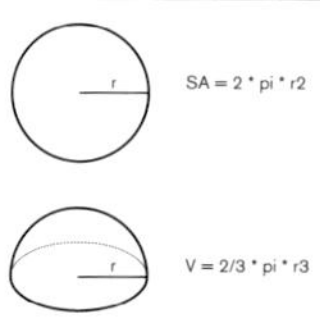

The greater the difference between outside and inside conditions, the smaller the shelter.

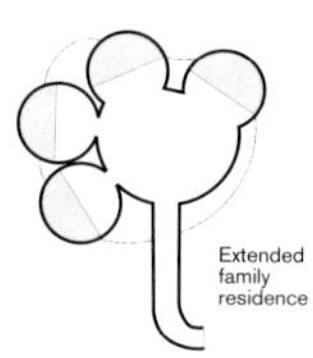

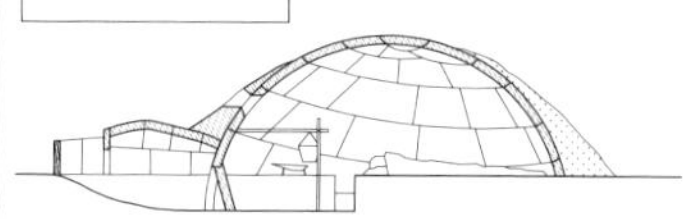

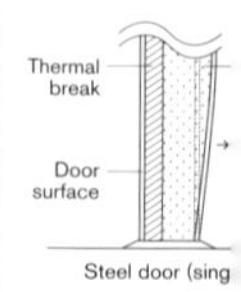

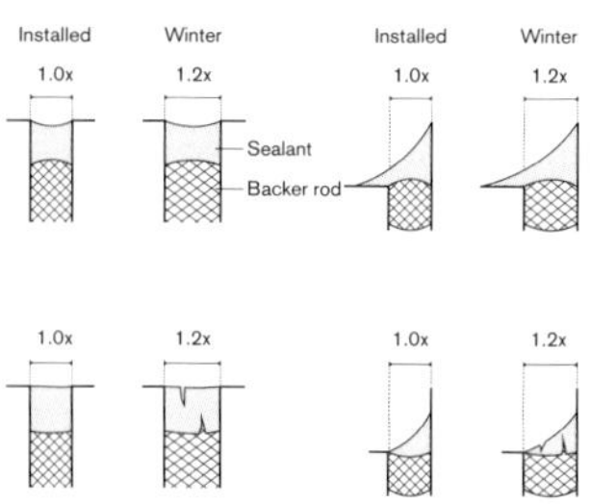

Although low angle sunlight has a minor impact on horizontal surfaces, vertical or steeply sloped surfaces catch sunlight at high angles of incidence. The surface temperature of the membrane may exceed +50°C.

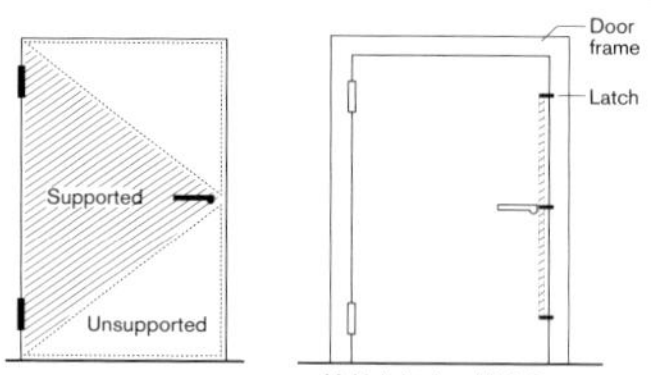

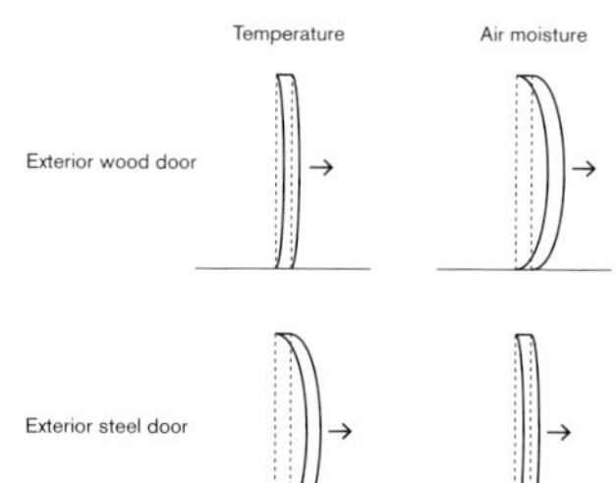

For joints t are subject movement, shape of the s is as importa the durability material.

Post-constru shrinkage of or green wo causes crack

Raised foundations help navigate unstable ground conditions.

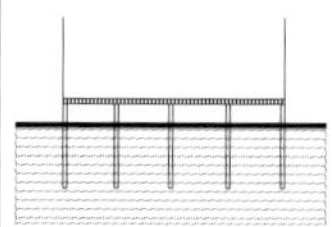

Wood is more reactive to air moisture content than temperature.

Temperature of the membrane may exceed +50°C in summer and fall below -40°C in winter. This variation in temperature causes more expansion and contraction than most membranes can stand.

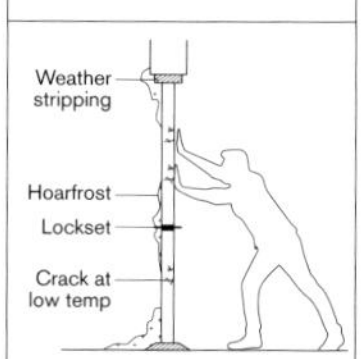

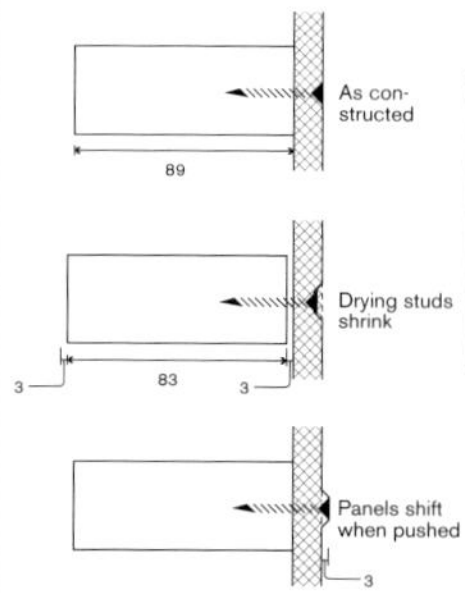

The door warps because of unequal thermal stresses on either side.

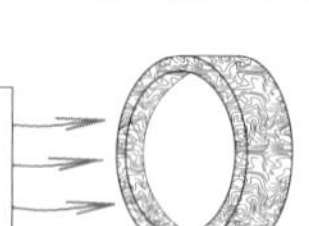

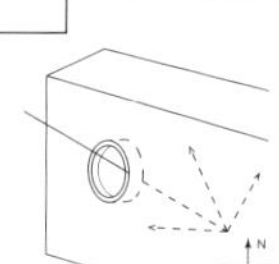

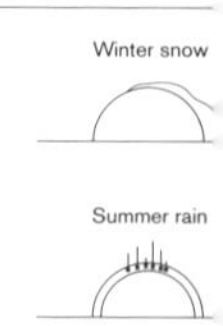

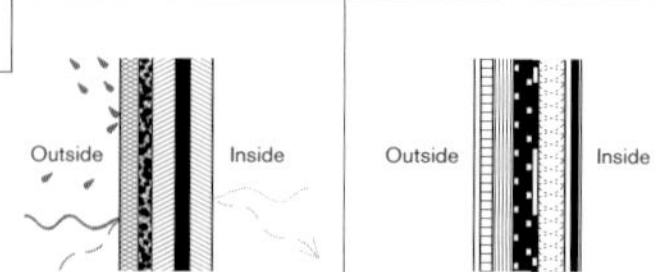

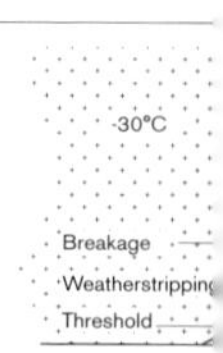

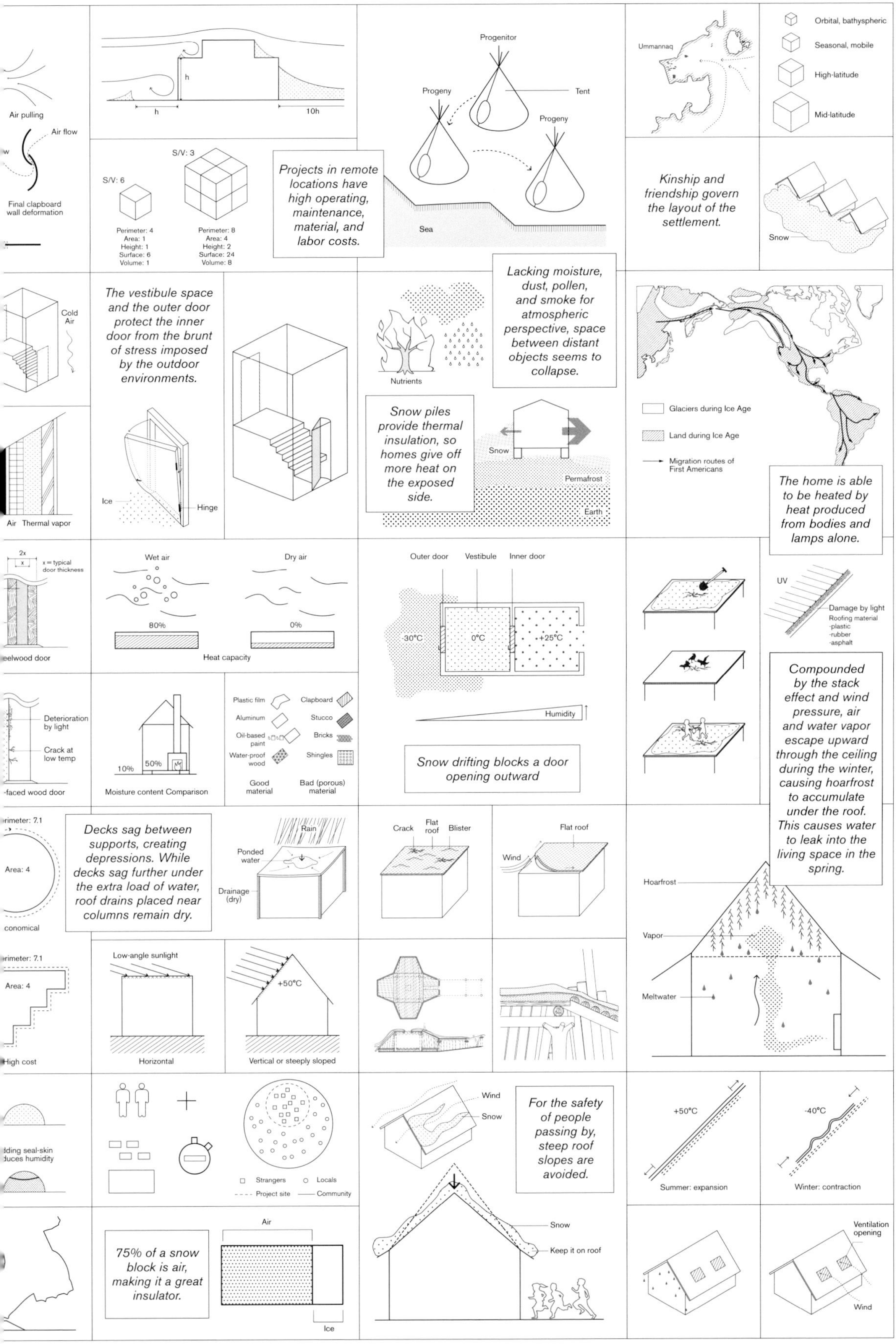

Projects in remote locations have high operating, maintenance, material, and labor costs.

Kinship and friendship govern the layout of the settlement.

The vestibule space and the outer door protect the inner door from the brunt of stress imposed by the outdoor environments.

Lacking moisture, dust, pollen, and smoke for atmospheric perspective, space between distant objects seems to collapse.

Snow piles provide thermal insulation, so homes give off more heat on the exposed side.

The home is able to be heated by heat produced from bodies and lamps alone.

Snow drifting blocks a door opening outward

Compounded by the stack effect and wind pressure, air and water vapor escape upward through the ceiling during the winter, causing hoarfrost to accumulate under the roof. This causes water to leak into the living space in the spring.

Decks sag between supports, creating depressions. While decks sag further under the extra load of water, roof drains placed near columns remain dry.

For the safety of people passing by, steep roof slopes are avoided.

75% of a snow block is air, making it a great insulator.

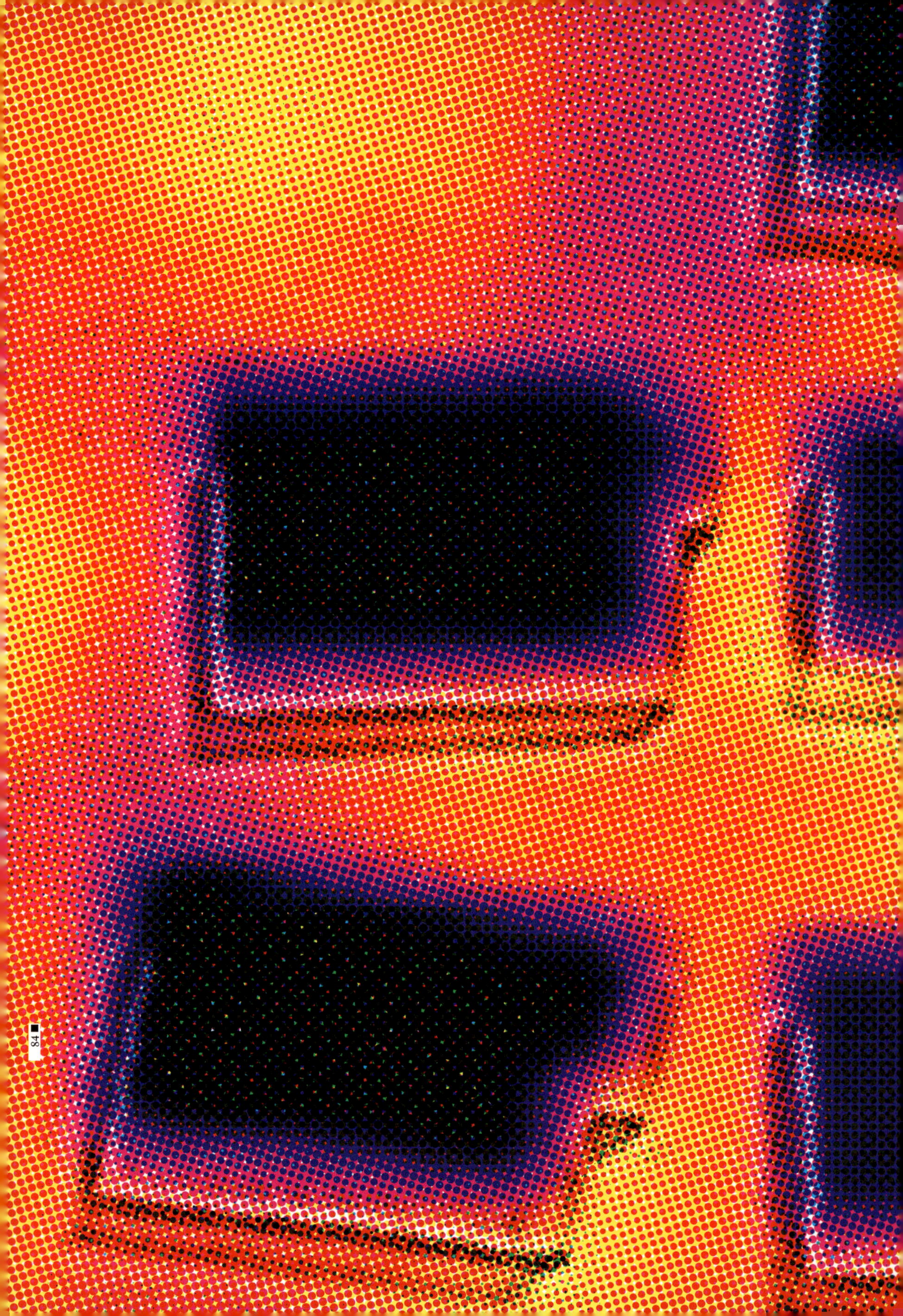

METHODOLOGIES FOR ENVIRONMENTAL RECALIBRATION

An important part of the Arctic Design Group's design research is a rigorous investigation into environmental systems, processes, and formations unique to the Arctic environment. Various mechanisms of living, abiotic, and phenomenological agents such as heat, light, wind, water, and permafrost, and their dynamics are studied, on the one hand, and are further tested materially, physically, and temporally for design at the human-perceivable scale, on the other. In this frame, we aim to understand the processes that govern and shape the physical environment, and explore the agency of design to reconfigure, transform, or regulate these conditions by strategically tapping into them. An example is studying the phase changes of water, from the mechanical effects of freezing and expanding, to the optical qualities of vapor and condensation. Although the five elements of heat, light, wind, water, and permafrost ground mentioned in the chapter are not independent from each other, we foreground the importance of each in several key topics of influence for future design development, such as indoor-outdoor, structure-ground, summer-winter, or water-land.

Drawing, physically modelling, and digitally simulating the often invisible, transient, and ephemeral qualities generate development of a greater intuitive understanding of their properties at the intersection of material effects and performance. What sets design research apart from science, albeit informed by science, is its ultimate emphasis to foreground human subjectivity and creative agency. A scientific experiment is an operation carried out under controlled conditions in order to support, refute, validate, or establish a hypothesis. In design, an experiment can be understood as a designed procedure capable of discovering and testing design questions. What evolves out of these studies is the development of design language that can be tested further in specific sites and conditions in Arctic cities. This investigation moves beyond the observational into the propositional. The process of translating the physics of the environment into a vehicle for design requires active and iterative abstractions and interpretations of those physical systems. The development of this knowledge delineates design concept and purpose—performative, programmatic, affective, and so on—grounded and specific to the Arctic environment, and continues to inform design process and refinement as additional layers of cultural contexts are considered.

HEAT

Life in the Arctic could perhaps best be described as a struggle for heat. Temperatures are below freezing for much of the year, and for most living organisms, survival depends on generating and storing heat. For humans, with a narrow range of body temperature between 97-99°F, living in buildings with indoor air temperatures around 70°F, an outdoor environment which drops below -40°F creates extreme challenges. Buildings are often spaces for survival. Moving from an interior warm, comparatively humid interior, to the dry cold, mid-winter, air of a polar night with a temperature differential of 100°F or more can be almost uncanny. Understanding the implications of such extreme thermal conditions, and the material and structural relationships that have evolved, both in the natural environment and from indigenous cultures, has important consequences and opportunities for design of the built environment.

The three modes of heat transfer–conduction, convection, and radiation–each play important roles in regulating thermal conditions. Conduction is physically expressed through a rich palette of materials that either retard or accelerate the flow of heat. Insulation has many forms – from fur to foam to vegetation, in multiple layers or as solid massive blocks that can have a wide range of sensorial effects. To observe "steam" that develops in -40°F air above exposed 28°F ocean water in the middle of winter in the Arctic ocean is to understand ice as a warm thermal blanket. Conversely, the intelligence of fur as a means to slow heat flow and create thickened thermal boundary layers becomes plainly evident. Convection, induced for example through cold vertical surfaces such as exterior walls or windows, creates three dimensional air or fluid cells, while the opposite - stable stratification - results in horizontal bands of warm air overlying cold in area areas of topographic variation, or in traditional indigenous homes. Heat in the form of infrared wavelengths of electromagnetic radiation emitted from the sun and other bodies at different temperatures, provides a third source of heat transfer and depends largely on albedo: bright and reflective vs dark and absorptive.

THERMAL FACTORS

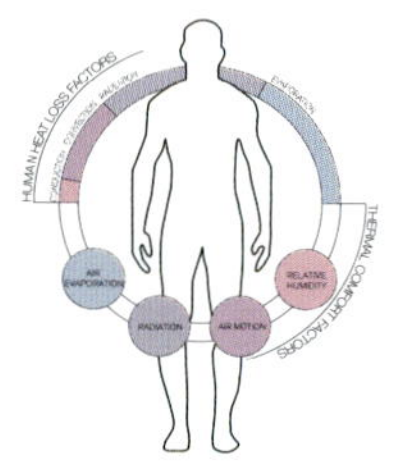

BODY TEMPERATURE

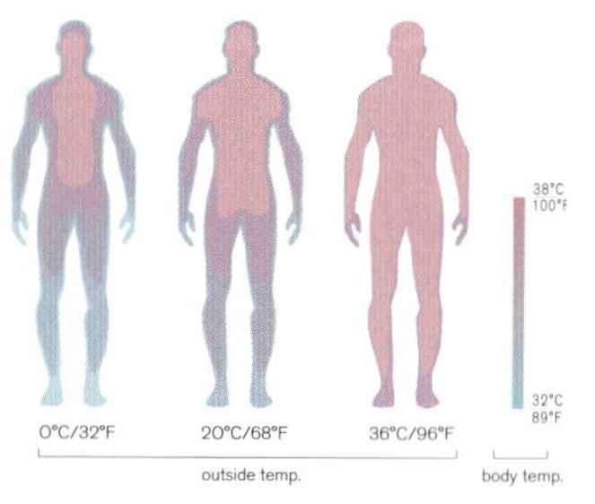

APPARENT TEMPERATURE

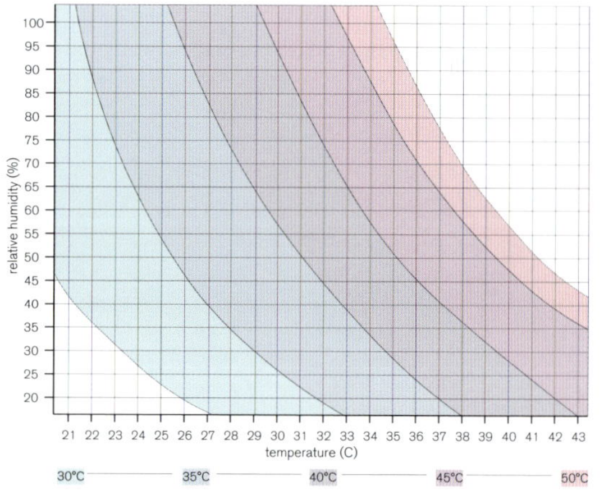

MECHANISM OF HEAT TRANSFER

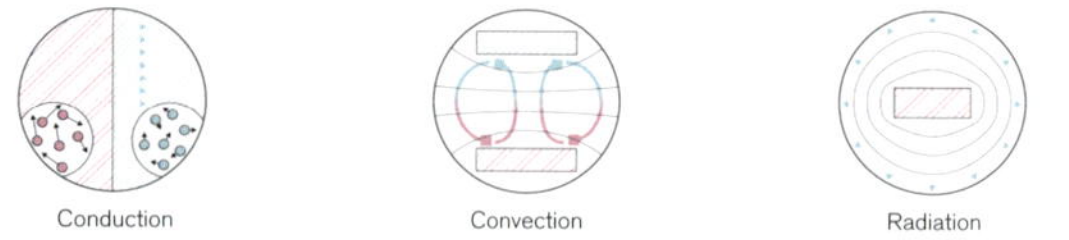

THERMAL DEFICIENCIES

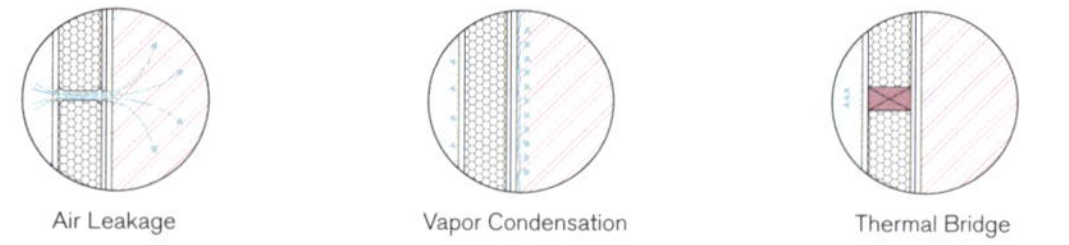

LIGHT

The naturally occurring visible and infrared light such as solar radiation plays an important role in the biosphere, transfer of thermal energy, visual perception, and human psychology. As the defining feature of the Arctic Circle, the presence or absence of light for portions of the year makes the polar regions unique on Earth. The high latitude of the Arctic has two primary effects on light, which are important for the environment. Much of the energy of incoming solar radiation is blocked by the atmosphere, and the angle of incidence of light is highly oblique, with the sun often low to the horizon, and shining during the summer from a full 360-degree position. Shadows are long and sunlight penetrates deep into buildings at low angle.

Changes in environmental characteristics have significant and specific effects on solar radiation. The albedo of ground materials varies between dark brown mud and gravel in towns, lighter green of low lying tundra vegetation, and highly reflective ground surfaces of snow and ice in winter. These properties, combined with the influence on optical conditions from gradients of temperature and air density at interfaces between ground, ocean, sea ice, buildings, and air create a multitude of visual and spatial effects. Consideration of indoor and outdoor material and spatial conditions can make use of these characteristics. The position of windows, the materiality of building envelopes, and condition of ground cover, can amplify or retard the absorption of energy, the illumination and visual qualities of space, and the health of occupants. On glazed surfaces the interaction with frost, fog, ice, and snow could become an entirely new design vocabulary. Periods of twenty four-hour darkness or sunlight during the winter and summer are equally important to regulate patterns of sleeping and waking. A shifting outdoor environment of reflected and indirect light on snow and ice transitions to continuous glare of sunlight through the seasons. Garbage bags taped across windows at night are a common sight during the summer to block out light. Artificial daylight lamps are common during the winter to promote health and well-being.

INSOLATION

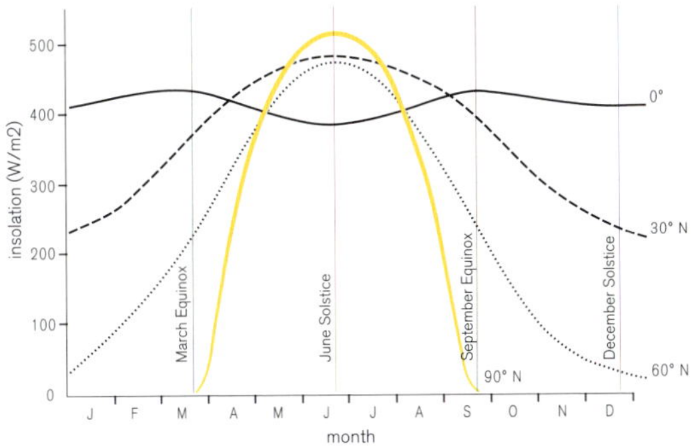

DAYLIGHT - TWILIGHT - NIGHT LENGTHS

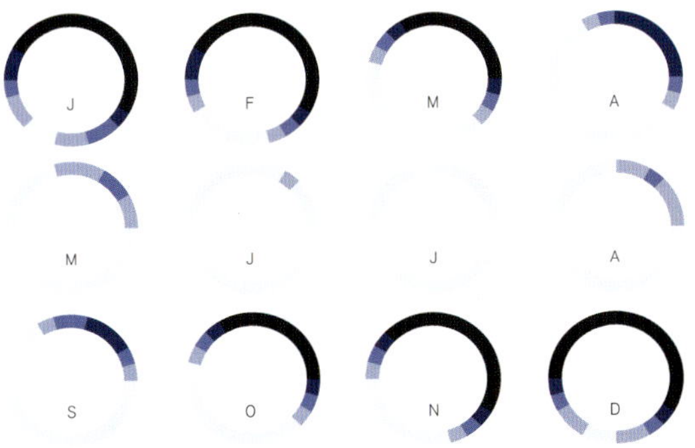

ALBEDO COEFFICIENT

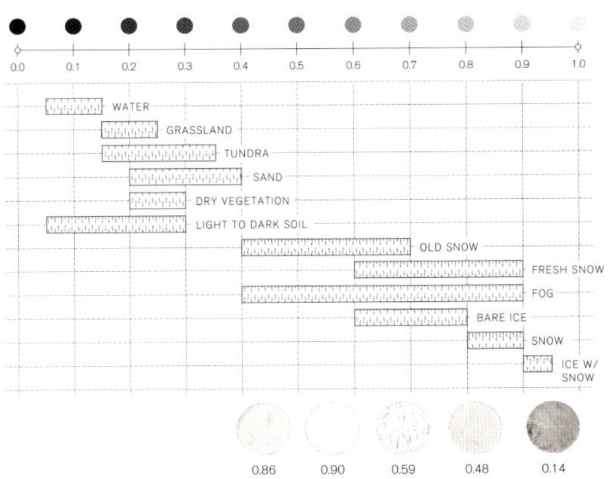

MESH
WHITE FOAM
MESH
FABRIC
BLACK FOAM
MESH
WHITE FOAM
FABRIC
WHITE FOAM
MESH
FABRIC
BLACK FOAM
FABRIC
WHITE FOAM
WHITE FOAM
WHITE FOAM
MESH
FABRIC
BLACK FOAM
WHITE FOAM
WHITE FOAM

FABRIC
BLACK FOAM
MESH
WHITE FOAM
MESH
FABRIC
FABRIC
BLACK FOAM
FABRIC
WHITE FOAM
MESH
FABRIC
FABRIC
BLACK FOAM
WHITE FOAM
WHITE FOAM
MESH
FABRIC

WIND

Living with wind is one of the principle features of life in the Arctic. In the largely treeless context of high latitudes, the flow of air is often unobstructed; wind plays a critical role in shaping the environment through either material or energy flows. Wind is the primary amplifier for heat loss by the efficient thinning of thermal boundary layers through advective transport. It is also the primary mechanism for transporting materials such as snow and dust, shifting sea ice and generating waves that erode shorelines and creating storm surges. Along coastlines, the frictional shifting from wind of a thousand miles of sea ice can pile up and inundate the shoreline. Close to the ground, the airflow regime can change from laminar to turbulent due to interactions with topography, vegetation, buildings, ocean, and sea ice. As the rate of air flow is reduced and disrupted, its ability to entrain material decreases, resulting in accumulation and deposition around obstacles. Even though much of the Arctic is a desert, the ability of wind to entrain small amounts of snow over vast distances can result in large snowdrifts. Indigenous people welcome wind as a means to scour away snow from communities, which can be aided by lifting buildings off the ground, as they are in regions of permafrost soil, allowing wind to pass underneath; such concerns are important for the maintenance of a town. European tendencies for town planning have been to block wind, in an effort to increase the comfort of residents outdoors. Such an approach can also reduce the loss of heat from exterior envelopes of buildings during the winter. But the consequences are snowdrifts, which can be unending and completely immobilize towns. To ameliorate this problem, snow fences are built around town perimeters, upstream of the prevailing wind direction, in order to slow down airflow and causing the snowstream to drop its entrained load before arriving in the town. Despite the challenges, wind is a readily available resource in the Arctic. Speeds up to 40-60 mph are measured monthly in northern Alaska, for instance, and this force catalyzes the shaping of the ground's geometry, the shorelines, and the boundaries between buildings and landscapes. Harnessing this resource is an important design element in Arctic towns.

LAMINAR VS. TURBULENT AIR FLOWS

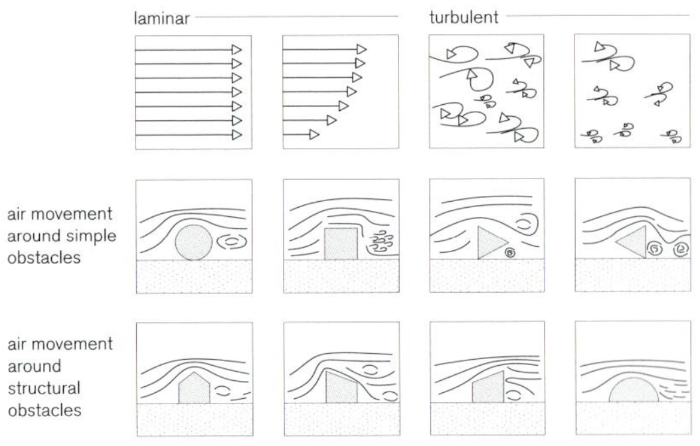

AEOLIAN TRANSPORT

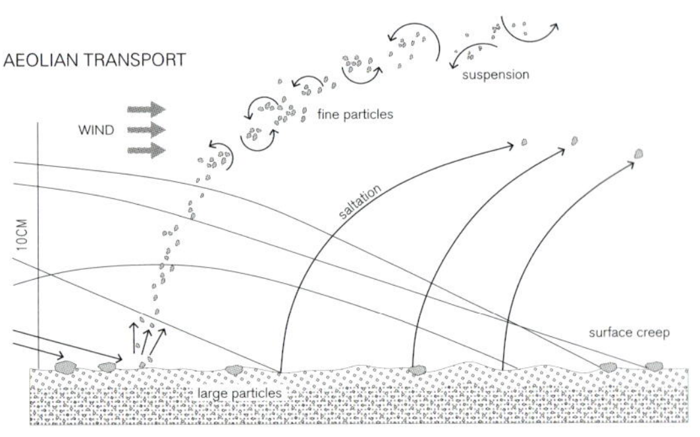

SNOW FENCE

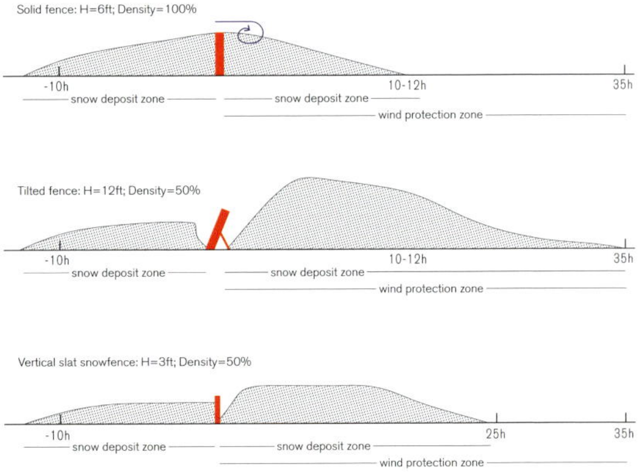

WATER

TYPES OF SNOW

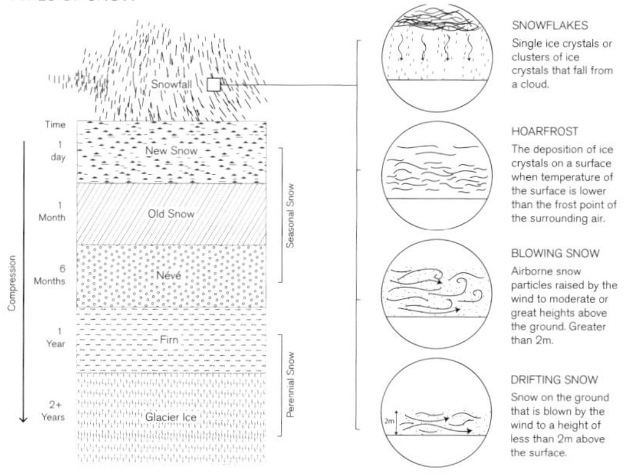

SNOW PROCESS

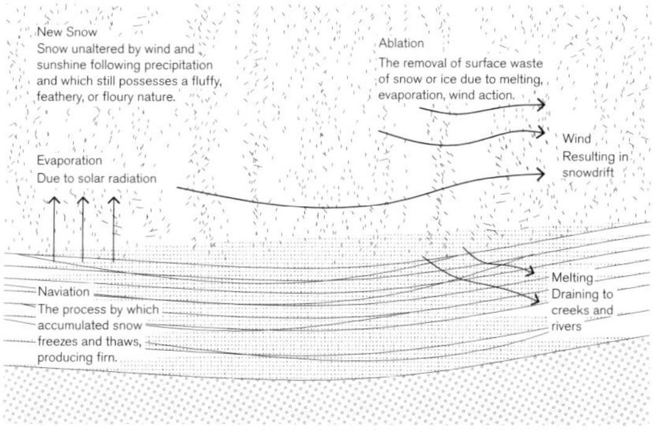

WATER DYNAMICS IN LITTORAL ZONE

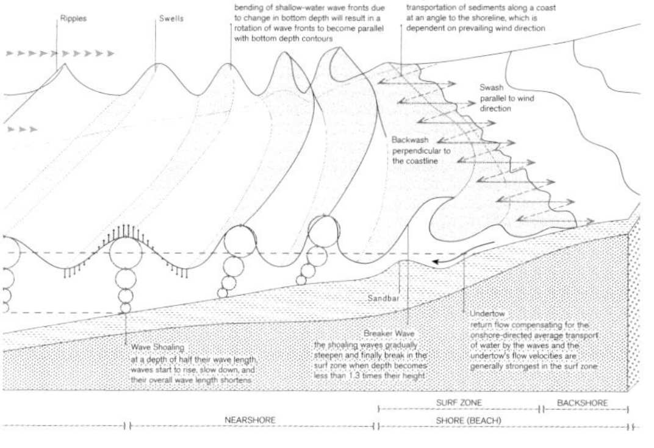

Despite large parts of the Arctic being classified as a polar desert, with less than ten inches of annual precipitation, and unlike deserts in hot climates, water is ubiquitous in oceans, lakes, rivers, streams, snow, and ice. In its various physical states of liquid, solid, and gas, water plays an aggressive role in continuously shaping and transforming the Arctic environment. In the extreme cold of winter, ocean water freezes, forming vast tectonic expanses of shifting, fracturing, and buckling ice that extends far beyond the horizon. The boundary between land and water is blurred and transformed into an endless landscape of ice and snow. Processes of freezing and thawing buckle the ground through the enormous forces that are exerted as liquid water expands when solidifying. Fractures in sea ice release clouds of water vapor as the relatively warm ocean water comes into contact with the cold atmosphere. The ground alternately transforms between concrete-like consistency and water saturated, spongy tundra or mud. In the form of snow it is an excellent thermal blanket, helping to provide habitats for animals and plants in frigid conditions.

The nearly unmatched ability of water to store heat energy in liquid form, means that it is an excellent thermal buffer to regulate air temperature. At the same time, freezing of water contained in buildings or utility corridors left unattended can explode pipes and tanks. Utilidors, above-ground utility conduits for drinking water, fuel, or sewage common in the Arctic, are therefore often heated to prevent freezing. As a gas, humidity of air is necessary for comfort, but at the same time sets up strong vapor pressure gradients with dry outdoor air through building envelopes, often leading to water and ice forming in improperly designed walls, ceilings, and floors.

Combined with its optical and acoustic properties – amplifying, transmitting, reflecting, and attenuating energy, it is a powerful constituent material of the Arctic. It could be said that almost every aspect of the built environment is in some way contending with water in its various forms, and the beneficial or destructive potential it holds.

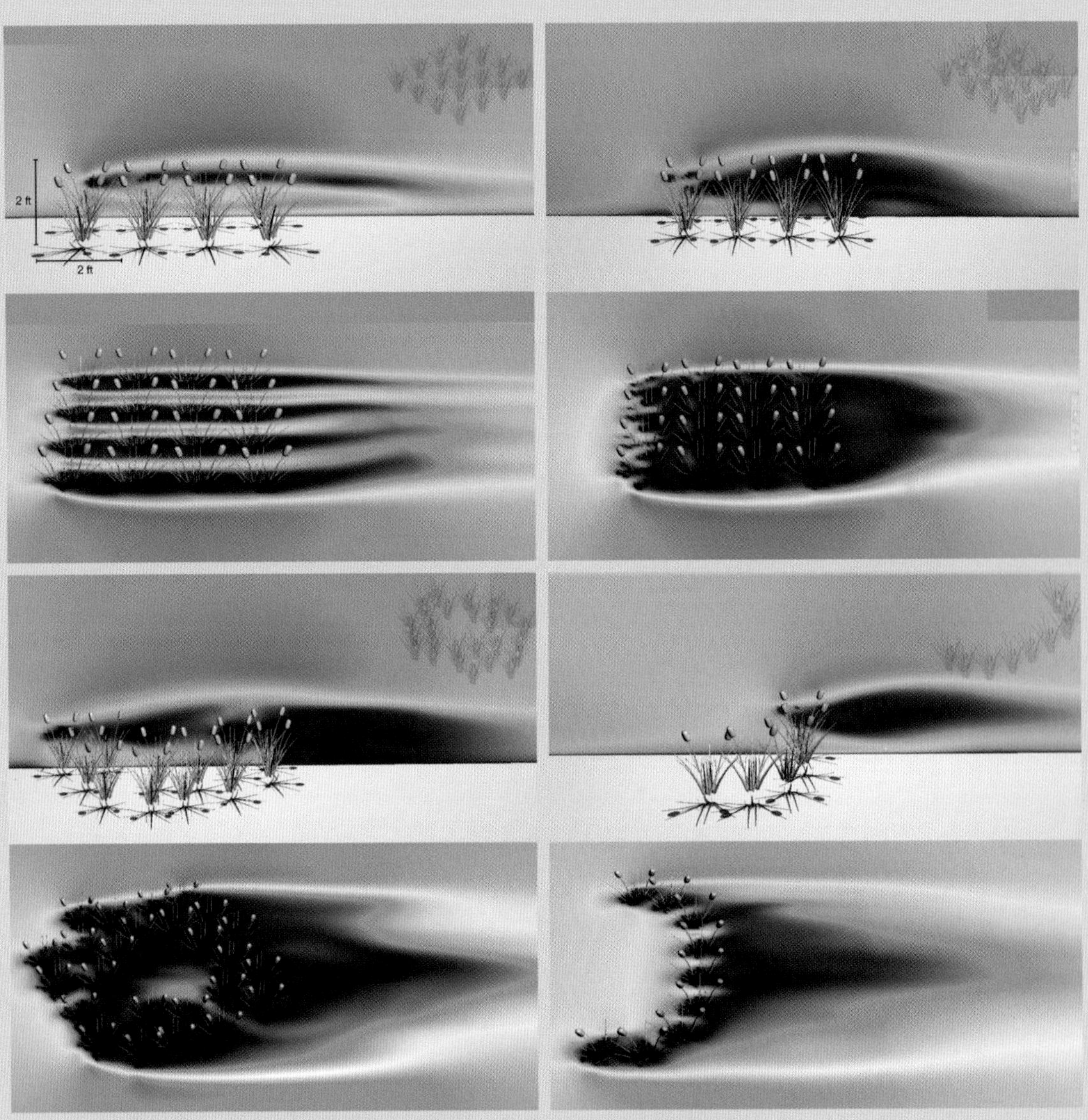
2 ft
2 ft

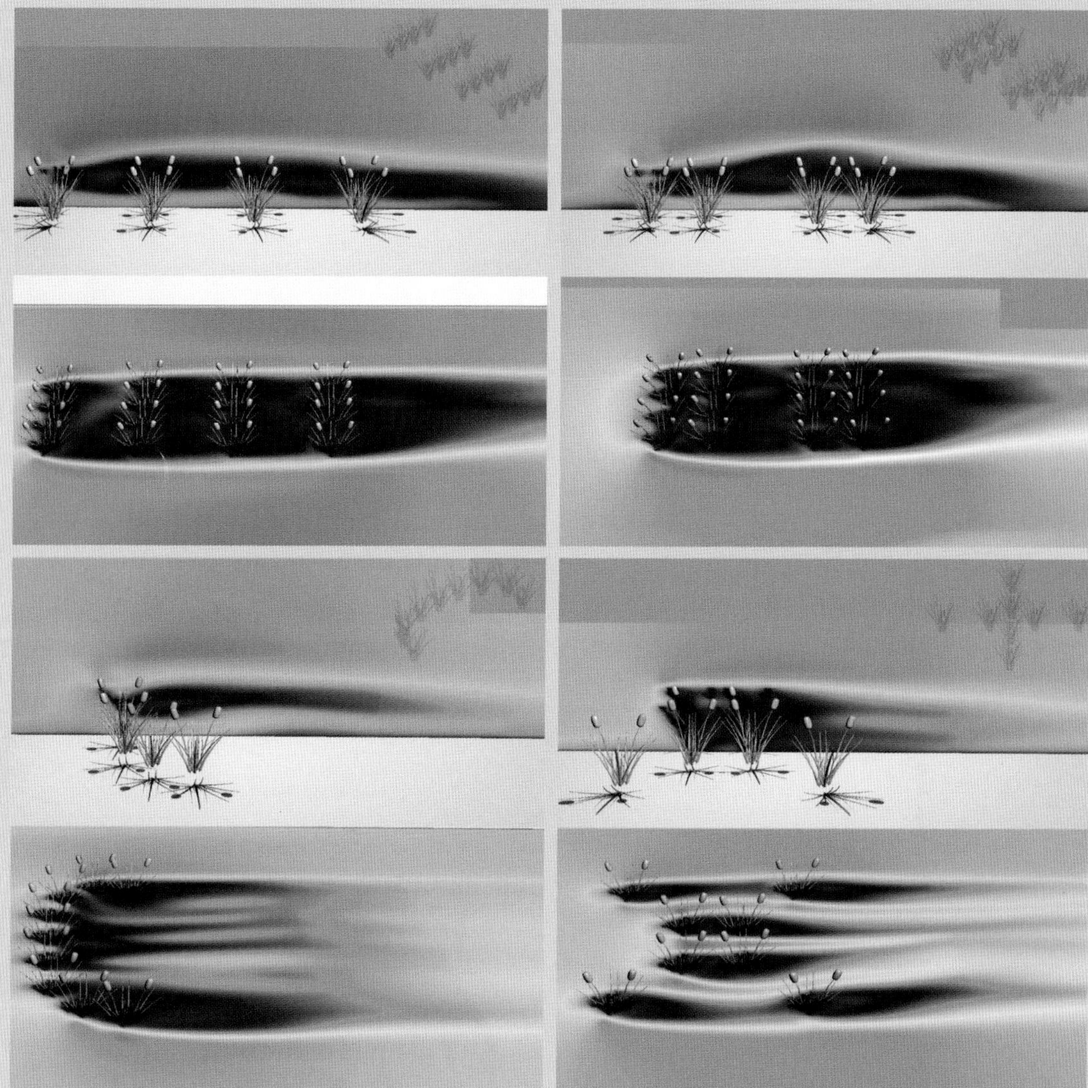

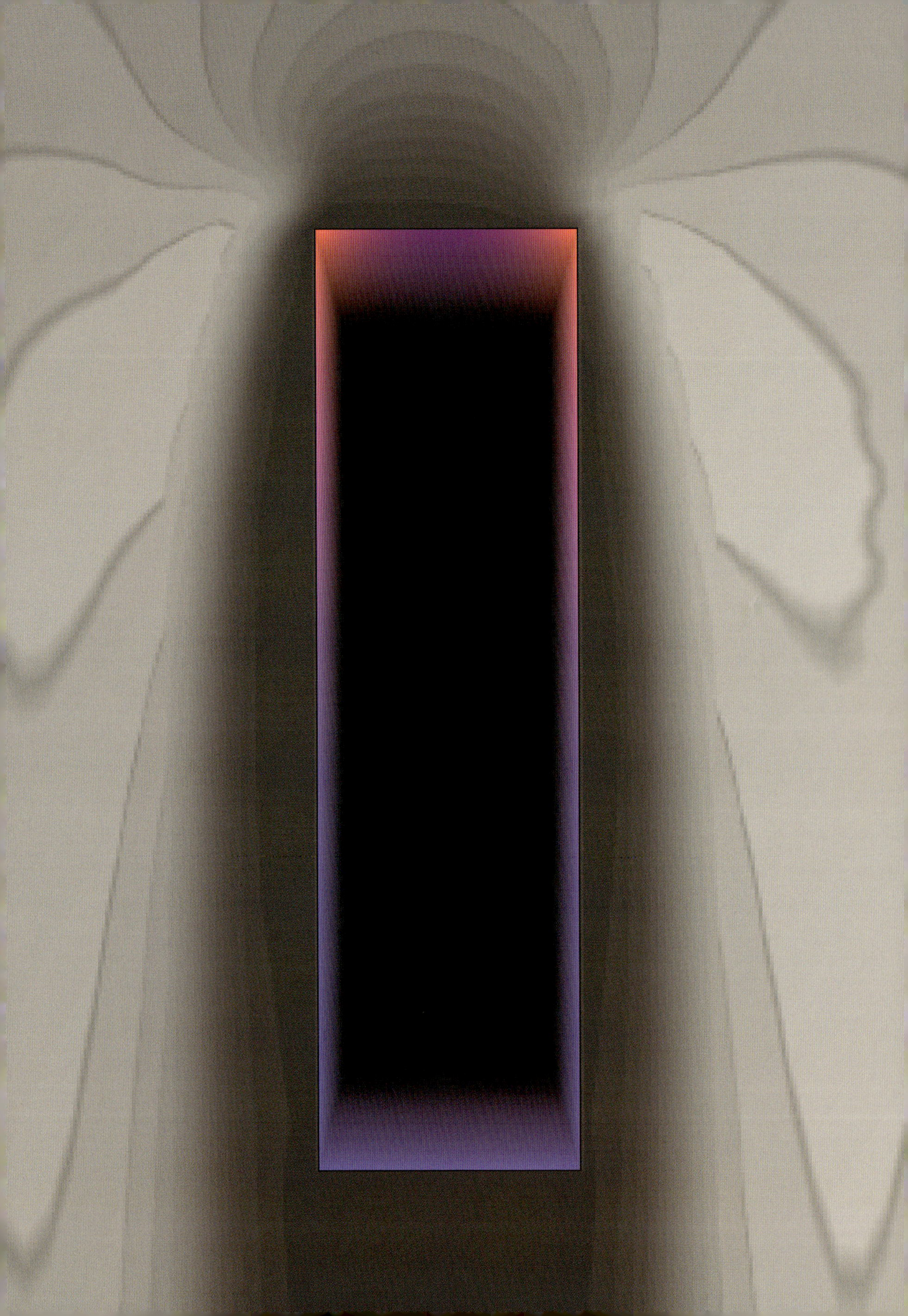

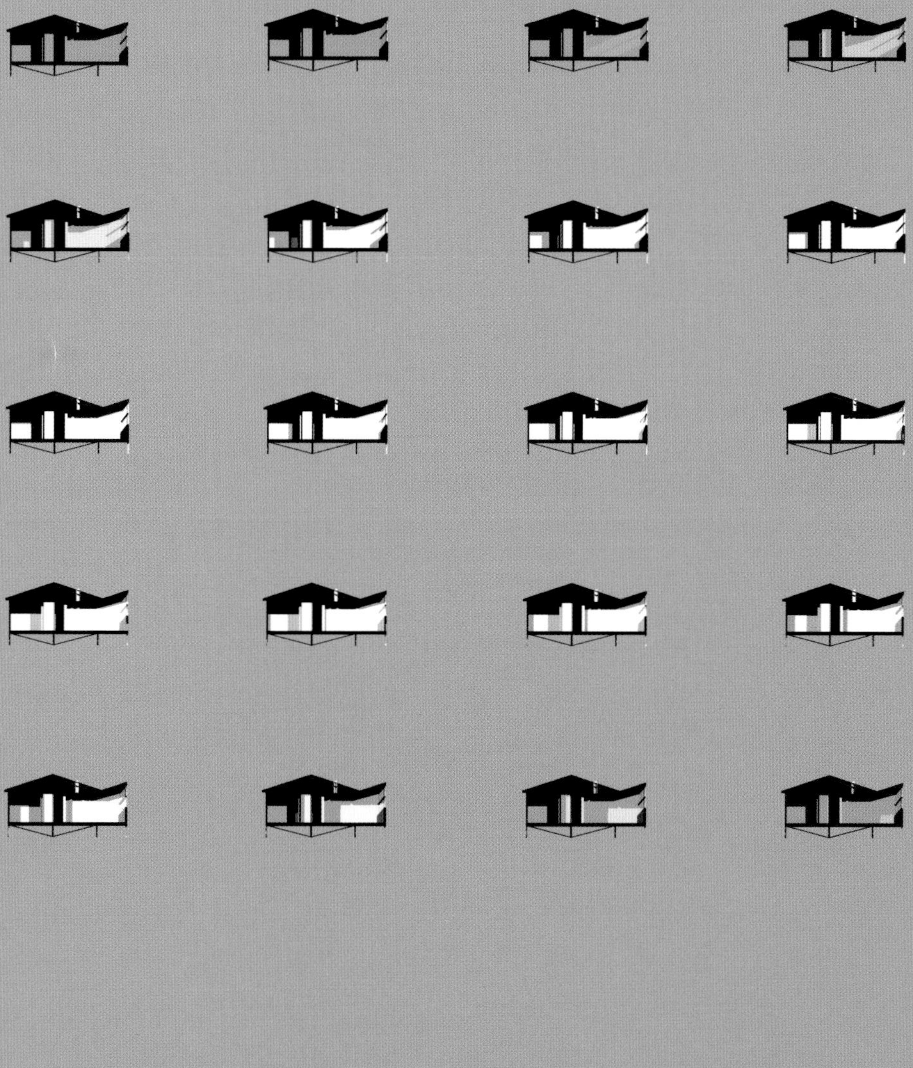

GROUND

The ground throughout much of the Arctic is characterized by permafrost–ground that is frozen, sometimes down to several thousand feet–overlain by an active layer that freezes and thaws annually. At high latitudes above the tree line, tundra ecosystems predominate, with low-lying vegetation, mosses and lichens at the surface.

The unique thermo-hydrological interactions that occur in tundra and the underlying active layer, creates highly dynamic and unstable conditions susceptible to small changes in air temperature, water content, and vegetation cover. In undisturbed areas of tundra, freeze-thaw cycles of water can lead to the formation of "patterned ground," which are distinct polygonal shapes made from sorted ground materials.

In cities and towns, freeze-thaw cycles create frost heave, forcing the ground upward and damaging roads, buildings, and infrastructure if not properly designed. Gravel is one of the essential building materials in the Arctic, levelling the uneven ground, distributing loads, acting as a thermal buffer, and helping to counter these freeze thaw effects. With seasonal changes, circulation within towns are remapped as movement along gravel roads is augmented by new networks of snowmobile trails that extend out over the land and sea ice.

Buildings must be elevated above the ground using piles or metal spaceframes to thermally decouple them from the underlying permafrost. Without this, heat emitted from buildings would warm the ground, affecting the thermal profile of the permafrost and causing it to weaken and shift, damaging the overlying buildings. This raising of buildings on pilotis creates a very specific character to Arctic towns, decoupling them from outdoor spaces and creating leftover spaces beneath buildings. In addition, it can make accessibility difficult for disabled or elderly residents. Strategies and appropriate programming responsive to the ground dynamics in the Arctic are however under-explored, and have potential to define a uniquely northern design paradigm.

GROUND ANATOMY

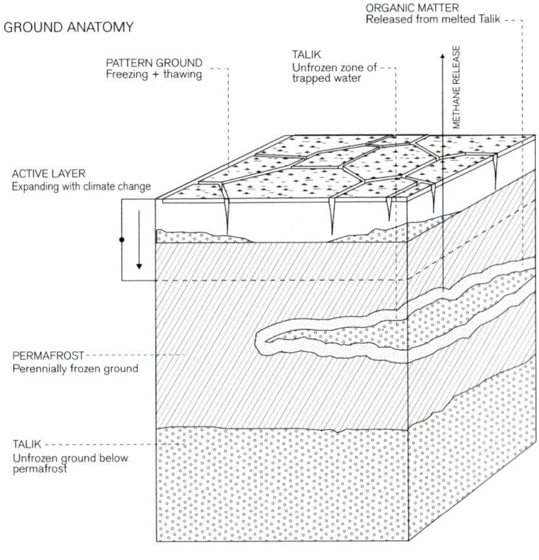

GROUND DYNAMIC

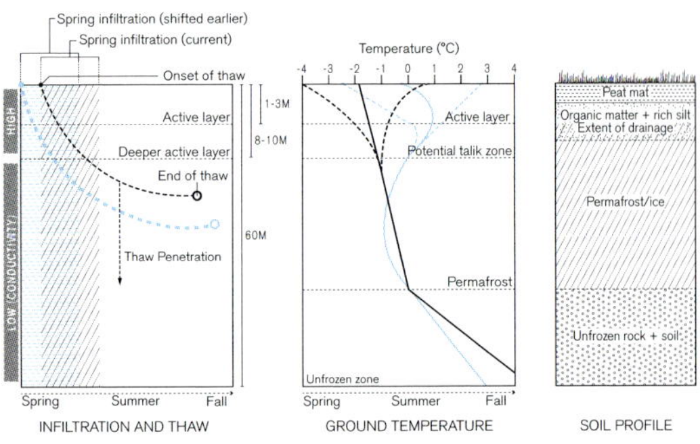

PATTERNED GROUND

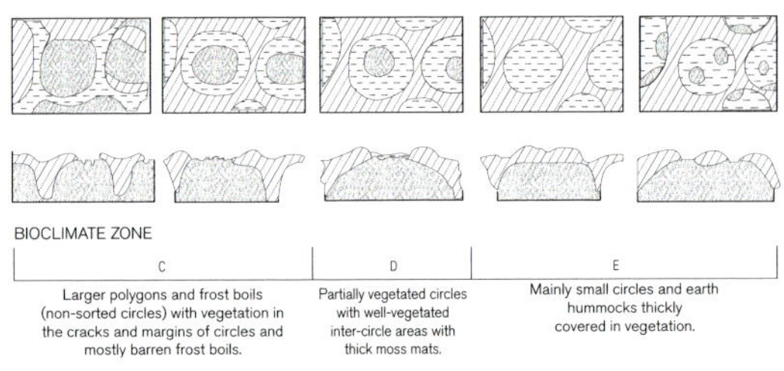

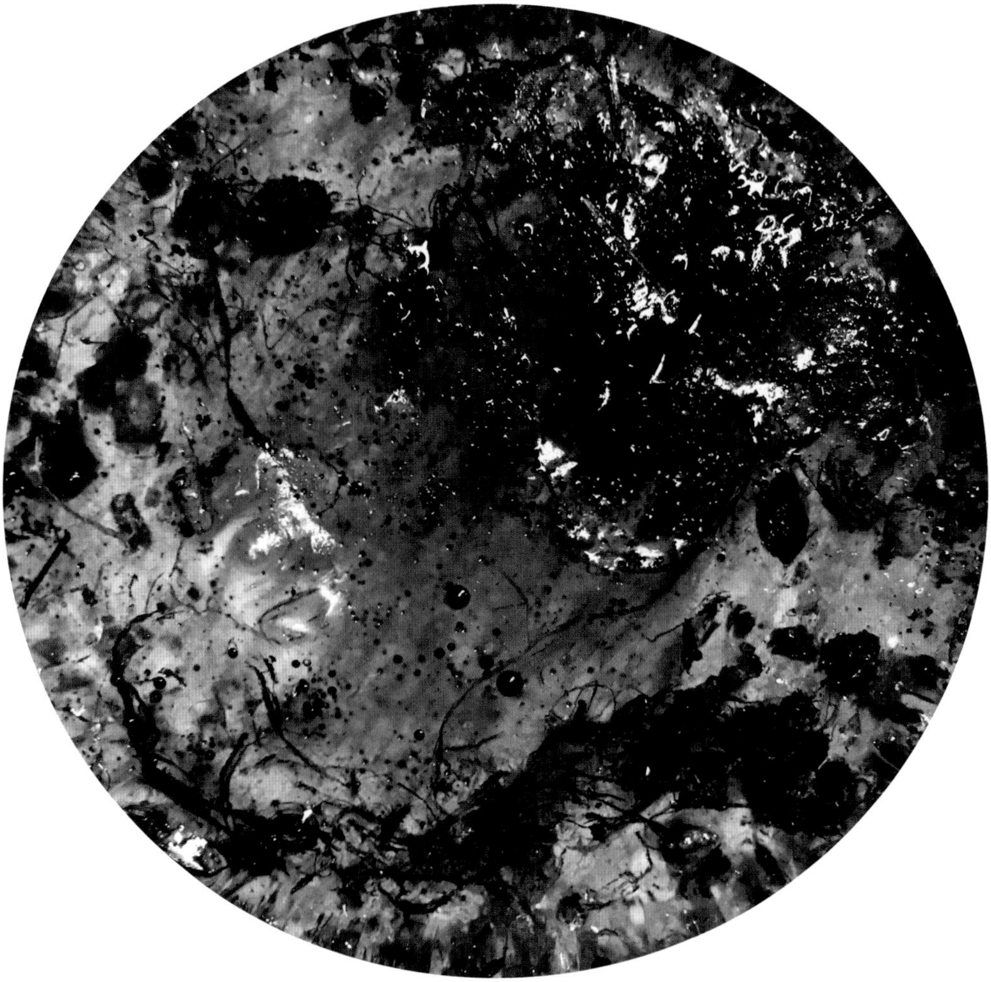

GROUND - VEGETATION DYNAMIC

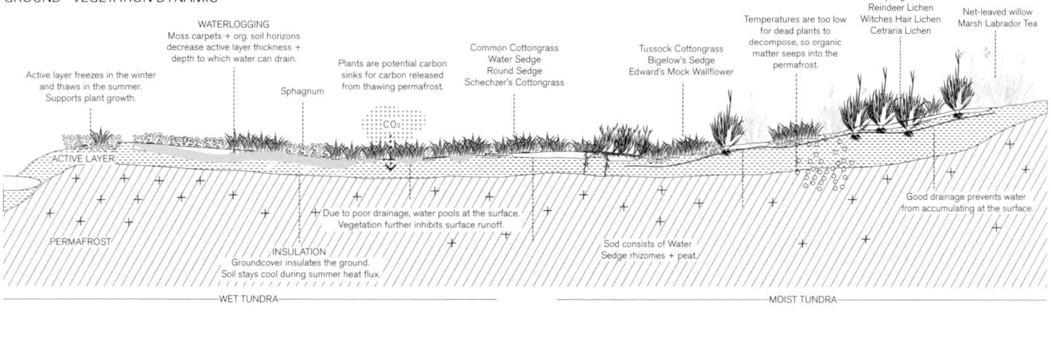

FREEZE THAW

We identified five environmental "agents"—heat, light, wind, water, and ground—to form a basis from which our students explored experimental design strategies and outcomes in the Arctic environment. A central feature of these experiments was to utilize a process that was simultaneously analytical and rigorous, while also creatively flexible. Principles of thermodynamics, material physics, ecology, and fluid dynamics formed a starting point to analyze, augment, and reconfigure environmental processes. Added to this mix was a set of operative keywords such as buffer, focus, amplify, diffuse, aggregate, layer, compact, filter, and redirect, to explore how the five agents could be transformed or interact with one another. After a crash course in physics, thermodynamics, and ecology, our students employed an iterative process of idea bombardment that led to a series of drawings, physical models, and analog and digital simulations to produce a catalogue of ideas - sometimes naive, other times impractical, while others possible – with a goal to uncover and speculate on new spatial or experiential potentials. Some examples of initial questions that guided these explorations were: How can a highly dynamic environment reconfigure the form and sequence of spaces? How can insulation become occupiable or provide additional functions? How does ground material morphology influence microclimates and ecologies that follow? How can the conditions of light in the Arctic be used to define space or alter perception?

The results of these experiments varied widely in scale and ambition. [1] One set of explorations proposed the building envelope as a possible dynamic interface between indoor and outdoor. As a dynamic boundary the building envelope could be transformed through passive mechanisms. For example, in winter, when maximum insulation is needed facing the wind direction, a porous/channeled surface could absorb snow to form a temporary insulating layer increasing the thickness of the thermal boundary layer. During the summer, the collected snow would melt, opening up the façade for light and ventilation. Building envelopes can be explored through the lens of expansion of water via freezing, which can create a mechanical force to open or close louvers. Further still, changes in temperature could be harnessed to deform an envelope through expansion and contraction, or possibly changing stiffness or flexibility, allowing variations in the transmission of air or light. [2] Another set of investigations explored insulation and possible building scale transformation. Ideas such as self-burying structures in snow drifts to contain heat in colder months reconfigure how buildings are entered and used differently during the winter and summer months. A nested series of spaces could be used as a thermal buffer that is fully occupied in the summer, and only partially occupied in the winter. The thickness and materiality of insulation could create a stronger phenomenological relationship that modulate light entering interior spaces or doorways. Highly reflective surfaces could preserve heat on the interior by redirecting thermal radiation like a foil blanket or redirecting and focusing light from the exterior. Dark surfaces could be used to absorb heat on the interior or exterior to create warmer zones and microclimates when the sun is above the horizon. [3] Rethinking the relationship between raised structures and underlying permafrost ground, a set of concepts suggests activating this in-between and often wasted space by raising the buildings up higher to insert a new public or semi-public space. Utilizing thermal stratification to stop cold air entering into the building and also reconsidering the common architectural feature of arctic entry, one can enter into a building from below. More radical in concept, another proposal suggests allowing some buildings to be dynamic and move with the ground altering the angle of floors inside, or shifting individual building segments vertically while its skin stretches and contracts. Informed by frost heave actions, artificial mounds can be created by injecting water into the permafrost's active layer, which then freezes and expands volumetrically in winter. These mounds could be utilized in a number of ways, for instance to amplify light reflectivity on snow or to create wind buffer or microclimates under raised structures.

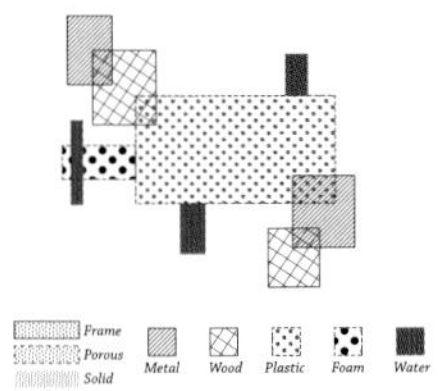

01

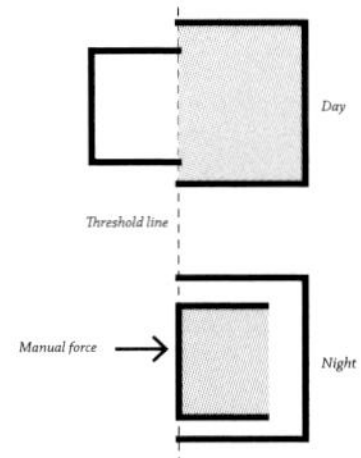

02

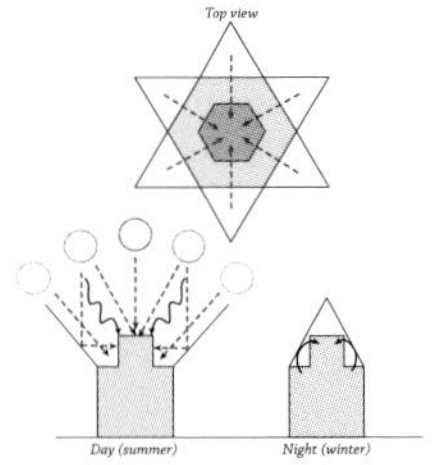

03

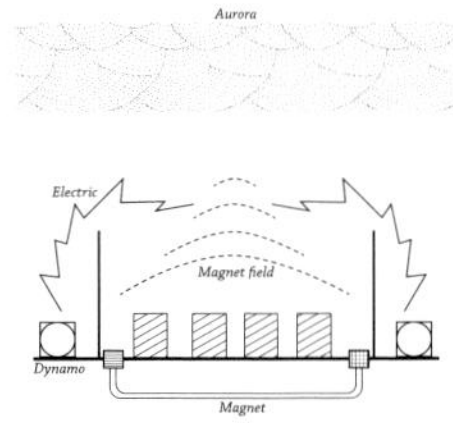

04

05

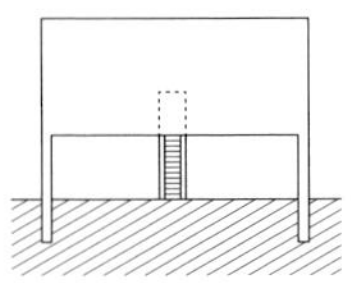
10

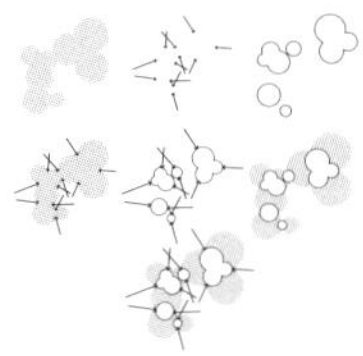
11

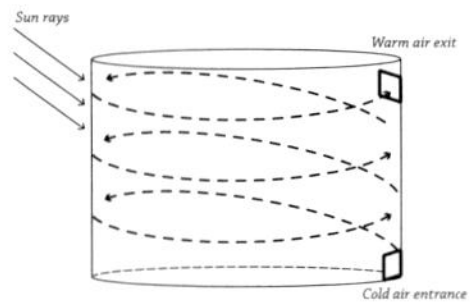

12

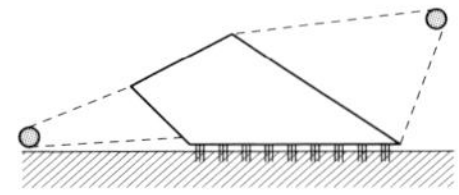
13

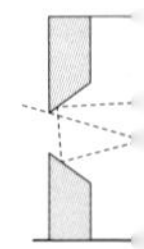
14

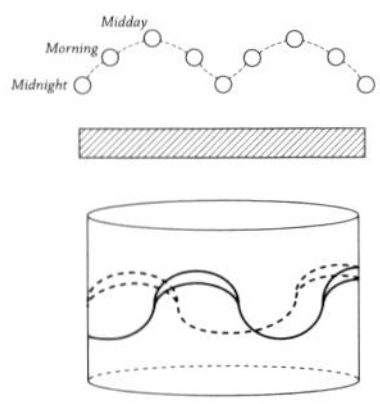

19

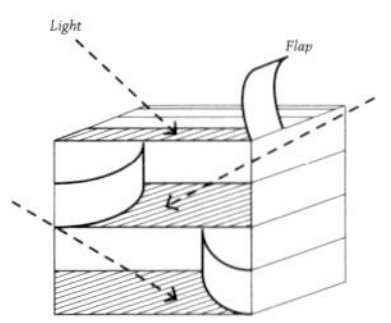

20

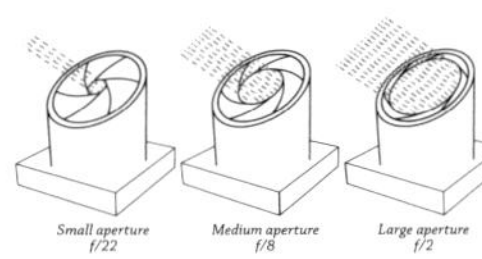

21

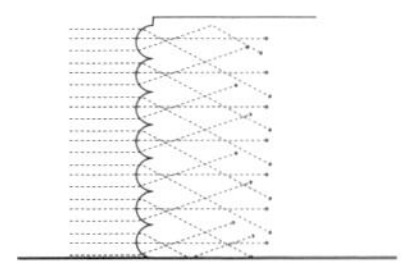
22

23

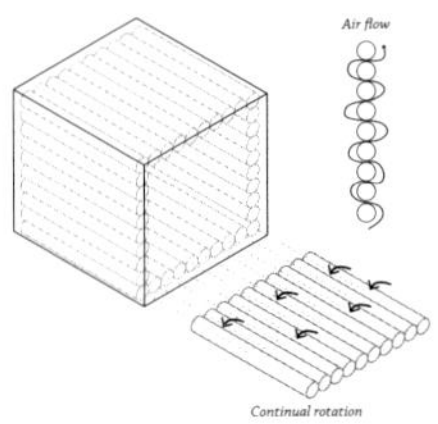

28

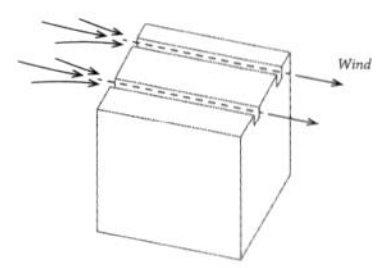

29

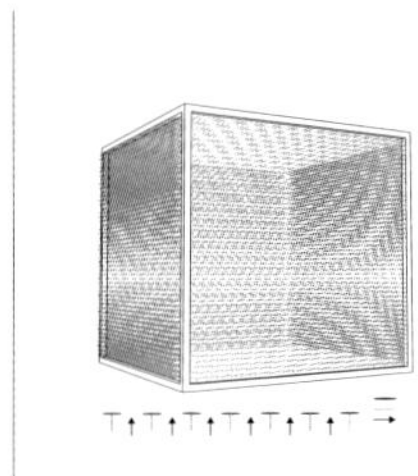
30

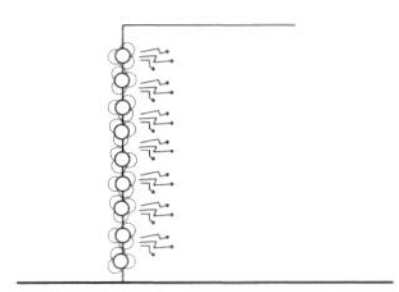
31

32

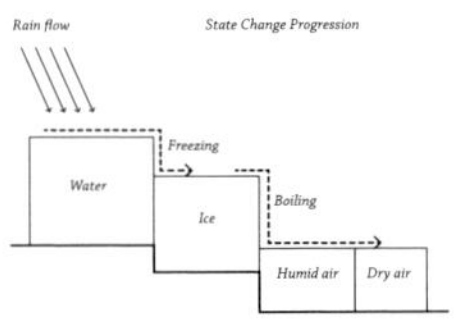

37

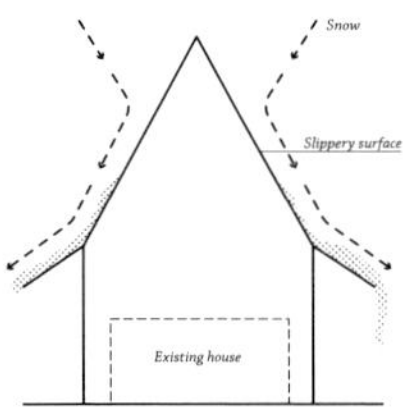

38

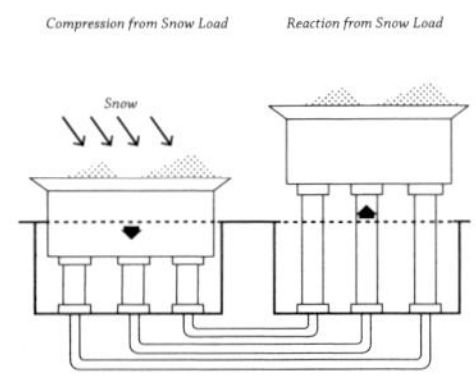

39

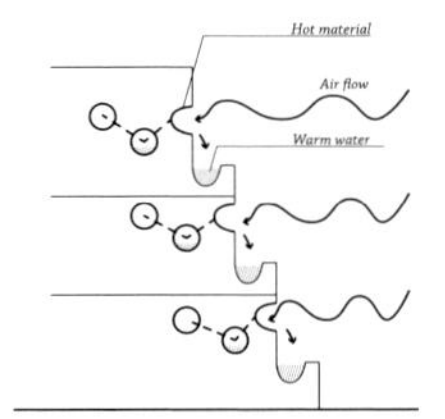

40

41

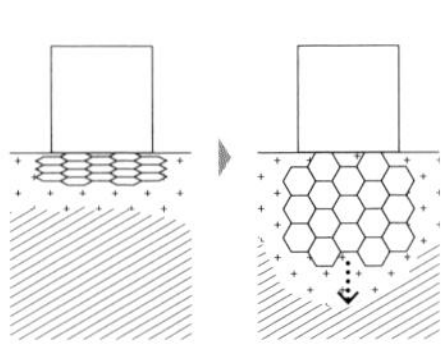
46

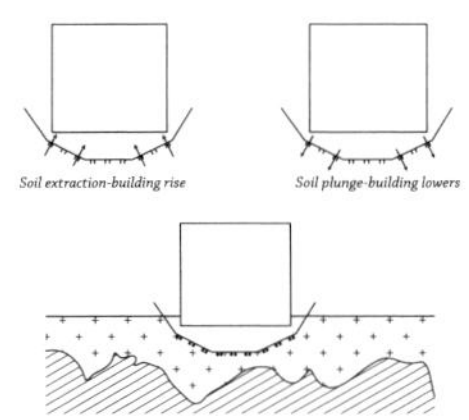

47

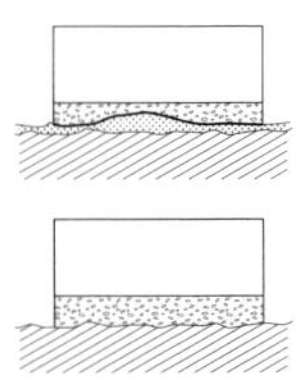
48

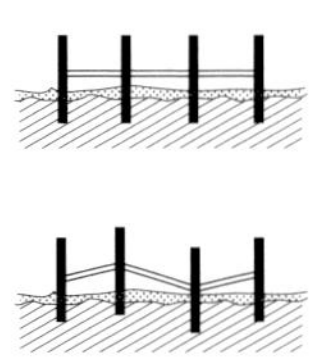
49

50

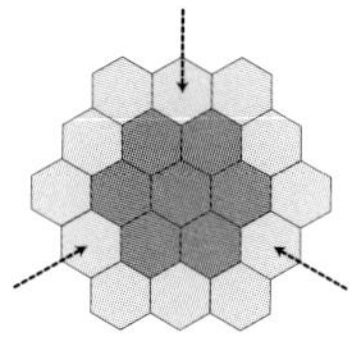

06

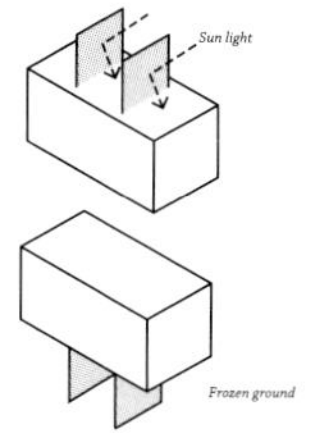

07

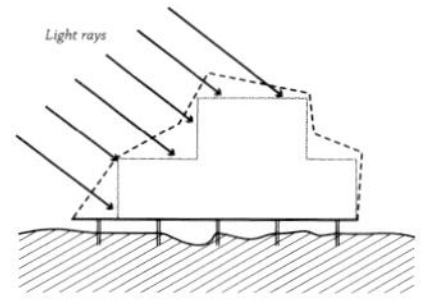

08

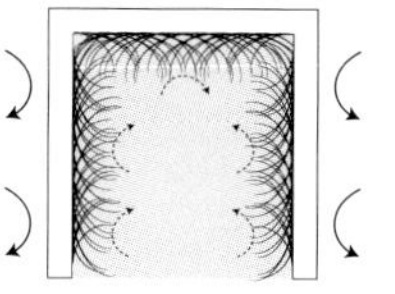

09

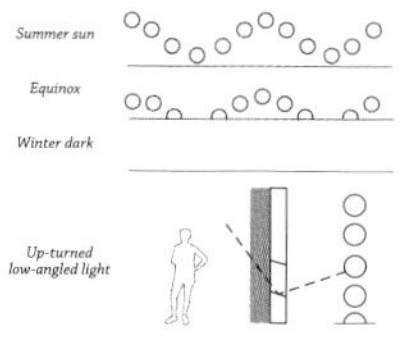

15

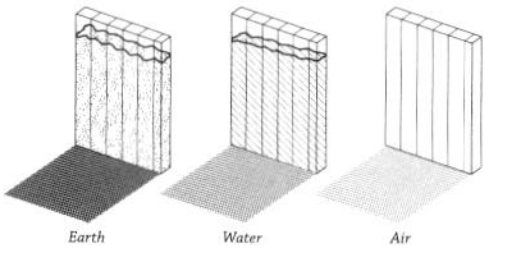

16

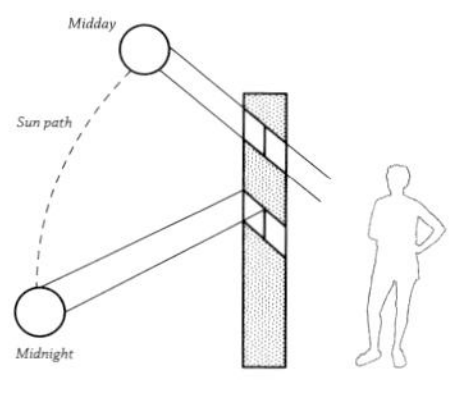

17

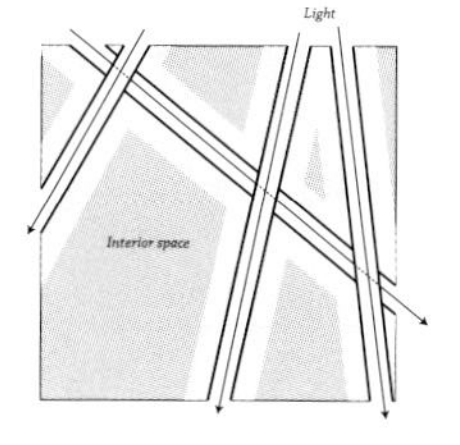

18

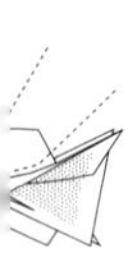

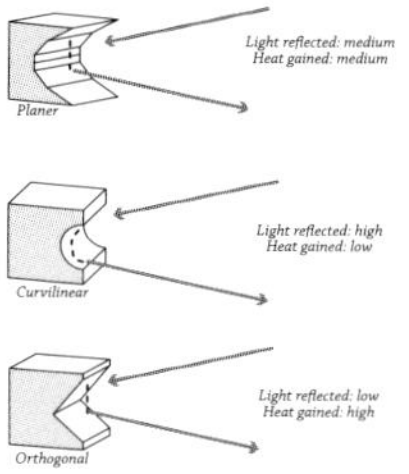

24

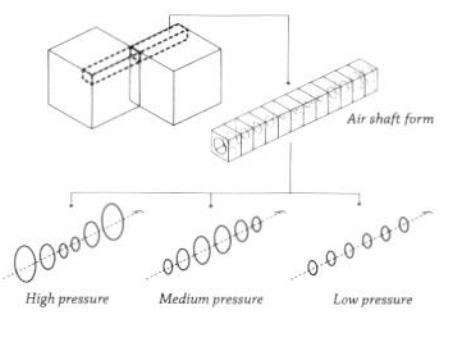

25

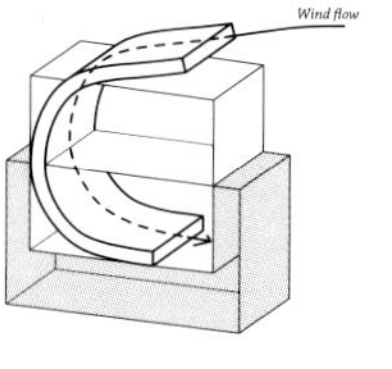

26

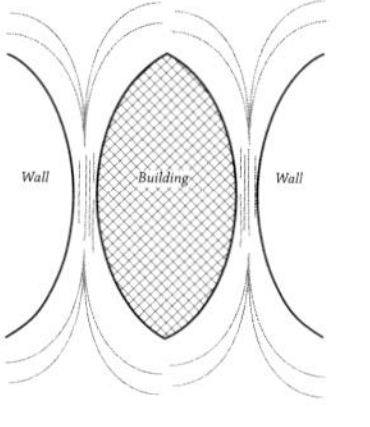

27

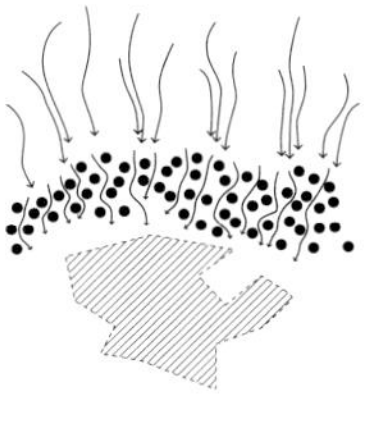

33

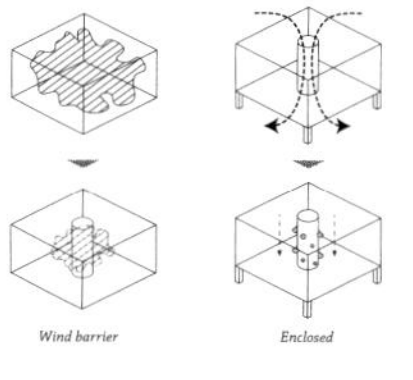

34

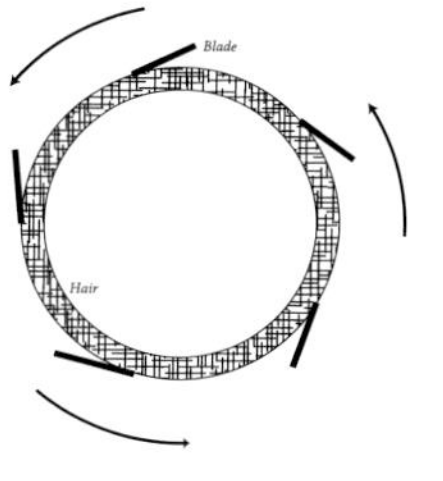

35

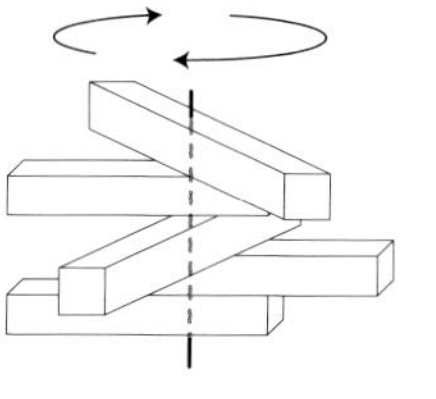

36

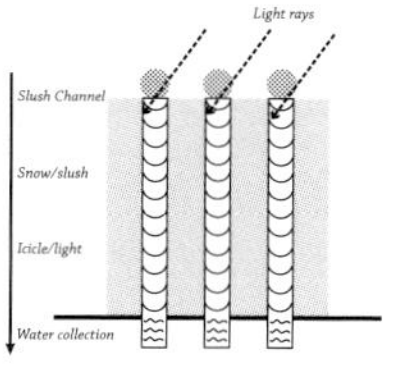

42

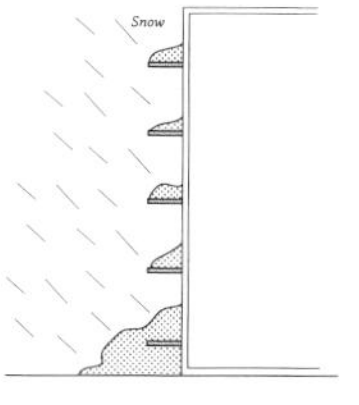

43

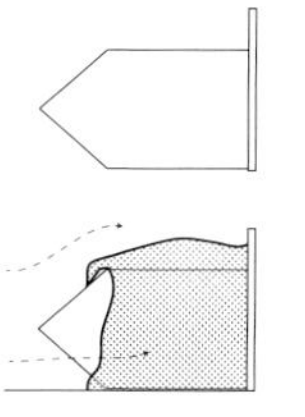

44

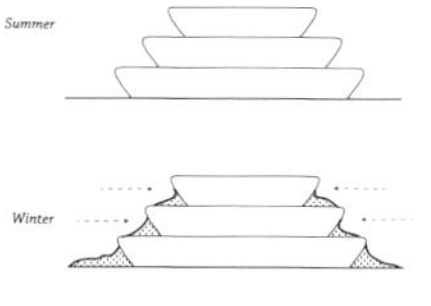

45

51

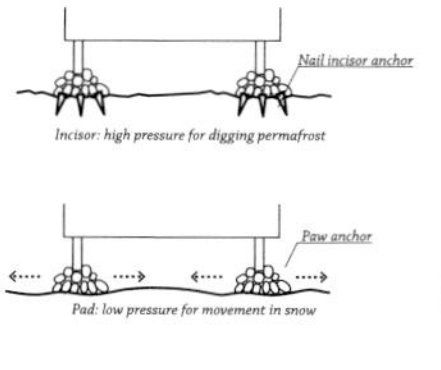

52

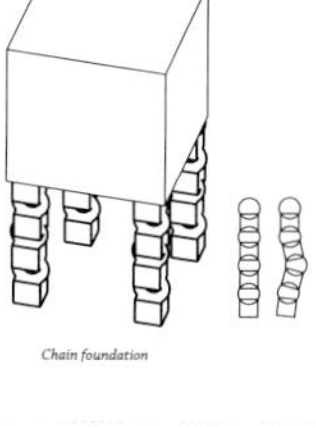

53

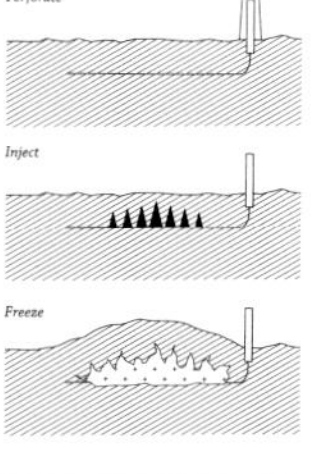

54

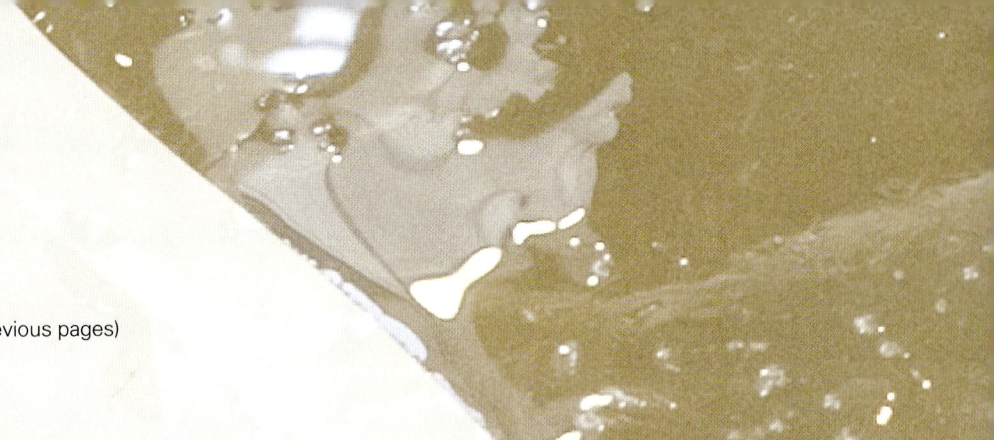

(drawings on previous pages)

HEAT

[01] Thermal Opportunism. Exploiting properties and differences in thermal conductivity and heat capacity, materials can be arrayed, combined, or aggregated to develop thermally efficient assemblages that also create spatial, visual, or haptic effects for occupants.

[02] Dynamic Volume. Buildings can alternately compact and expand to modulate heat exchange in response to diurnal and seasonal environmental changes.

[03] Learning from Plants. Biomorphic spatial concepts can be based on survival techniques of Arctic flora in extreme environmental conditions. Arctic vegetation grows close to the ground and close together; some Arctic structure reflects and concentrates solar to the interior during the day and retracts at night.

[04] Electromagnetic Antidote. Aurora can cause unwanted electrical currents in communication and power lines, pipelines, and produce disruptions in communication, electrical outages, brownouts, and fuel leaks. Tuning into nature and tuning out of digital technology.

[05] Buried for Warmth. Ocean water in the Arctic in the middle of winter can be more than 60°F warmer than the air. Situating a building underwater, underground, or under snow can take advantage of relatively warmer and stable temperatures with air temperatures that can range from -40°F to 100°F.

[06] Matryoshka Living. A sequence of nested envelopes can buffer against changes in environmental conditions, alternately blocking and facilitating the passage of heat and air.

[07] Modulated Boundary Layers. Surface ridges and textures can modulate albedo, redirect infrared radiation into (or away from) a building interior, modulating albedo, disrupt advection of heat, and thicken or thin exterior thermal boundary layers.

[08] Buffer Spaces. Double skin envelopes can utilize infrared solar radiation to create a thermal buffer zone between interior and exterior, while also creating microclimate niches for outdoor use.

[09] Fuzzy Exteriors. Dynamic exterior fibers in the form of "furry" envelopes can slow cold air and trap warm air, similar to polar bears.

[10] Stable Stratification. Thermal stratification can be exploited to avoid inundation of cold air in the interior of a building. Placing an entrance underneath a building – particularly in areas of permafrost where buildings are elevated, reduces heat loss and door bowing due to strong winds.

[11] Venturi Bubbles. Constricting and expanding passages for airflow in towns and near building entrances can alternately reduce and increase wind speed, disrupting advective heat transfer in key locations.

[12] Solar Chimney. Following a thermal concept developed by architect Alvar Aalto, cold air travels upward through a vertical stair solar chimney, gradually warming from sunlight before entering a building interior.

LIGHT

[13] Low Angle Light. Building form and envelope can be developed to capitalize on the high angle of incidence of sunlight and attenuated solar radiation at high latitudes.

[14] Aperture orientation. Orientation of openings through a thickened building envelope can be used to reflect, redirect, or focus sunlight and solar radiation into the interior.

[15] Thick Skin Geometry. Thickened wall sections in cold climates create opportunities for reflecting or redirecting sunlight into a building interior.

[16] H_2O Multiphase Optics. Water exists readily between solid, liquid and gas in cold climates. In each phase it has different optical properties from clear to opaque.

[17] 360-Degree Sunshine. During the polar summer, "midnight sun" (low angle sunlight) can be blocked from entering interior spaces by angling window apertures.

[18] Internal Sunlight. Light tubes can illuminate interior spaces with natural light, while also providing drainage pathways for water from rain or melting snow.

[19] Ribbon Window. Windows are designed as a continuous sequence according to a 360-degree sun path, narrowing at low angles of incidence and widening at high angles of incidence in order to transmit or retard transmission of sunlight during the day and night.

[20] Wall Window. An integral building envelope and solar shading device that can variably reduce heat loss at a windows thermally weakest point – the window frame.

[21] Adjustable Iris. A dynamic, light sensitive building aperture/diaphragm automatically allows for varying amounts of light to enter, similar to the shutter on a camera.

[22] Optical Aesthetics of Ice. Light transmitted through variable opacity and optical clarity to create a glowing ambient light.

[23] Biomorphic Microclimates. Based on the form of an arctic poppy, the structure directs light and solar radiation to the center, creating warm pockets (microclimates) of air.

[24] Dazzle Patterns. Surface geometry can influence the albedo of building surfaces, redirecting light to create visible markers or local external microclimates.

WIND

[25] Passive Suction. With continuous high latitude winds, varying aperture size in building envelope design can modulate air pressure via a Venturi effect, creating ventilation possibilities for interior environments.

[26] Boundary Dynamics. Curved or angled forms can redirect wind to create either laminar or turbulent flow regimes. This can affect the creation of microclimates and zones for social interaction.

[27] Automatic Clearing. Building volumes can be situated in relation to each other to enhance wind speed preventing snow accumulation around the building. Self –burying buildings can create protected envelopes during winter.

[28] Functional Wind Chimes. Exterior screens comprised of cylindrical elements can rotate, generate electricity, while also creating a buffer for heat loss from a building exterior.

[29] Slippery Exteriors. Channels in a roof or exterior wall can redirect airflow and either thicken or thin thermal boundary layers, increasing or retarding cooling.

[30] Polar Bear House. A dynamic envelope consisting of fibers that selectively extend or retract can modulate air flow around a building envelope.

[31] Energy Harvesting. Aeolian vibration from wind passing through screens or structures can create kinetic energy that can be converted to electricity or heat.

[32] Microclimate Zoning. Towns are designed in sequential layers or zones with larger buildings blocking or redirecting wind from residential areas. Residential buildings are placed close together to reduce heat loss and create microclimates.

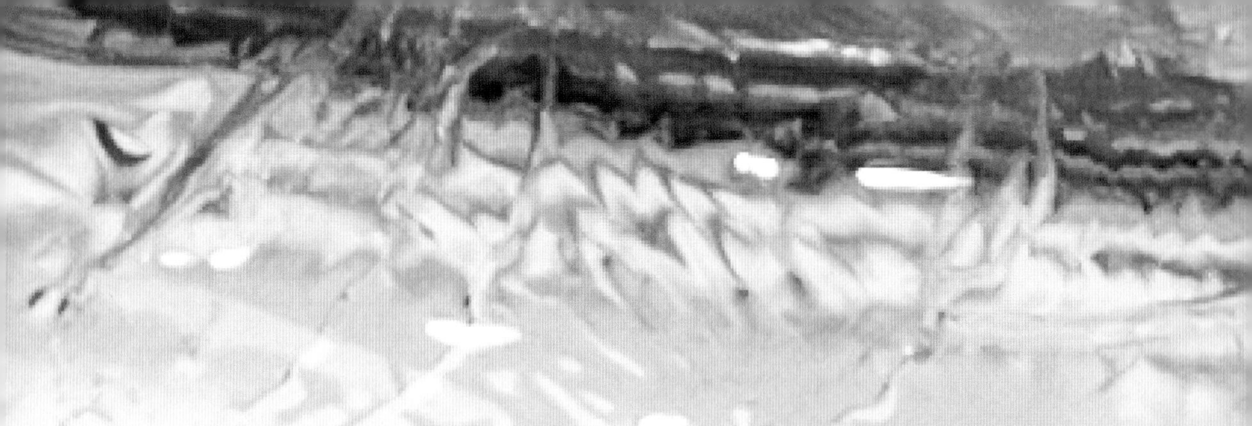

[33] Wind Dam. Design of landforms or infrastructure outside of a city can act as a barrier against winds or entrained snow loads.

[34] Automatic Dehumidification. Intentional thermal bridging into an interior can modulate indoor humidity through condensation in areas of high humidity such as bathroom or kitchen.

[35] Wind Heat. Wind-powered turbines create friction, heat, and electricity.

[36] Front Yard for a Day. A building decoupled from the ground could be allowed to rotate to align with the wind direction, reducing the area of the leading face of a building and creating serendipitous building alignments.

WATER

[37] Water Thermal Buffer. A building that collects rain or snow can use the stored forms of water for insulation, as a thermal mass in liquid form, or purified into clean drinking water.

[38] Dynamic Exterior Insulation. Exterior screens or double skin envelopes can redirect or capture snow creating a thermal buffer.

[39] Snow Load Redux. The weight from snow loading can be used as a driving force to actuate a mechanical system or modify an interior or exterior spatial configuration.

[40] Water Catcher. A porous façade can absorb and collect snow or water, retarding air flow through the envelope in the winter and allowing ventilation in the summer.

[41] Dry Climate Reprieve. A greenhouse can create a concentrated humid environment during dry winter conditions, possibly allowing growth of fresh food and creating a healthy community space.

[42] Ice Kaleidoscope. The accumulation and drainage of snow and ice (and its different forms: slush, icicles etc.) on a building exterior can be designed to modulate the transmission of light into the interior and views to the exterior.

[43] Snow Burial. A building envelope can be designed to accumulate snow for insulation as well as thickening the thermal boundary layer by disrupting air flow.

[44] Ground Maintenance. The form of a building can be designed to adjust the location of snow drifting, reducing maintenance of exterior roads or paths, creating play areas, or possibly zones of water accumulation for tundra vegetation.

[45] Embracing Snow Drifts. Exposed edges and gaps can be designed to fill with snow during the winter, creating opportunities for modulating light or airflow between interior and exterior, as well as opportunities for microclimates.

GROUND

[46] Spreading Building Loads. A distributed lattice for a building foundation can distribute building loads and mediate subsidence and deformation in regions of thawing permafrost.

[47] Active Layer Floating. A structural bathtub could support a lightweight structure that floats in a melting and deforming ("liquefying") zone of melting permafrost.

[48] Underbelly. The space beneath an elevated structure can be designed to become a functional microclimate metaspace for people. Or simply storage.

[49] Seasonal Dynamics. A building foundation relaxes and floors are flat during the summer when the active layer is thawed, but are deformed vertically and laterally when the active layer freezes.

[50] Crumple Zone. A collapsible support system adapts to the freeze-thaw cycle by deforming and absorbing changes to the ground, limiting the effect on an overlying building.

[51] Flexible Buildings. The building structure is designed to move and change shape with the shifting ground. The skin of the building stretches or contracts, and adapts to these actions.

[52] Walking Houses. Foundations can be alternately anchored in place or movable depending on needs of the user, requirements for relocation, and the state of the ground freeze/thaw.

[53] Building Jacking. Flexible pilotis can adjust to changing ground conditions.

[54] Induced Frost Heave. Frost jacking can be achieved to synthetically modify the local topography of the ground by injecting water into the subsurface, creating artificial ice lenses.

First Measures: Approaches and Pedagogies in the Far North

DAVID GARCIA

Associate Professor & Master Program Director of "Architecture and Extreme Environments"
Royal Danish Academy of Fine Arts School of Architecture, Denmark

The projects I'm going to show you are student works and their efforts in the Arctic. On this journey, we'll deal with ways that we can engage with the Arctic before we engage with architecture. So, I can already say to you, you're not going to be seeing any buildings. I come as a practitioner, but also as an educator. We recognize when we teach our students that they're looking endlessly at their computer screens. We also do this in our practices when we work. But we want to encourage them to add a layer of action to their tables. We want them to make. We want them to also take initiatives and be inventive, and of course, research to engage with territories, question through mapping, and communicate their work beyond the traditional architectural drawing. So what do we do? We send them to the ends of the world – to Chernobyl to Fukushima and to deserts with their constructions where they test their ideas and give them physical shapes. And it's because we feel that when they have physical shape, they engage with the community. They're forced to stay and test them out. And of course, one of the areas which we're very active in is the Arctic. So today we'll venture into northern territories not so much guided by geographies, but by challenges, effects, and actions, the journey of implications through cartographies of hits and misses that are derived from the desire to engage and survey, but especially to make.

Figure 1: Arable land and soil management in Iceland.

The Arctic is not pristine. This is perhaps the first realization that our students meet when we take them to these regions. They have an idea of what the Arctic looks like and it's very far away from what we have been told. We've been charting mines and crashes of airplanes in Greenland and one of the most noticeable events was the Broken Arrow in 1968 at the Thule Air Base where four thermonuclear bombs crashed. The crash spill and a clean-up and cover-up still ensue in state matters today. While B-52s were flying over Greenland with nuclear bombs, Iceland was loading DC-3s with seeds, bombing their own island with foreign seeds in an effort to recreate a landscape which was lost. Enter the Soil Conservation Service of Iceland created in 1907. It was formed to transform their landscapes into a arable land. Due to volcanic activity and extensive and aggressive agriculture in the past, most of Iceland is literally a desert. It lacks CO2 and nitrates. But they managed to turn it into this [Figure 1] in the past sixty years, amongst other things, by bombarding it with seeds. We met with scientists that told us how they catalog, since the 1940s, hundreds and hundreds of soil specimens to chart their CO2 and nitrate levels.

To this, we had a very curious student, Marius Costan who decided to breathe CO2 into these areas [Figure 2]. He was carrying for weeks his device that allowed him to collect specimens and breathe his own CO2 almost like an extension of his own lungs. He was carefully placing seeds into the soil samples, exhausted of his own breathing. Another student, Ivo Tedbury, designed and unfolded a shelter with seeds, which were placed in the fabric of his construct [Figure 3-4]. He rolled up the fabric during the night and carefully took care of his seeds by spraying them and heating them with his own body heat as they slowly grew around him during the days he was living and traveling with his shelter, until it encompassed him during the night. Finally, he would start to cut his harvest and cannibalize his own architecture. He would eat and sell his harvest in Iceland. Seeds have a very strange relationship to the Arctic when we think that they didn't have any place in the Arctic. But they keep popping up. Enter Svalbard, and zoom into Longyearbyen where we have seeds, not bombarded this time, but shipped from all over the world to be archived in a vault for eternity, burrowed in a mountain in deep tunnels and chambers where the seeds are packed and cataloged. But one is in doubt if this cenotaph of diversity is actually a moral kidnapping of the Arctic. I mean, what better way to guarantee sovereignty over a territory than to be the protectors of the world's seeds. They're very careful of their seeds. They want to know where they come from. Students sometimes do thesis projects by removing your shoes as a tourist and trying to find out what seeds you bring with you.

It's easier for you to come into Svalbard as a human being than it is as a seed due to the Svalbard Treaty. Signed in the 1940s, it allows almost any individual to go to the archipelago without a visa. And as long as you have a job and find a place to live, you can stay. You won't be protected by social security, but you can absolutely stay. From Afghanistan to Saudi Arabia, individuals can just come. Our taxi driver was actually from Seattle. But tourism has an impact in these communities. The Costa Luminosa, one of the many ferries and cruise ships that dock on Longyearbyen during the summer, brings 2,200 tourists, doubling the population of Longyearbyen in a single hour. Often people do their natural necessities everywhere but in public spaces – there's just not enough toilet services for them.

Figure 2 (top); Figure 3 (middle); Figure 4 (bottom).

Energy is a very big issue as well. For example, a monster truck was driven endless times a day by a single driver for the past fourteen years, bringing coal from Mine 7 to the town's power plant. They are 12 kilometers apart from each other. We could see in the distance a daily supply of coal, feeding this isolated, arctic town with an emergency load that would only last seven days. So, what happens after those seven days? A lot rides on this single driver one could argue. But one could also argue that it is the most sustainable community that we know of. Albeit coal, its energy resource is only 12 kilometers away.

Julian Nolan, a student, did not think so, of course. He devised his own battery system, a façade which was driven by snow and salt [Figure 5]. He would slowly trickle between copper and zinc and illuminate this construction every night in front of the power plant, a gesture for an alternative energy source or fantasy. Stine Bundgaard engaged with a very different way of using heat source loss [Figure 6]. With Peltier tiles in an area of heat sinks, she would literally turn cold bridging into energy, a parasitic entity that thrived in the arctic landscape of heat loss as she entered people's homes and lit their rooms, aimed to redefine the traditions of a window through a technological weed, not killing, but thriving on an efficient design.

Figure 5 (top left); Figure 6 (top right); Figure 7 (bottom left); Figure 8 (bottom right).

About killing – you're not allowed to die in Svalbard. Mining heritage has left a range of buildings, beautiful structures in the landscape made out of wood. Svalbard's heritage policy prohibits restoration. It also prohibits further human intervention on those structures. There's actually an architectural euthanasia – one could argue for, almost a breach of the Hippocratic Oath of architecture. So, architecture is allowed to die, but you're not. You're not because you'll be buried in the permafrost. Your body will be just kept frozen forever. But even though you're not allowed to die, you can certainly be killed. Polar bears are a big issue in this territory. There's about 3,500 polar bears and about 2,200 inhabitants. The governor will literally not allow you to leave the town boundary of the red zone without a rifle. But at the same time, you're not allowed to shoot the rifle within the black zone. What happens if you do is always very dubious. But you are really recommended to take a rifle. And so much so that the students that come to the world's northernmost university, everything is the "northernmost" in this locality. They have the northernmost bank, the northernmost post office, and the northernmost university. But the first image you see is a polar bear and the first thing that you're taught in this university is to kill, which is very interesting since Svalbard is actually declared a demilitarized zone. You're trained to shoot polar bears. How is this threshold with the wild negotiated? How does one manage a weaponized routine of the everyday? But accidents do occur, and sometimes with casualties on both sides creating a cartography of trauma and a map of forensic tragedy which is taken very seriously in Longyearbyen. So, I engaged with a polar bear alarm as a project and what is the frontier condition between the wild and the settlement and what is "wild." And I set out to encourage the discussion in the community and engage different stakeholders from the miners, tourist services, children, and designed it to trigger and send a signal to the authorities and the locals instead – in case of a breach. Where actually are the limitations and where is the frontier? This is defined more often than not by emotional grounds. And their discourse shifted back and forth according to experiences and habits and the disagreement on placing limits defining the danger triggered debate. It's interesting. Nobody had ever asked the locals how they deal with the polar bears until we did. When a polar bear goes into town, somebody sees it, they run into their house. They call the governor. They come with a police car and usher it out. That's why all the doors are actually left open in Svalbard so you can quickly take refuge. We wanted to take part in this discussion with a technological device and encourage the community to also consider this.

But the wild is also a source of inspiration. A polar bear's fur is hollow. It not only traps air, but it allows light to go through it and reach the black skin of the polar bear, almost like a natural version of fiber optics. Its black skin allows that light to literally heat its body. And obviously we had a student inspired by this. Astrid Litchfield, a biomimicry tour de force, recreated an electronic version of a polar bear skin, imagining and envisioning buildings that could be made out of furry façades trapping air and light. Could this be an arctic façade? As she measured and charted the results and the temperature – we feared that her biological reference may lay patent claim and we looked behind us fearing for polar bears.

Due to a three-day snow storm and a whiteout, we got stuck for a couple of days in Iceland. Building in the Arctic, as it has been referenced, has been very problematic. We often literally copy and paste building typologies and solutions from one place to the other without taking into account different scenarios. Although we try and fail, we simulate and digitize our way out of natural challenges as the designs of the UNIS building in Longyearbyen aimed to do. We shape around what is otherwise in constant motion with more or less success. Fascinated by this process and the properties of ice and snow accumulation, our architect and DJ student, Anders Nottveit, turned to sound, aiming to understand the granular qualities of snow and acoustic vibration to shape and craft a natural code [Figure 7]. Through the use of high frequencies, his aim was to manage ice and snow cracking, ever so slightly by asking if he could use his device on the roofs of local's houses and to see if they could shake the snow off the roofs. They suggested that he do it in garbage containers. Is there a danger of vibrating a house from its snow, but also from its structure or foundation? Maybe. Sara Gøtze was also fascinated with structure, architecture and building in the Arctic. She managed to transport a twelve-foot-square cube to the edge of the north pole and stretch fabric daily to freeze it, spraying it into rigidness with water that would instantly freeze and then rotating a new shell, almost like a life sized 3D printer, bringing up the question, "Do we always need to build permanently in the Arctic?" and "Does all constructions need to be forever?" [Figure 8]. Local engineers were interested in ice particle densities in the air regarding the impact of snow accumulation, which triggered in us the construction of this snow scanner. Literally, this laser would spin up into the air and we could gather and scan slivers of split seconds of spin drift, turning black night into galaxies of sonic drift in a strange revelation of what was normally invisible.

I call these "First Measures." It's a journey that strives to argue for methods that engage in arctic territories as participatory, as bold, as embracing inventions, always engaging with site, allowing for failure and success as a shared project with the local community. They make evident the challenges of the Arctic in small physical interventions as potential design tools for architects to come. But perhaps few projects make my point more clear than these interventions. In the isolated northeast of Iceland, in the middle of a very barren landscape, this autonomous quaint box [Figure 9], which tried to be as domestic as possible and invite individuals to put a coin in, and as it slowly wakes up, this tiny monster would light up and you would be rewarded with a chocolate bar. A parody of contradictions in the Far North, but at the same time it becomes a very strange revelation of how small actions can start to bring big questions into play.

Figure 9: An autonomous box rewards individuals with chocolate after they insert a coin, waking up the dormant creature.

Designing a Resilient Future

JUDITH GRUNAU
Project Manager, Cold Climate Housing Research Center, USA

I work at the Cold Climate Housing Research Center in Fairbanks, Alaska. CCHRC is a private, non-profit organization that was started by a group of builders who were fed up with the lack of durability of the houses being built in Alaska. Much of the boom in building, especially in the urban areas, occurred with the oil pipeline being built. So, in the late '70s and early '80s, a lot of building materials and housing stock was brought up from the lower forty-eight states. They weren't designed for the Arctic and sub-Arctic environments. Builders wanted a way of testing building systems. So, they teamed up with some scientists to test and see what systems and technologies worked, before they were put into houses.

Alaska is the largest state in the U.S. And if you were to overlay it on top of the U.S., you would realize that it covers nearly every climatic zone in the U.S. Fairbanks is in the very center of the state in what's known as the interior. It's below the Arctic Circle, but has discontinuous permafrost. One thing that's great about working in Alaska is the different climatic zones that we get. So you can test things out in a rainy area as much as you can test them out in a dry tundra area or the Tanana Forest. Another great thing about working in Alaska is the converging ways the traditional wisdom and traditional values are just colliding right now with modern technology and the Internet age.

Figure 1: Sod igloos were inhabited in the Anaktuvuk Pass as recently as 1963. These vernacular structures are useful precedents for contemporary prototypes.

This is Anaktuvuk Pass, 1963 [Figure 1]. Many of the children who lived in these sod igloos are still alive. We have quite the living history. This is Anaktuvuk Pass fifty years later complete with a grid system, houses that look like they would be anywhere in America, satellite dishes, high speed internet utilities. This grid system is placed in most rural villages. And it doesn't really pay attention to the best land. It doesn't pay attention to wind direction. It doesn't pay attention to how close they are to the ocean. Most of the time, in the villages the grid was put down based on where the school or the post office was and everything was built around it including the utilities, since the utility companies only wanted to establish their systems in a grid.

In Point Lay, this has been detrimental because it is a land that's made of ice wedge polygons which is a type of permafrost that's frozen in a polygon shape and all around it is a natural drainage pattern [Figure 2]. But when you put something in like a road or utility, that has run off and also collects heat, you end up dealing with melting of the ice-rich soil that is not in the geometric pattern of the polygon and ponds of water begin to form. That similar effect is happening underneath most of the houses in this village. It's called subsidence. And it's undermining the foundation of these houses. It's collapsing their water and sewer systems. But if you're going to build there, you have to stay on the grid. Because then you just extend the roads, the utilities, you put in nice driveways, you divide everyone into equal spacing and you give them all their own house or they build their own house.

When we plan for areas like this, it would be wise to go back and look at what was done before the grid system came in. And instead of placing houses the way they have been placed for the last fifty years, maybe look for the best land. Build on the highest part of the polygon wedge. Try building houses in a cluster where they can share utilities instead of being on a large grid system. Use the land more wisely and hopefully the land can sustain it longer. This quote really describes it all: "We structured our grids to that port. The next two generations, our children will be forced to locate their houses based entirely on where they can defecate. I think as humans we are capable of much more than that." This was said by a Canadian resident. Very smart comment. Not only is this infrastructure limiting us to where we can build and not letting us pick the best site, but it's also incredibly expensive.

Figure 2: Regular freezing and thawing of the ground forms ice wedge polygons, revealing some of the difficulty of building in the arctic and sub-arctic.

When we look at hooking up the house to the existing water and utilities, we're just talking about pulling it off the main water or sewer line down a short driveway and it's costing fifty to seventy thousand dollars just to do that. Housing is extremely expensive in this area and this would add to the cost. The first prototype home that we worked on, the housing authority brought us in because they couldn't get a bid from a construction company to do it for less than $700,000. We have heard about a 1,200 square foot home costing $1.2 million in some areas of Alaska. So if you want to be off the grid and you are in wetlands or on permafrost, your next best solution for sewage utilities, according to what Alaska has been doing for the last fifty years, is a honey bucket. Some of you have experienced this in the rural parts of the north, you probably know what this is, but for those that who don't, it's a five gallon bucket with a toilet seat lid. And when it fills up with waste, often it's the youngest child's job, because they're the grunt of the family, to take that bucket and put it into a dumpster outside that's specifically for the honey bucket waste. Then these guys that are pretty much dressed in hazmat suits come and collect the waste and take it to a sewage lagoon where it's treated before it goes out into the ocean again.

Figure 3: A Separett Toilet separates liquid and solid waste, allowing solid waste to dry out and become non-toxic.

There must be better ways to get off the grid. Due to soil conditions, we often can't use leach fields or outhouses. So we're looking for other solutions. As an architect, you're going to have to think about the things that your client doesn't want to think about. So as a result, I think about poop a whole lot, and where it goes and how it's treated. But when you can present the residents with an alternative to a honey bucket that actually works, and teach them how to use it, they're thrilled. It may not be indoor plumbing. They don't have running water in this village, but we put in a Separett Toilet [Figure 3]. This is a dry toilet system that separates the solid waste from the liquid waste. It places the solid waste into compostable bags and dries it out with a fan making it inert, not toxic. You can then dispose of this as trash or burn it. It's not a definite answer, but it's a step in the right direction and we need to take all those steps we can. We also hooked this toilet up to our home heating and ventilation system so that the waste air would not back-draft into the house, but be forced out of the house continuously.

Another solution that we've used is a household water sewage treatment plan, designed by Lifewater Engineering. They're also located in Fairbanks. This system uses microorganisms that exist in solid waste to digest and process the waste. And then before it is considered fully treated, it goes through a UV filter which makes the water DEC certified for groundwater discharge. We are using this system to treat the wastewater at our research facility. The building is on permafrost and we use this to treat the wastewater quite successfully.
This is another great quote. "We used to build our homes underground where it was warm and lay our dead

up to rest in the air. We were told that was uncivilized. And now we have to build our houses on stilts up in the wind and bury our dead in the ground and we've been cold ever since." This was said by a gentleman out of Newtok, Alaska. Newtok is in the far southwest part of the state. It is dealing with a lot of coastal erosion and the residents are talking about moving the village. We hear this quote, and very similar quotes to this everywhere we go. And although the idea behind putting a house up on stilts was to create that Venturi effect, it's not the only solution that we have. Maybe we can provide ways to build more traditionally. Now I'm not saying that we should go back into sod igloos because God only knows, every spring they would flood inside because the snow would melt. They were only supposed to be a winter place of habitation. In the summers, the people would move into more tent like structures and oftentimes they would follow whatever it was they were hunting whether it was in the ocean or whether it was on land.

Figure 4: Snowdrift blocks the egress windows of these houses in Newtok Alaska, potentially endangering residents.

One of the things we can learn from sod igloos is snow drift. These houses are in Newtok, Alaska [Figure 4], which actually doesn't get much snow. But due to the type of construction or how close they are to their neighbor's house, the snow piles up and blocks the egress windows creating a place that's unsafe in the winter; if there was a fire, these people would have a really difficult time getting out if they could get out at all. Looking at that sod igloo, specifically its form, this wasn't as much of a problem. This is a house that we designed in the shape of an octagon. The wind scoured the snow from around the house, it had no need to be shoveled out. Just by the pure shape and form of that building, it was able to clear the snow drift around allowing access around the entire house. Another way we've looked at snow drift is the roof of the building and how the wind can scour it and dump snow away from the house.

Another thing we can learn from sod igloos is the long arctic entry ways. The longer you create your entrance, the less heat is going to get into the house. Typically, a lot of these houses have an entry way that you open up and you really can't close that door behind you before you have to open up the next one. In igloos, they would often not only make entryways long, but they would dip them down into the earth to create a cold trap. We have tried to emulate that where we can by creating long entrances to get into the house so that one door has to be closed or even if it's not closed, at least not that much heat is going to get out of the house. In this case, we also put the outside walls of the arctic entryway on the side that gets the most wind-driven rain and snow to try to keep the house warmer, to make it more efficient to heat.

The open plan design is also driven by the communities. Households are often multi-generational and include extended family. They like to know where everyone is, for safety and community. Another thing that we've learned a lot about from looking at the past is subsistence food storage. Lots of times, food, whether it be caribou or whale - was stored in the ground or in a cold area. If we design our houses so that there's a cold area and a hot area, it's not all the same temperature throughout, then we can actually create a space where that subsistence food storage can occur. In the case of the Anaktuvuk Pass Prototype, we made the cold on the right side of the house and we created a soil berm around it. This enabled the space to maintain a temperature of forty degrees or colder.

In a place where there are no trees, you're not going to find wood as a building material. Local resources must be used. This place has great gravel, but a lot of places don't have gravel. There are not a whole lot of building materials that you can get locally, so you need to be creative. You may think sod is not really a resource, but sod is actually a great resource. It allows you to berm the soil up around the house, or you can put it on the roof. When we were constructing the Anaktuvuk Pass Prototype, the elders walked by and told us how to do it. The Sun, or solar gain, can actually be a great resource for reducing your heating loads and for use of photovoltaics. And often the local people are your best resource. They can build, they can learn, they can instruct your design.

So, what can we learn from the current housing? We know that often times it's failing. This is a house in Quinhagak, Alaska. Once again, it's on the southwest coast. The housing stock here was brought up in the '80s. They barged up kit homes or modular homes. They were built, and shortly thereafter, people realized that they were way too cold. They weren't retaining the heat. So, in the '90s, they decided to put two inches of insulation on the outside of these houses, but they didn't increase the roof overhang. So now you have really cold temperatures outside, an overcrowded house inside where they cook, boil water, and take showers. There's a lot of moisture and vapor being driven into these walls causing mold within the structure. In addition to this, rain coming off the roof is now going down between the house wrap and the siding and rotting it. So now you have rot coming in from both directions. It's deteriorated the foundation beam. It's making people sick. It's causing problems with breathing and health, in addition to structural problems. What we can learn from this that it's important to insulate your buildings well, but you need to do it the right way.

These are two of the designs that we've been working with. The first one is an integrated truss house [Figure 5]. It uses a continuous insulation all the way around the entire house extending foundation, walls, and roof. You've got to think beyond just your walls, think about the entire building envelope, and have enough insulation that you can separate your condensation point from the structure. In most places in Alaska it's a rule of thumb to keep one third of the insulation on the inside and two thirds on the outside of the structure. It's not a rule all over the state, but it definitely is the farther north you get. This ratio pushes that vapor and condensation point outside of the structure to the drainage wrap that can handle the moisture.

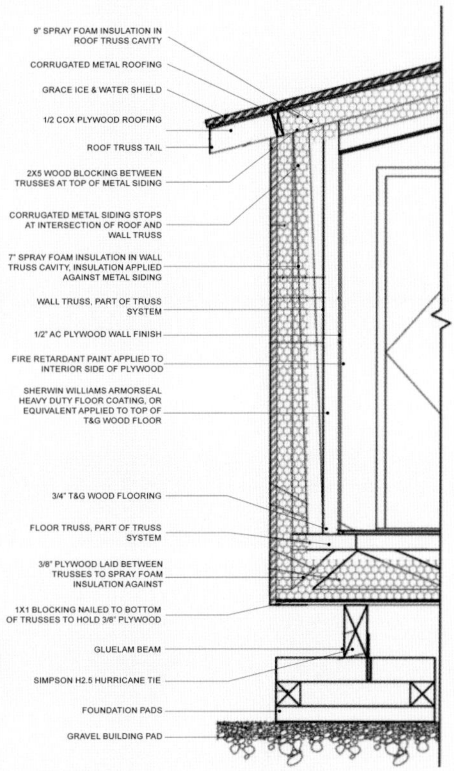

Figure 5: Wrap The Building: Integrated Truss House with Spray Foam Insulation.

The second one is the arctic wall design by Reina Properties that we've been testing and modeling – it's a cellulose wall [Figure 6]. It uses no vapor barrier. Typically when you have a super insulated house, you want to make it tight. The solution up to this point has been to put a vapor barrier on the inside of the walls of the house. Essentially, that's like putting someone in a plastic bag. You're not really letting the house breathe. This wall demonstrates a way to let the moisture dry to one side or the other. By putting enough insulation outside of the structural wall the condensation point is occurring right on the edge near the rain-screen where the air temperature is very cold and it almost dries immediately. We're testing this right now. It's working great in the interior and it's modeling great for a lot of other places, but we have yet to test it in a maritime climate.

When you build a tight house and you insulate it well, you really need to make sure that you ventilate it properly. It's very common in Alaska to use a heat recovery ventilator. It pulls the moist, stale air out of the house past a heat exchange plate. The heat from the indoor air then tempers the fresh, cold air being brought in from outside, so that you're warming the negative-forty-degree air before bringing it into the house. The older versions of this didn't really warm the air very well. So people tended to shut the unit off, especially in the rural areas where they weren't taught how to use them. So in order to get around that and basically help people have healthier homes, we've combined the HRV with the boiler system so that the air is not only tempered, but brought up to the temperature of the house using the boiler, then it's circulated through duct work around the entire house. If you want heat, you get fresh air. There's no two ways about it. This system is also great because we're able to hook it up to solar thermal and do the same thing with the water heating, a typical water heater is often the thing consuming the most electricity.

So, what can we learn before it's too late? Everyone here is aware of climate change and how it's affecting the Arctic. We know the glaciers are receding. We know the permafrost is thawing. But the most immediate needs are the housing crisis. There's a huge lack of housing in Alaska. I don't know how this is across the entire Arctic. I know the Canadians are dealing with a lack of housing as well.

The housing issue is one thing. Coastal erosion is the other. Due to climate change, there's a lack of sea ice. Sea ice used to protect coastal villages from storm surges coming up the coast. It's either no longer there or it's forming later in the year. As a result, villages are getting flooded. So what little housing they have is getting wiped out by storm surges. What are things that we can do besides building storm shelters and sea walls? We can consider designing houses that can be moved. In Point Lay, we assisted on the design of various systems in a house. We modified the foundation of houses designed by the housing authority, TNHA, and we could lower the house down using the adjustable brackets and the foundation beams become skids. If they ever need to move, they can pull their house on the snow and move it to a new location.

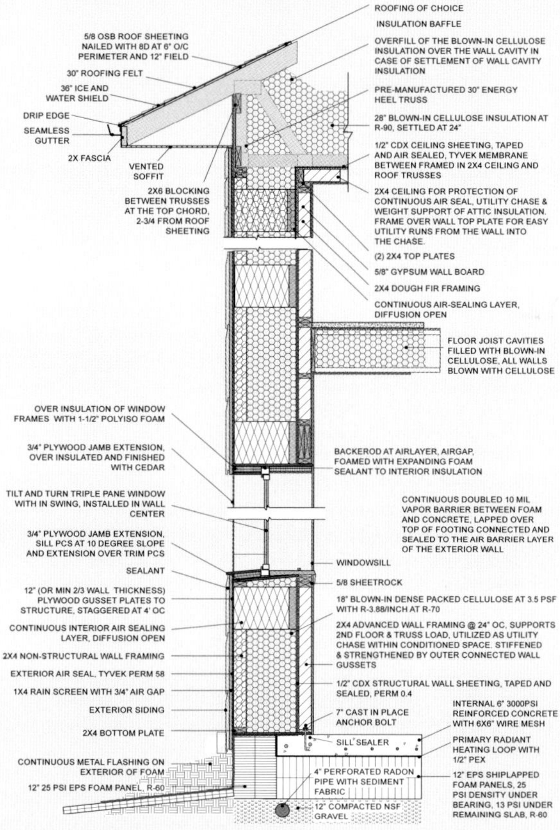

Figure 6: Superinsulated R-70 Arctic Wall and R-60 Slab Detail.

We need to think about the ability to construct houses quickly. Not only to get more housing in place, but also if there's ever a disaster we are able to build houses more quickly. In Alaska and the Arctic, the building season is very short. In most places it's May to September. Sometimes it can go a little beyond that. Many places have no roads to them. Sometimes materials can be sent on barge, sometimes they have to be flown in. An integrated truss system [Figure 7] combines a roof truss, a wall truss, and a floor truss into one structure that can be tilted up by a crew of four, 24 inches on the center. A house can basically be roofed in one day. If you can get the house enclosed before it gets too cold, you're in good shape to have people in there before winter. A lot of people don't think about the cost of transportation. We think about the cost of oil. Many people think that since Alaska produces oil, the oil would be cheaper in Alaska, but we don't refine much oil there. We export our oil and a lot of our raw natural goods to be refined in the Lower 48. By the time it has been shipped down and back, it's incredibly expensive. This greatly affects transportation costs. The typical housing package to bring materials up to a project is about one third of the cost of a house. If you can figure out a way to put all of your building materials on one flight to a village that is fly-in only or maybe one barge load, then you're going to save yourself a lot of money.

The most important thing when working in the Arctic is working with the local people. Often, the locals do not get a say in what housing is built. Before we design or build in a community, the village or tribal council or the housing authority has asked us to come in and collaborate on what's going to work with their culture and their needs. It gives them ownership of it, and it makes the projects more successful. Involving the local residents in every aspect is vital. What's the good of building a prototype or a house if you're not teaching them how to build the houses and how to order the materials and how to continue to make this happen, creating a sustainable economy? We all think about the next generation. But let's ask ourselves, "What are they going to remember?" Are they going to look back and say, "Remember when we used to live on the coast?" Are they going to say, "Remember when we used to live in a dilapidated house?" What's their memory going to be? We take note of that. Make it the immediate challenge to address.

Figure 7: Integrated truss system combines a roof truss, a wall truss and a floor truss into one structure.

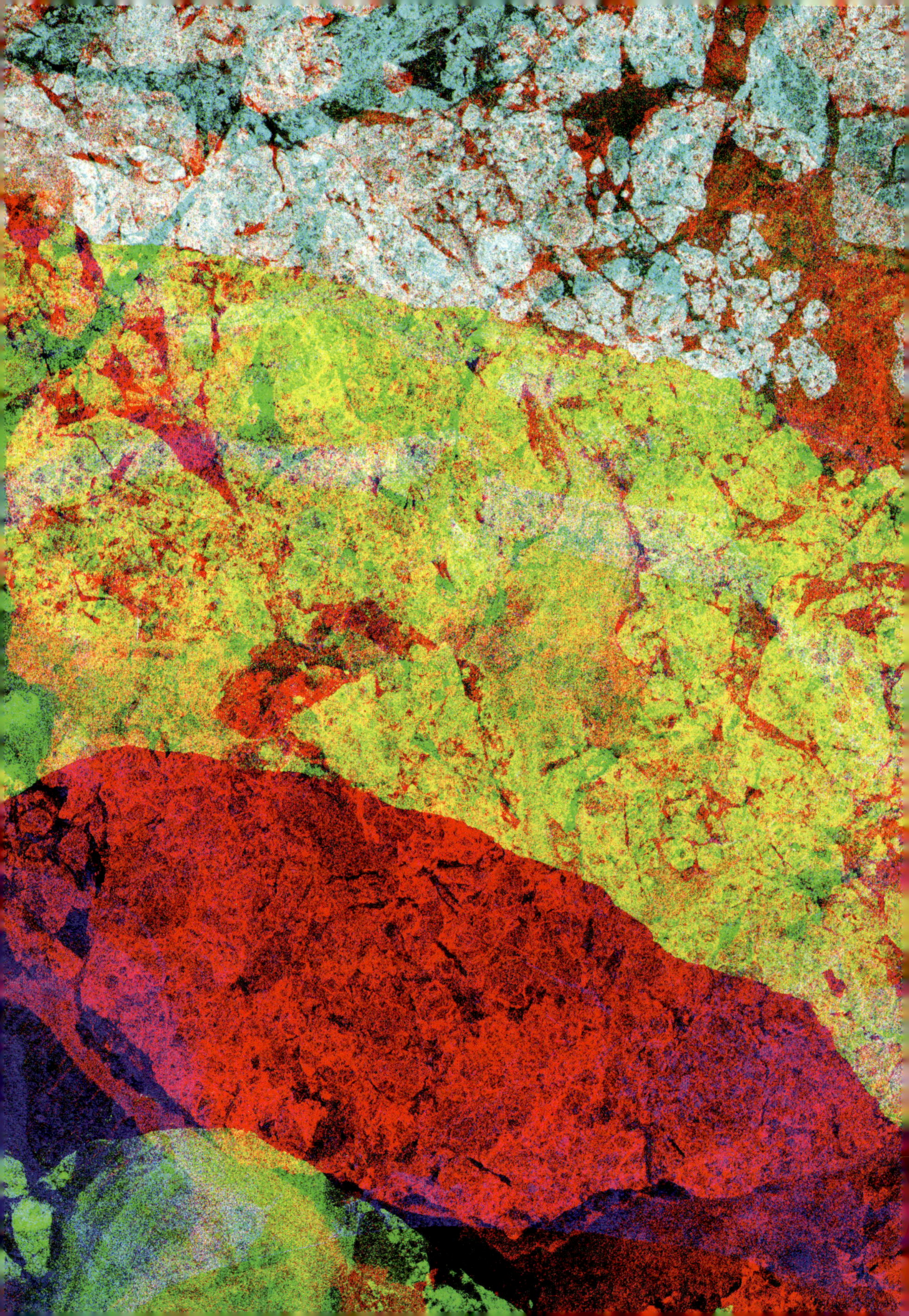

Propo-
sitions

TOWARD A NEW CULTURAL PROJECT

The integrative ambition to work synthetically and spatially across multiple disciplines at a wide range of scales is at the core of the research of the Arctic Design Group (ADG). This chapter comprises a selection of design research projects carried out by students at the University of Virginia School of Architecture under the direction of the ADG. The work is from two Alaska studios: "Altered States: Experiments in Cold Climate Design" (2017) and "Shishmaref: What does it take to move a village?" (2016). Both studios directly engaged with environmental, cultural, and economic conditions in the arctic and sub-arctic Alaska in order to explore how the design of the built environment–from wall to building to landscape–can mediate the extreme environment, and the critical changes many communities are currently experiencing. Each project is grounded in an analytical foundation and critical position to develop an innovative design agenda. Together, they present spatial and material propositions to meet the challenges of Alaskan communities that are also common in other Arctic cities and further probe underlying assumptions, overlooked opportunities, and misplaced priorities in design within a parallel context of extreme environment and climate change. In this particular selection, research topics range from food practices, building envelopes, and communal spaces to novel technologies, culminating in tactical or long-term design strategies for houses, public spaces, schools, and landscape management.

5074B

The two studios operated under different prompts, but several emerging themes and the challenges they tackled are comparable and cross-threaded. The "Altered States" studio explored fundamental thermodynamic, environmental, and material characteristics that define conditions in extreme climates as well as currently prevalent construction techniques in response to these conditions. Using this knowledge as a design foundation, the projects position the peculiarities of Arctic environment as an opportunity, not hindrance, to the making of the built environment while foregrounding community needs and indigenous cultural practices in design. The "Shishmaref" studio examined the complexities of community relocation in the context of climate change and its mechanisms such as cost, funding, and phasing. Situating the relocation within the contested history of colonial legacy in Alaska, the projects question the limits of the current relocation paradigm and underscore inseparable ties between the Native Alaskan culture and concepts of climate and home. Both studios, on the one hand, act as a magnifying glass to reveal existing issues in rural Alaskan communities that have often been overlooked and, on the other, aim to build up long-term community resilience and agency in times of shifting environmental, economic, and social structures. Echoing Mike Hulme, they aspire to use the extreme environment and the ideas of climate change as a vehicle to "re-think how we take forward various political, social and economic projects over the decades to come" rather than simply addressing them as one-off problems to solve.[1]

1 Mike Hulme, "Four Meanings of Climate Change," in *Future Ethics: Climate Change and Apocalyptic Imagination*, ed. Stefan Skrimshire (London; New York: Continuum International, 2010), 54.

METHODOLOGIES FOR DESIGN SYNTHESIS & SPECULATION

The methodology for "rethinking fundamentals" described in the previous chapter acts as a preliminary research for on-site fieldwork. It provides a partial but important lens through which we can understand how structures are built—or not built—and have evolved, while offering a critical insight into material potentials unique to experiencing the dynamic polar environment.

Operating in the Arctic, it is especially important to visit the working sites and communities, and absorb nuances of a place that cannot be discerned and traced by studying them remotely. Based on our students' fieldwork and trip logs, it is patently clear that experiencing the unfamiliar terrain of the Arctic in person provides renewed understanding for the design and maintenance of cities, both at home and in the North. In late September of 2017, over the course of ten days and charting a south-to-north transect through Alaska, the "Altered States" studio visited Anchorage, Fairbanks, Minto, and Utqiagvik (Barrow), crossing three different climate zones and rapidly changing seasons. The objective was to study the built environment at a wide range of scales and climates, and identify a purpose, site, and program that would engage with current design challenges in Alaskan communities.

Fieldwork plays an essential role in examining the condition, situation, or value of the site and place, and querying the landscape in question in order to collect quantitative and anecdotal data for analysis and interpretation. Daily activities such as surveys, interviews, guided tours, workshops, and lectures are documented in text, sketches, photographs, and short videos, edited and choreographed with intention. Together they capture factual, sensorial, and spatial narratives from the visits. Most importantly they reveal the stories of people in communities and their desires, sensibilities, and encounters in daily life. It is an overwhelming experience no matter how well one has prepared for it. But through this experience, we define issues we must address, and identify what is at stake, why it is important, and how it addresses the needs and potentials for future living in response to the Arctic's environment and its changes. Elaborating on them requires recalibration of previous work on the fundamentals, and clarification of assumptions guiding design directions.

As the largest state in the United States, Alaska covers ten different types of Köppen climate systems, ranging from warm-summer Mediterranean continental to tundra and ice-cap [Figure 1]. A collection of mountain ranges, glaciers, active volcanoes, huge tracks of forested lands, and tundra makes Alaska's landscape culturally and ecologically diverse, while 85% of the state sits on "permanently frozen grounds" extending as much as 2,000 feet below the surface on the arctic coastal plain [Figure 2]. Topography varies sharply among the six distinct regions too, covering flat coastal plains to mountain peaks of 10,000ft including the tallest mountain peak (20,310ft) in North America, Denali [Figure 3]. The diversity of its people and major changes in the state since the 1960s have resulted in social, political, economic, and educational contrasts that are no less remarkable. The state's discovery of oil (1968), the Alaska Native Claims Settlement Act (1971), the building of the trans-Alaska pipeline system, TAPS (1974-7), and decentralization of the state school system (1975), among others, have had significant impacts upon the everyday life of Alaskans.[2] Over the past three decades, the population of Alaska has grown by more than 40%. Despite the rapid population growth in the Anchorage Municipality, the state remains predominantly rural, with three major cities, Anchorage (298,695), Juneau (32,756), and Fairbanks (32,751) as well as much smaller but economically significant cities such as Valdez (4,000) where TAPS terminates [Figure 4]. Only twenty-six of the state's 352 communities have populations of more than 1,000 people.

2
Carol Barnhardt, "A History of Schooling for Alaska Native People," *Journal of American Indian Education* 40, no. 1 (January 2001): 4.

While the major cities such as Anchorage offer modern amenities, well-developed transportation system, and fully-equipped homes, the smaller towns and villages are accessible only by air and in some cases by water [Figure 5, 6, 7]. Rural Alaska, typically refers to any region in the state not connected to the North American road network or readily accessible by the state's ferry system. Beyond a roughly triangular area connecting Anchorage, Fairbanks, and Valdez as well as the north-to-south Dalton highway between Deadhorse/Prudhoe Bay oil fields and Fairbanks, land-based transport infrastructure is scarce and scattered, resulting in a sharp contrast between the western and eastern regions. A large proportion of Native Alaskans live in rural subsistence-based communities. Most small villages are disconnected from each other except by boat, snow machine, or light aircraft. Likewise, moving food and supplies to and from these communities is no easy feat, especially to its rural outreaches, and is often far more expensive than outside of Alaska. Most items coming into Alaska pass through Anchorage (by ship or air cargo) before being delivered to other destinations in the state. Barges arrive to small communities generally twice a year during the navigable seasons, but many depend on aviation for access and mobility.

Within the geographic and environmental boundaries of the Arctic [Figure 8], these bush communities and small hub cities, which are often located on coastal or riverine edges, make up most of the Arctic settlements in Alaska. The contrasting degree of development and infrastructure in small arctic Alaskan communities coupled with environmental extremes, colonial legacies, and indigenous subsistence practices presents a significant challenge when the factor of climate change is introduced. The effects of coastal erosion, flooding, sea ice reduction, and thawing permafrost are not new, and many villages have been identified at a federal level experiencing imminent danger from these changes.[3] Shishmaref, a small Inupiat community for instance, has been pursuing complete relocation since 1976 and has been engaged in relocation, evacuation, and emergency preparedness planning for the past forty years with varying degrees of success.[4] Over this period, the community has continued to shrink with erosion eating away over 200 feet since 1969. A few storms have eroded 25-30 feet of land from a single night of storm.[5] The circumstances of Shishmaref are equally complex and challenging on a logistical level given the lack of existing or well-functioning infrastructure such as roads as well as policy framework and funding to assist relocation and long-term efforts towards environmental adaptation.

3
U.S. Government Accountability Office, *Alaska Native Villages: Limited Progress Has Been Made on Relocating Villages Threatened by Flooding and Erosion*, GAO-09-551 (Washington, DC, 2009), 16.

4
Alaska Department of Commerce, Community and Economic Development, *Shishmaref Relocation Site Selection Feasibility Study*, by AECOM (Anchorage, AK: 2016), 1-1.

5
Ibid., 1-1.

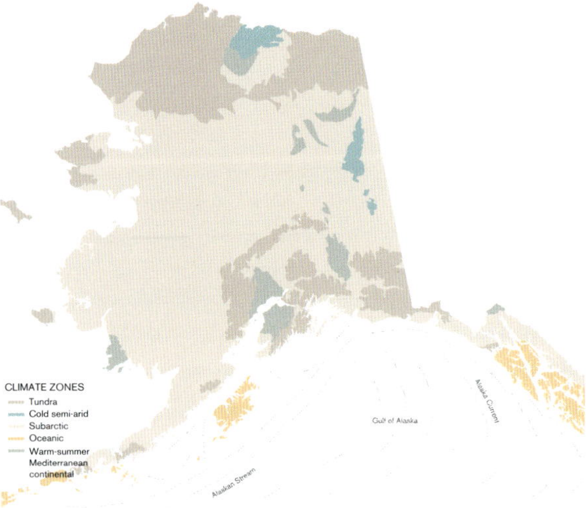

Figure 1

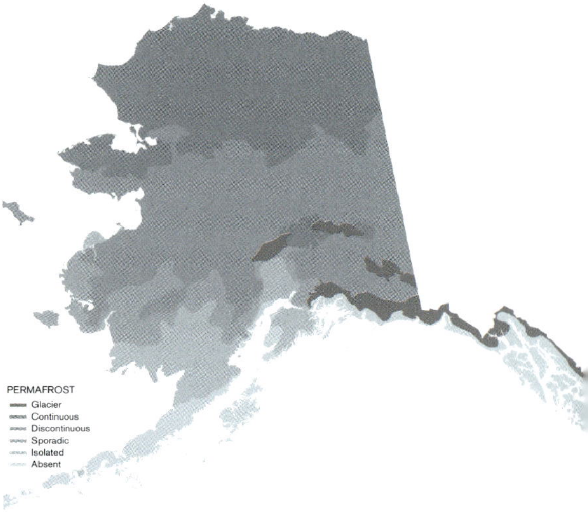

Figure 2

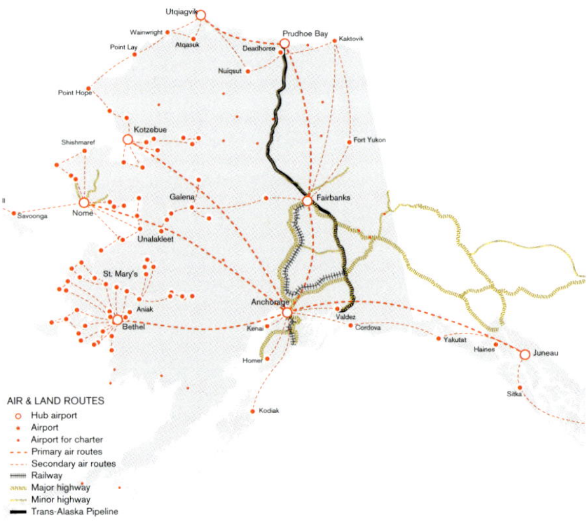

Figure 5

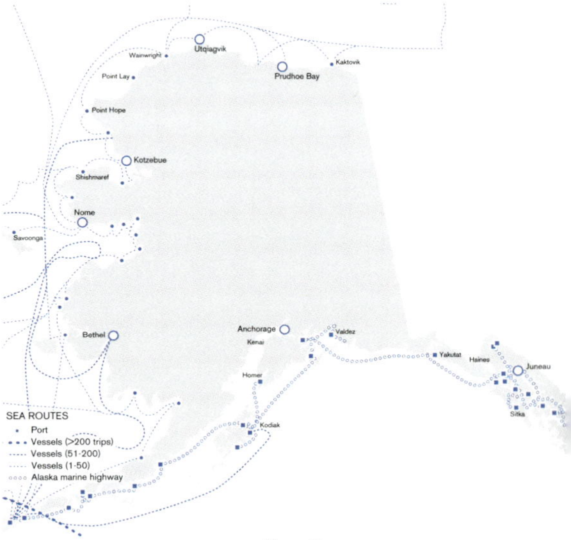

Figure 6

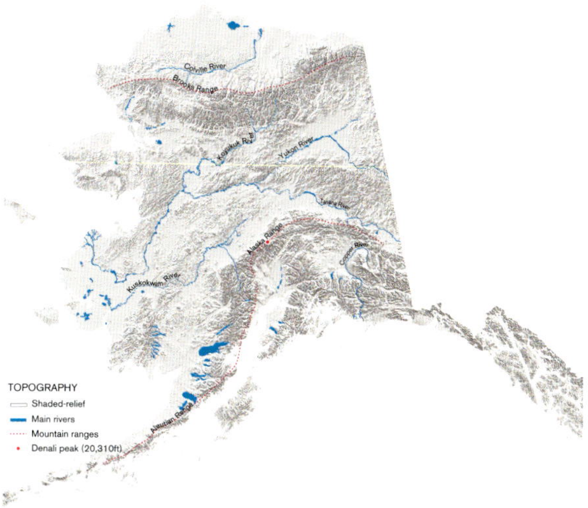

Figure 3

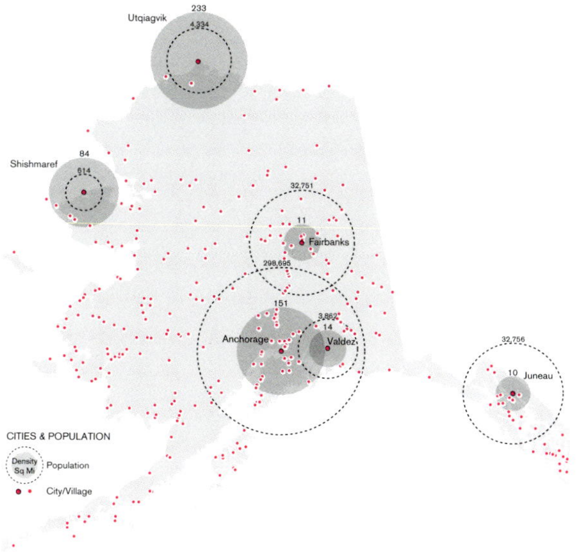

Figure 4

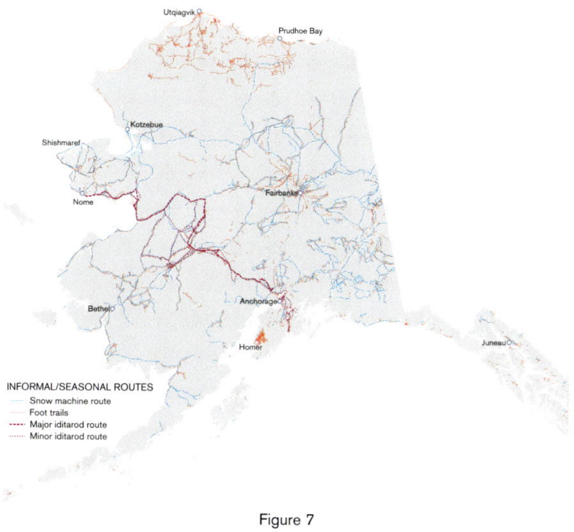

Figure 7

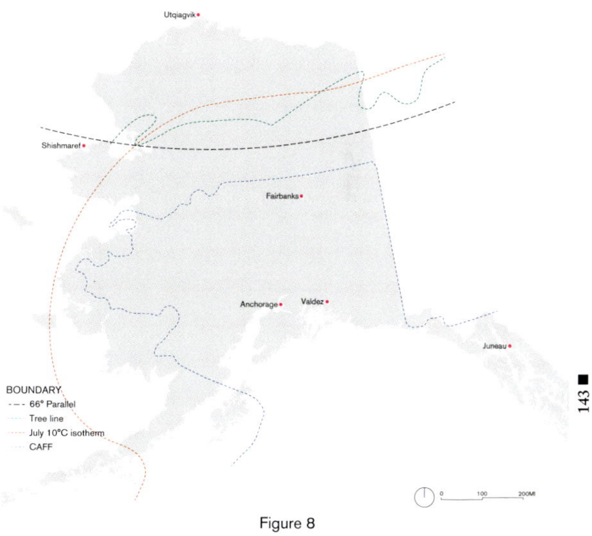

Figure 8

HOUSE

According to the U.S. Department of Housing and Urban Development, the overcrowding and physical housing problems of Native Alaskans remain strikingly more severe than those of other Americans.[6] Circumstances of tribal rural settlements such as "remoteness, lack of infrastructure, and complex legal constraints related to land ownership make it difficult to improve housing conditions in those areas."[7] Cities and villages the ADG has engaged with in the past two years—Anchorage, Utqiagvik, Minto, Fairbanks, and Shishmaref—are at the forefront of these concerns and the conditions of houses are exacerbated by aging infrastructure, eroding, and thawing ground, and lack of climatic and cultural considerations in design. All buildings in the Arctic must consider strict rules of environment, economies, and efficiency such as constructability (e.g., permafrost, short construction season), logistics (e.g., cost of shipping building materials or exporting waste), and environmental performance (e.g., heat exchange, wind, and snow drift). The majority of houses in rural Alaska are modular units designed and shipped north from the Lower 48 under the auspices of the U.S. Department of Housing and Urban Development (HUD). The HUD houses, as referred to in Alaska, have been built through a southern, non-Arctic lens, transplanted and often maladapted to the Arctic climate. The resulting interior spaces are too often deprived of natural light and poorly ventilated. Many homes are old and drafty and energy inefficient, burdening residents with high costs.[8]

6
U.S. Department of Housing and Urban Development, *Housing Needs of American Indians and Alaska Natives in Tribal Areas: A Report From the Assessment of American Indian, Alaska Native, and Native Hawaiian Housing Needs: Executive Summary*, by Nancy Pindus et. al. (Washington, DC, 2017), 1.

7
Ibid., 1.

8
Cold Climate Housing Research Center, *2018 Alaska Housing Assessment: Statewide Housing Summary* (Anchorage: Alaska Housing Finance Corporation, 2018), 23.

GROUND

Buildings and infrastructures such as utility pipelines often hover over the ground in Arctic regions and rest on wooden stacks, metal scaffolding, or some variation of wood or steel pillars. They are raised to minimize permafrost disturbance caused by heat emanating from the structure's interior, or snow drift. The freeze and thaw cycle of permafrost is a seasonally occurring natural phenomena in the Arctic and is one that catalyzes remarkable geomorphological and ecological features. From an engineering perspective, however, it is a powerful destabilizing force for any structure built within and above it such as foundations, roads, and utilidors, and is a condition that is increasingly becoming unpredictable due to warming temperatures. This ubiquitous Arctic engineering technique, although essential in this region, often disconnects architecture from the ground and curtails dynamic social and ecological exchange that occurs at the ground level. While engineers and researchers are increasingly experimenting with new building supports to prepare the Arctic for rapid shifts in permafrost and ground stability,[9] pillar constructions and innovations are rarely discussed in the social and ecological contexts of living environment –such as the qualities of outdoor space adjacent to, and microclimate–dependent urban ecology of the "underneath" space that these engineering techniques produce. The layer between the structure and the earth is where distinctively "northern" design problem occurs, and to this extent, where great potentials exist for claiming uniquely Arctic architecture and urban landscape.

9
Laura Poppick, "Engineering new foundations for a thawing Arctic," *Eos, Trans, American Geophysical Union*, no. 98 (August 22, 2017), https://doi.org/10.1029/2017EO080435

LUKE TITUS
GYM

SCHOOL

Historically, schools have held a contested role in Native Alaskan communities. The assumptions that people's needs are best served through schools that promote "civilization" and Christianity has continued to be a powerful theme throughout the history of Alaska Native education,[10] and to that extent, how communities are organized. For instance, the development of Shishmaref began with the construction of a post office in 1901, a government school in 1906, and a Lutheran mission in 1930.[11] Infrastructure development through schools and missions, and policies that required children to participate in school programs, resulted in the sedentarization of seasonally migrating indigenous family groups and consolidation of winter villages to the centralized and permanent location.[12] In the ongoing relocation efforts for Shishmaref and Newtok/Mertarvik, schools continue to play a strategic role in regards to phasing of the move as they trigger and unlock various funding streams at the state and federal levels. Today, many schools in Native Alaskan towns struggle with the combined legacies of governmental intervention, environmental under-performance, and southern architecture models. Despite this complexity, schools are an integral part of communities in the Arctic, and often the most important communal space in small rural villages. Basketball in school gymnasium, for instance, is a highly important social event. Interpersonal ties and sense of community are the overarching concern and priority for many Native Alaskans, and school is viewed as a critical infrastructure capable of strengthening traditional knowledge transfer, social cohesion, and safety in case of emergency.[13]

10
Elizabeth K. Marino, *Fierce climate, sacred ground: An ethnography of climate change in Shishmaref, Alaska* (Fairbanks: University of Alaska Press, 2015), 51.

11
Ibid., 52.

12
Ibid., 53.

13
Victoria Herrmann, "Investing in community: conceptualizing inclusive school design for America's Arctic," *Polar Geography* 39, no. 4 (November 2016), 239.

LAND

Alaskans' connection to the land is both powerful and complex as the story of Shishmaref shows. The notions of land and variegated practices of living within it, such as rugged individualism and subsistence lifestyle, define the cultural foundations and identities of Alaska, and are closely linked to the broader historical construction of Arctic as a place. More recently, the Arctic has taken on profound environmental significance as a bellwether for changes to come elsewhere. The transformations brought forth by warming temperatures, however, are more than just physical; they are deeply connected to the accumulated and layered histories of the landscape where people's connection to it will be confronted by changes as well. The elements of house, ground, and school discussed earlier, as well as a host of other spatial practices in the Arctic such as hunting, summer camps, and ritual grounds, are deeply enmeshed in the overall and often competing notions of land, too, and they cannot be fully discerned or addressed if the study of the built environment in Alaska and in the Arctic is decoupled from this relationship. Jack Hébert from the Cold Climate Housing Research Center captures this sensibility eloquently: "A house is not home, a house is a place within home. The land is home." In rural Native Alaskan villages, people's connection to their land reverberates through every corner, and as much as it is complicated, it is at least in part "rooted in a subsistence tradition that is about food, practice, skills, and connection to family and place."[14] The difficult challenge for designers is beyond physical and spatial problem-solving; it is the remediation of deep bondage to land expressed or hidden in the built form that is becoming uprooted due to multiple factors of change.

14
Marino, *Fierce climate, sacred ground*, 82.

Ford

PAMIILAQ
ALMAR

DESIGN APPROACHES AND PROPOSITIONS

Design in the Arctic calls for a radical attunement to its climatic and cultural identities. These identities are multivalent, contingent, contested and evolving at the nexus of the past and the present. Likewise, the key design challenge in the Arctic is a creation of design intelligence merging the modern technology and engineering of the extreme and rapidly changing environments with the traditional spatio-material practices. Given these physical, technical, and social challenges, the Arctic Design Group's design approach is grounded in a multi-layered and hybrid process that ultimately emphasizes the qualities of living and the agency of local inhabitants. We use the combined domains of architecture and landscape architecture to interrogate the relationships between, for example, indoor and outdoor, structure and ground, personal and communal, cultural and technological. This relational approach extends to the design of a house, public space, urban blocks, landscape infrastructure, and its management regimes. The issues many Arctic communities are facing cannot be solved, or even be understood, by one disciplinary perspective alone; they require a multiplicity of views, and it is with this humbling awareness that we have engaged with indigenous community leaders and residents, environmental scientists, anthropologists, school teachers, and engineers in the design process. In the case of climate change, our approach has also been beyond physical and technical problem-solving. We use the idea of climate change forensically to reveal issues that have long existed in the communities, such as colonial legacy and food insecurity, and to closely examine undermined opportunities within the current paradigms of relocation discourse.

Student projects such as "Framing Logics," "Full Spectrum Symbiosis," and "Thermal Thresholds" aspire to generate this synthesis and a greater sense of belonging in three different locations in Alaska – Shishmaref/West Tin Creek Hills, Utqiagvik, and Minto. Each design–a house, park, and school, respectively–utilizes natural thermal hierarchies to site and organize programs. The architectural components unique and prevalent in the Arctic such as integrated trusses, underground ice cellar, arctic entry, and raised foundation are reconceptualized while maintaining their profound ties to the indigenous practices and landscapes. As such, extreme environmental conditions are positioned as an opportunity to highlight cultural identity, conceptual expansion and technical design inventions, while addressing the everyday needs of residents.

Moving the community to a higher ground doesn't necessarily ameliorate its vulnerabilities that climate change has exposed. "Hacking the Homestead" asks, in essence, how else we should approach relocation beyond the limits of short-term engineering, funding, and logistical complexity. It foregrounds the deep cultural ties to the climate, land, and subsistence practices in the relocation and new town planning as critical to the sustainment of community. Other projects in the studio have also critiqued the absence of material and ecological frameworks in the current relocation discourse, and called for creating long-term barrier island management as part of the relocation planning as well as harnessing material and logistical byproducts of relocation as a resource to strengthen community's economic autonomy "beyond the move."

Safeguarding and, at times, rebuilding resiliency is vital to the future of Arctic communities. Resilience is the capacity to deal with change, and, when pushed past a threshold, to transform. It is the capacity to use the disturbance like climate change and weather extremes to spur renewal and innovative thinking and to adapt to a different set of meaningful socio-ecological interactions. At the heart of this, and also voiced in all of the sampled projects, is the question of human agency – who defines that threshold, who transforms it, and who ultimately benefits from that adaptation.

Whether it is a house or a trail, a school or an entirely new village or city, what has motivated the work of the ADG Alaska and our students in their explorations is the humanist undertaking in design – its capacity to engage, listen, provoke, imagine, and empower, and to restore authority, remediate rituals, and to unleash a new cultural project that is equally long-term and transformational for rural Alaska and for the Arctic.

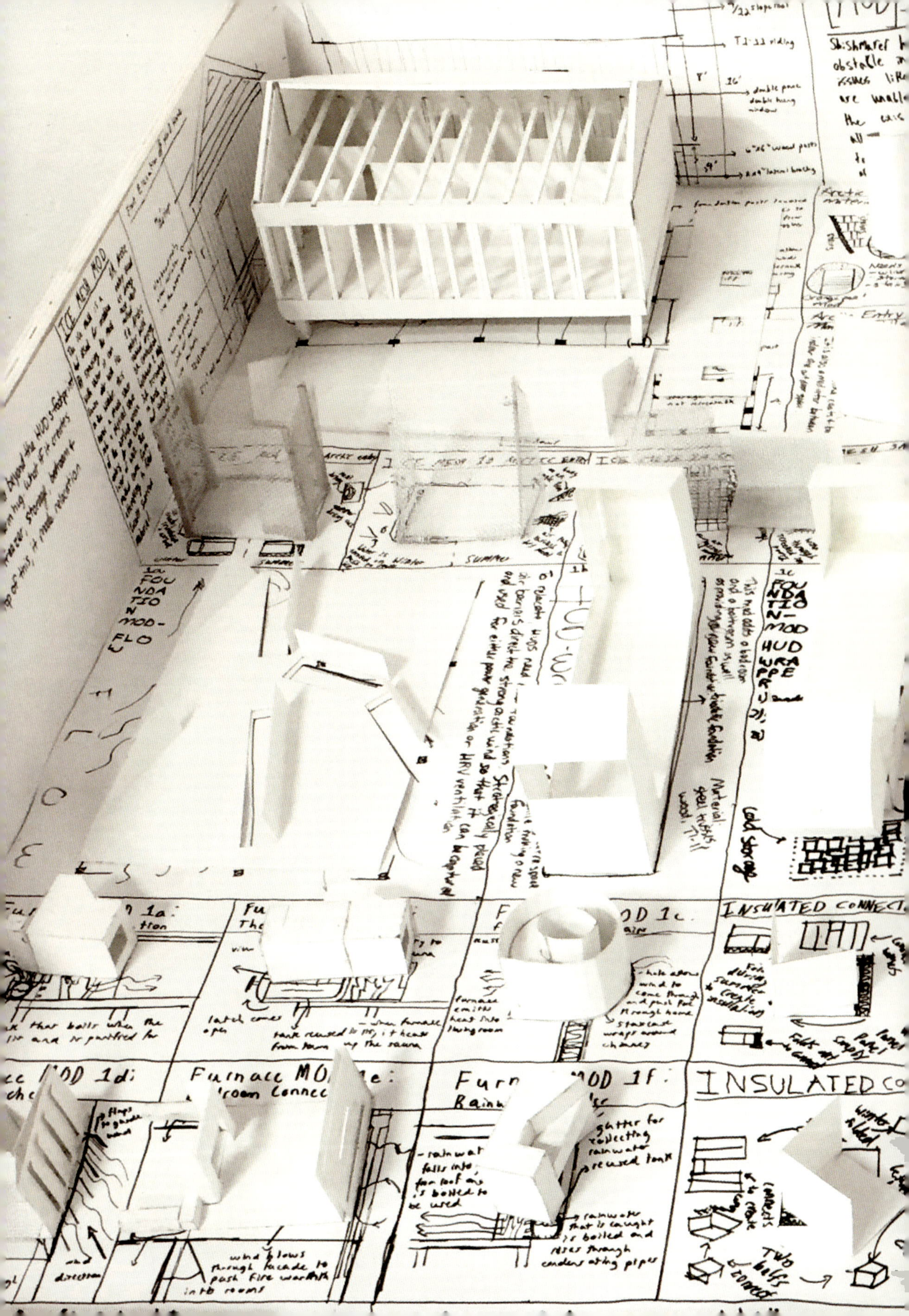

T1-11 siding
double pane double hung window
ICE MESH MOD
FOUNDATION MOD FLOW
FOUNDATION MOD HUD WRAPPER
Arctic Entry
Material: steel, HUD, wood, T1-11
cold storage
INSULATED CONNECT
Furnace MOD 1f: Rainw
INSULATED CO
gutter for collecting rainwater reused tank
rainwater that is caught is boiled and rises through condensating pipes
wind blows through facade to push fire warmth into rooms
SUMMER

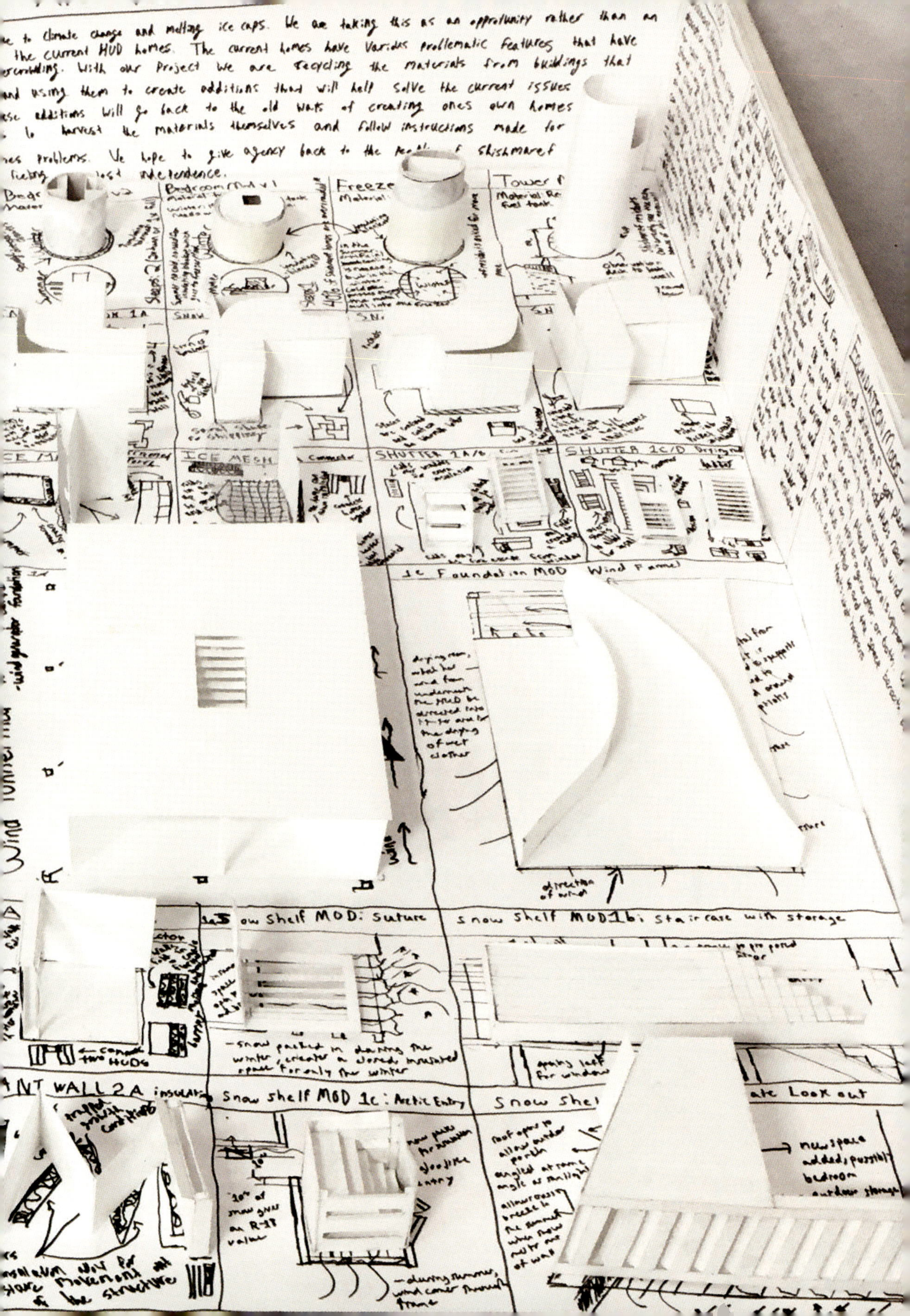

e to climate change and melting ice caps. We are taking this as an opportunity rather than an
the current HUD homes. The current homes have various problematic features that have
ercrowding. With our project we are recycling the materials from buildings that
and using them to create additions that will help solve the current issues
ese additions will go back to the old ways of creating ones own homes
to harvest the materials themselves and follow instructions made for
es problems. We hope to give agency back to the people of Shishmaref
Freeze
Tower
ICE MESH
SHUTTER 1A/B
SHUTTER 1C/D
1C Foundation MOD Wind Panel
Wind Tunnel
direction of wind
ow Shelf MOD: Suture
Snow Shelf MOD 1b: Staircase with storage
—snow packed in during the winter, creates a closed insulated space for only the winter
NT WALL 2A
Snow shelf MOD 1c: Arctic Entry
Snow Shel
Look out
new space added, possibly bedroom
—during summer, wind comes through frame

View to Shishmaref Island
Barge Access Location
allowable density
buildable area
soil ice content
Zone 1
Gravel Access Road
Zone 3
Zone 2
View to Ear Mountain
50
50

Program: House
Location: West Tin Creek Hills, AK
Ziggy Chen, Ben DiNapoli, Austin Edwards, Tyler Mauri

FRAMING LOGICS

This project envisions a flexible housing framework driven by passive and efficient energy systems on the one hand, and Inupiaq cultural practices of intergenerational and subsistence-based living on the other. Addressing the failure to resolve critical issues related to the changing climate and relocation, a flexible housing framework is necessary to adapt to an array of environmental, social and economic conditions. Can the house itself operate in a way that embraces the extreme climate of the western Alaska region, replacing the need for expensive technical solutions? Can the building technique in the Arctic foreground sensorial and physiological aspects of inhabitation? Given the legacy of HUD houses in Alaska and operating under the scenario of relocating Shishmaref to West Tin Creek Hills – one of the inland site alternatives studied by AECOM (2016), the project offers a new model for housing attuned to the Arctic climate, Inupiaq family structure and their environmental interaction, and allows the villagers to use a set of tools to address their individual preferences.

The prototype house provides new construction systems capable of growing and shrinking depending on the family needs and size. The internal microclimate system further regulates program sequence from cool to warm; air filters from fresh to stale; humidity is channeled from dry to wet. Light becomes accessible even in winter months, and insulation is a result of form, not merely technical specification. Material layers of polycarbonate sheathing, plywood sheathing, and rigid foam insulation create different thickness of insulation, coupling specific uses within a house with varying thermal properties. By introducing an interstitial semi-climatized space, and by re-sequencing the programs within the house to follow their natural thermal hierarchies, the house becomes integrated with function, climate, and culture including the possibility of storing subsistence goods in the underground ice cellar. This interstitial space contributes to increased passive ventilation, moisture reduction, heat exchange and thermal comfort.

The primary activity across all spaces in a house is a direct result of the confluence of seen and unseen phenomenological forces. Importantly, the strategies emphasize restoring authority and ownership of house for Inupiaq families, and use the relocation as an opportunity to rethink the future model for housing in rural Alaska.

LOGICS

Critical junctures in the relocation strategy of Shishmaref

- × biased factors
- • comprehensive topics
- • site-specific
- O key intersections
- □ objectives

Relocation Options

R1 *Shelter-in-place*
R2 *Vote to relocate*
R3 *West Tin Creek Hills site*
P *Prototype*

I ECOLOGICAL
SUFFICIENT SPACE FOR COMMUNITY OF 800 PERSONS
STORM SURGE VULNERABILITY
RIVER FLOODING VULNERABILITY
SHORELINE EROSION VULNERABILITY
SITE DRAINAGE AND WETLANDS
SOILS (ICE CONTENT)
VULNERABILITY TO HIGH WINDS
WATER SUPPLY (SOURCE AND QUALITY)

II CONSTRUCTIBILITY
GEO TECHNICAL CONSTRUCTIBILITY ANALYSIS
SEWAGE DISPOSAL AVAILABILITY
EASE OF WATER STORAGE AND DISTRIBUTION
SOLID WASTE DISPOSAL AVAILABILITY
GRAVEL REQUIREMENTS TO DEVELOP SITE
BARGE ACCESS DISTANCE TO SITE
SITE FOR AIRPORT WITH CROSSWIND RUNWAY
COMMUNITY EXPANSION POTENTIAL
EASE OF MAINTAINING TWO SITES DURING CONSTRUCTION
PERMITTING OBSTACLES

III ACCESSIBILITY
DISTANCE TO CURRENT VILLAGE SITE
ACCESS TO OCEAN
ACCESS TO SHISHMAREF LAGOON
ACCESS TO SUBSISTENCE CAMPS AND TRADITIONAL USE AREAS
LOCATION OF BOAT/GEAR STORAGE
POTENTIAL FOR CELLAR CONSTRUCTION
GENERAL COMFORT WITH SITE
LAND STATUS

IV COST IMPLICATIONS
SITE PREPARATION COSTS
ACCESS ROAD DEVELOPMENT COSTS
OPERATION AND MANAGEMENT COSTS
COST OF LIVING (HEAT/POWER)
FUEL COSTS FOR ACCESS TO SUBSISTENCE AREAS, AIRPORT, DOCK

V SITE SPECIFIC CRITERIA
LOCATION OF PERMAFROST SUBLAYER

VI SHISHMAREF
COSTS ASSOCIATED WITH PROTECTIVE INFRASTRUCTURE
HOUSING RETROFITS
MAJOR INFRASTRUCTURAL IMPROVEMENTS OF EXISTING SYSTEMS

VII WEST TIN CREEK HILLS
REQUIREMENT FOR PILE FOUNDATIONS AND BUILDING ELEVATION
PILE-SUPPORTED BOARDWALKS FOR PEDESTRIAN ACCESS
REQUIREMENT FOR ABOVE-GROUND INSULATED WATER PIPES
REQUIREMENT FOR ROAD BED AND GROUND INSULATION

VIII OLD POND
REQUIREMENT TO FILL SITE WITH GRAVEL TO RAISE ABOVE FLOOD LEVEL
BUILDING SITE SURCHARGE FOR INSULATED SHALLOW FOUNDATIONS
NO SUPPORT FOR PILE FOUNDATIONS
ALLOWED USE OF BURIED ARCTIC INSULATED PIPES
CULTURAL ARCHITECTURE

IX NATIVE HOUSING NEEDS
MODULAR ADDITIONS FOR ELDERS' HOMES, EXTENDED FAMILY
POLICIES THAT RESPECT CULTURAL VALUES
MAINTAINING PROXIMITY TO EXTENDED FAMILY
ABILITY FOR SELF-MAINTENANCE
OWNER EDUCATION ON HOUSING SYSTEMS
STANDARDIZATION OF BUILDING MATERIALS
CERTIFY AND TRAIN LOCAL COMMUNITY MEMBERS
REDUCE OVERCROWDING
RESTORATION OF NATIVE HOUSING OWNERSHIP

X SPATIAL OBJECTIVES
UNIVERSAL COMMON SPACE
THERMAL TRANSITION ZONE
INTEGRATED STORAGE CAPACITY

XI ARCTIC STRATEGIES
EFFICIENT STRUCTURAL SYSTEMS
FLEXIBLE FLOOR PLANS

XII CLIMATIC ARCHITECTURE
INTEGRATED BUILDING PROCESS
OCCUPANT-DRIVEN SPACE
SENSORY AND PHYSIOLOGICAL TREATMENTS OF BUILDING TECHNIQUE
THERMAL PROGRAM SEQUENCE
PASSIVE AIR HEAT EXCHANGE AND FILTRATION
HUMIDITY CONTROL
PASSIVE COOLING AND HEATING STRATEGIES
PROGRAM-SPECIFIC INSULATION

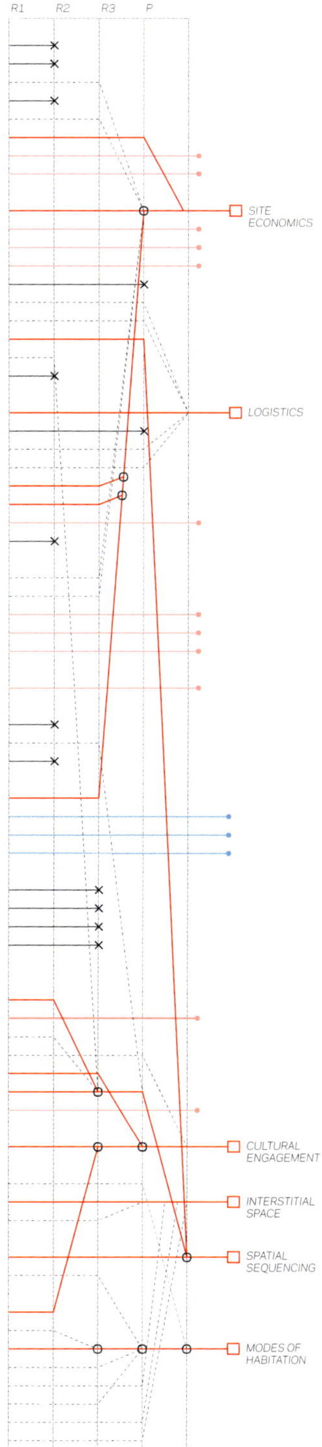

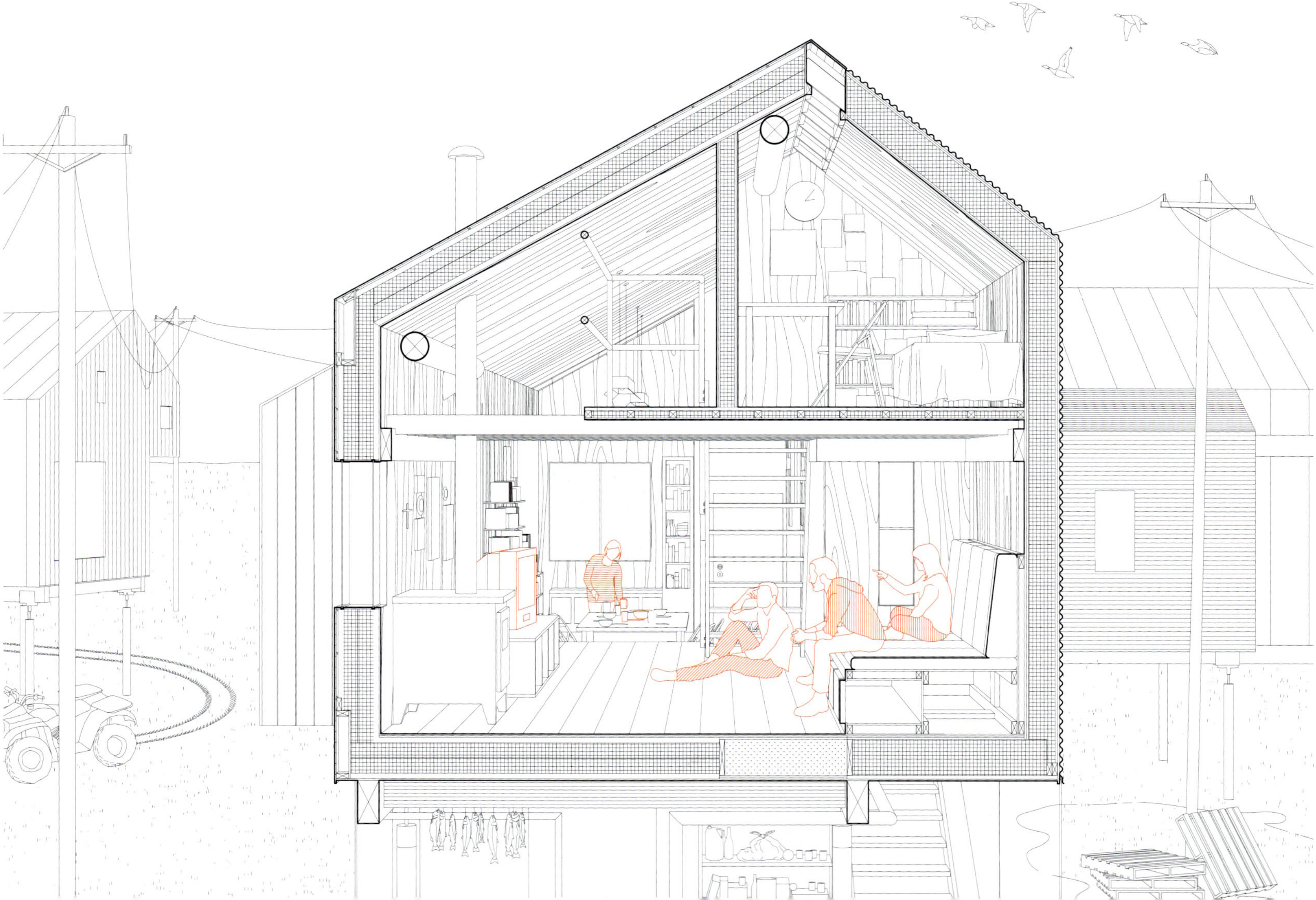

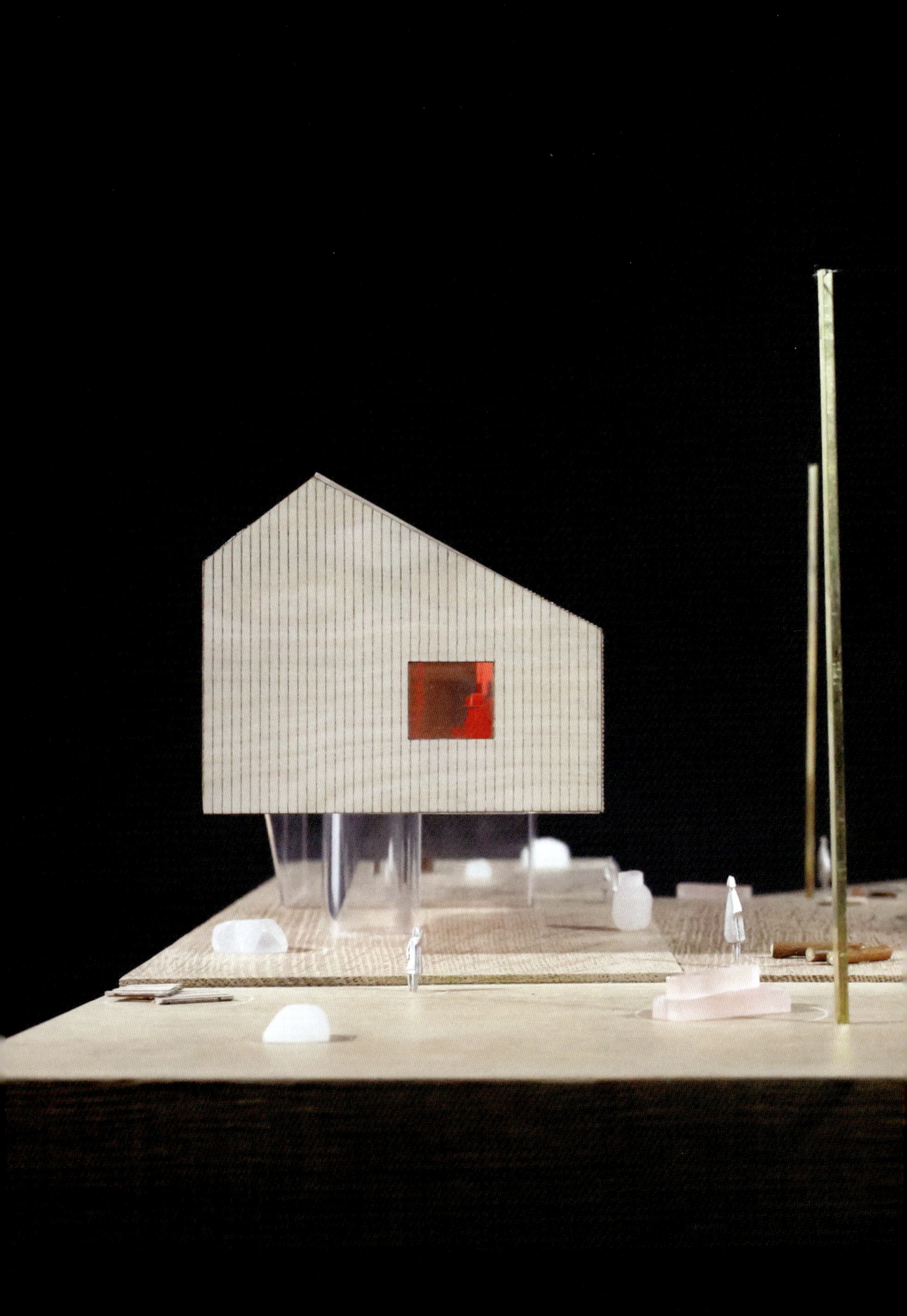

Program: Park
Location: Utqiagvik, AK
Yue Han, Xinxin Huang, Han Yu

FULL SPECTRUM SYMBIOSIS

Utqiagvik, formerly known as Barrow, exhibits an extreme geological and meteorological condition. At this high latitude, attenuated solar radiation due to atmospheric filtering and seasonal occlusion, combined with continuous permafrost create a cold and moist climate regime. With little natural variation in topography, human settlements can significantly alter local ecosystem in the open tundra. Raised road beds and elevated building structures reshape the radiation distribution and air-flow patterns at ground level.

How can this important space between structure and ground in the city be reconsidered and integrated into daily life? Could this decoupled and often wasted space catalyze generative linkages between environment and humans, human and non-human species? How can a wide variety of spatial and material typologies at the building-ground interface create a full spectrum of interaction - a new "socio-environmental matrix," within which people and the dynamic environment could make a step toward greater symbiosis?

This project calls for a new design paradigm in the Arctic by envisioning a park–an uncommon typology in small Arctic cities–that runs through three typical urban conditions in the center of Utqiagvik: infrastructure, school, and houses. Each zone, defined as "Market," "Melting Water Garden," and "Playground," is designed with a different set of parameters related to scale, program, and materiality of buildings, underlying permafrost, and surrounding outdoor spaces.

The proposed park utilizes local plant species, natural and artificial ground materials, structural supports, and building volume and massing in order to re-introduce social and ecological interaction into the heavily engineered landscape. The radical seasonal changes the city undergoes are incorporated into the design of the park that is dynamic throughout the year. By claiming sunlight, snow accumulation, melt water, wind shadows, and heat from buildings as design media for the park, the city becomes integrated with the environment and transforms the neglected spaces into an active ground for experience.

vegetation type 1
vegetation type 2
vegetation type 3
gravel
paved road
naked ground
ice
thawing ice
design area sheltered space
design area enclosed space
design area protected polygon
design area vegetation type 1
design area vegetation type 2
design area vegetation type 3
design area gravel
design area paved road
design area paved runway
design area snow drift
design area muddy soil
design area airplane

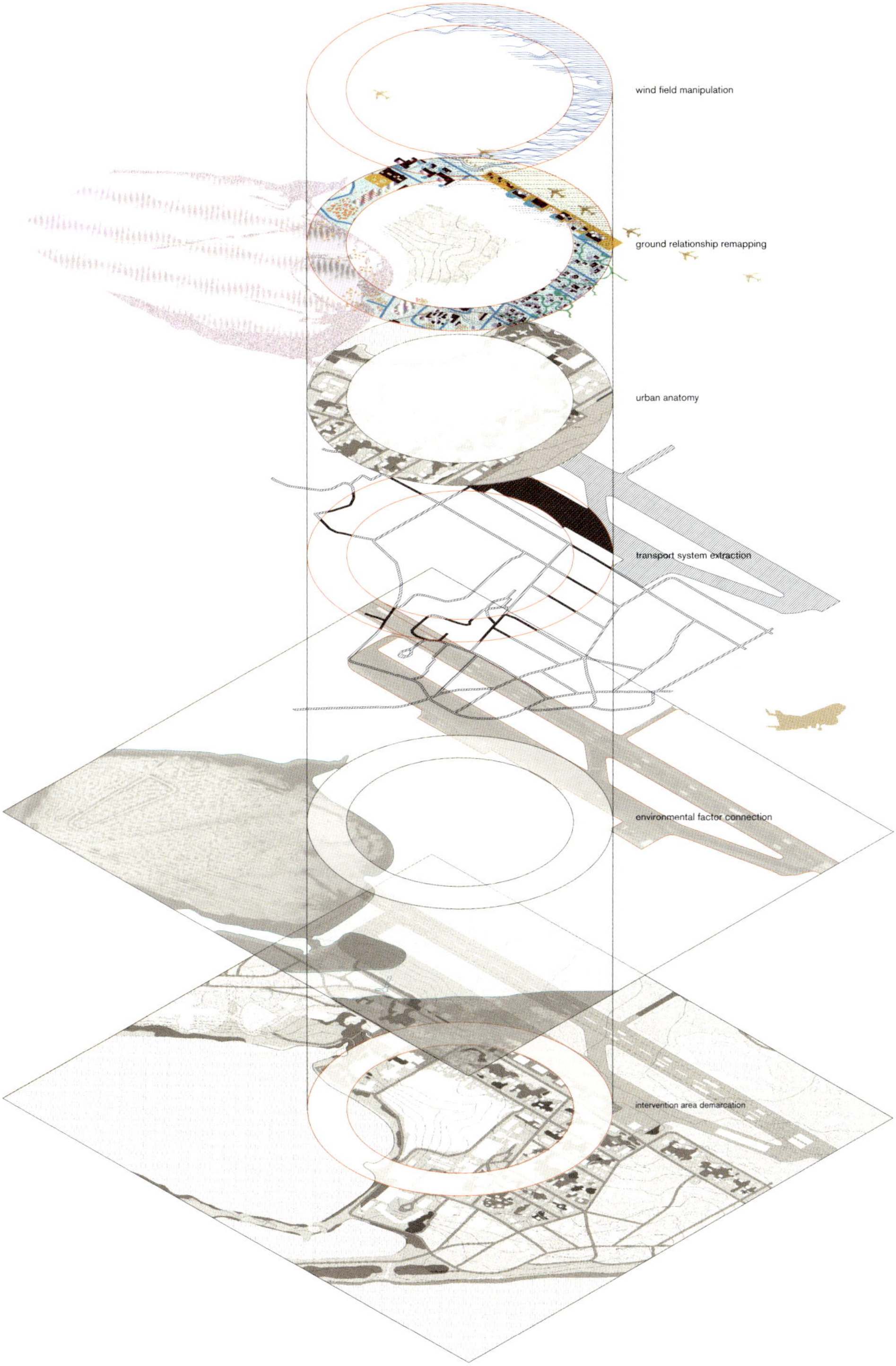
wind field manipulation
ground relationship remapping
urban anatomy
transport system extraction
environmental factor connection
intervention area demarcation

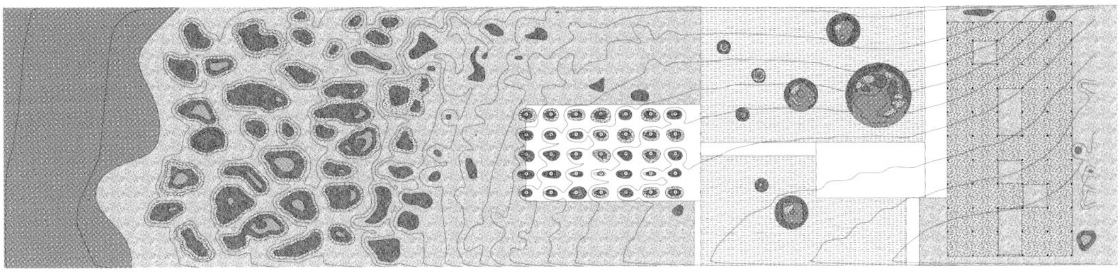

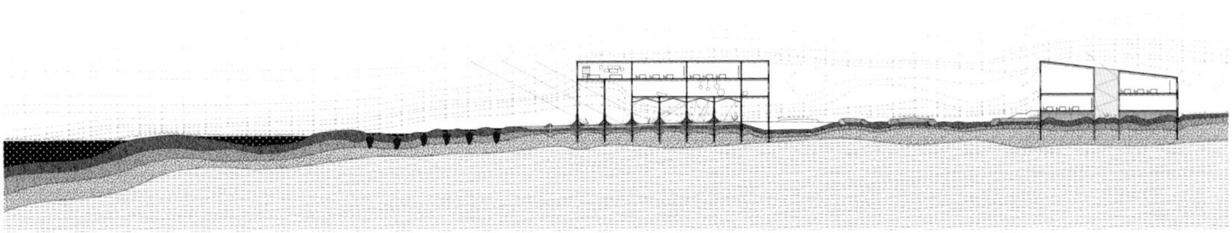

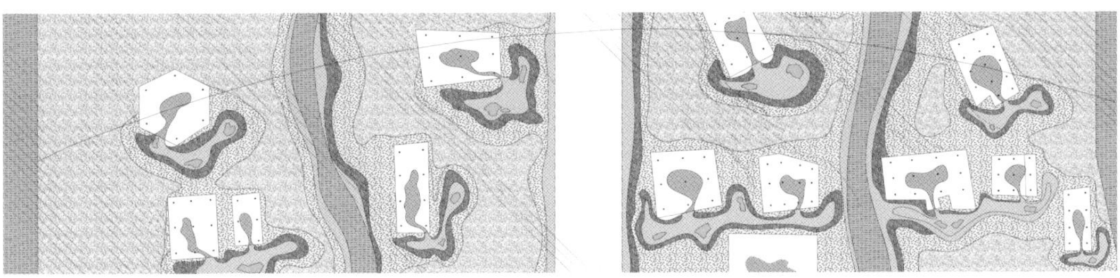

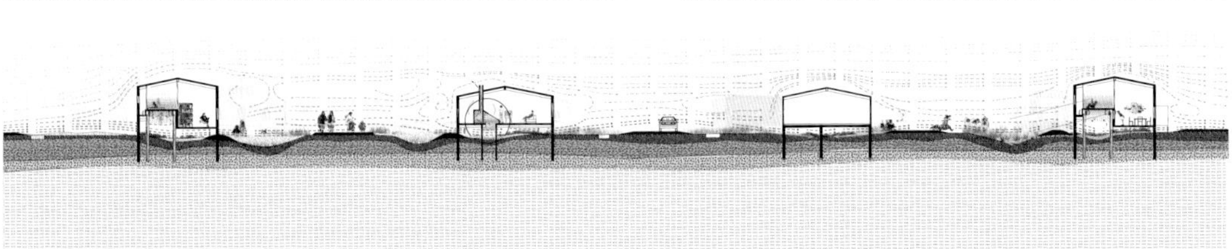

"We used to bury our homes in the ground and our people in the sky; now we bury our people in the ground and put our homes in the sky, and we have been cold ever since."

Eugene Brower
Former Mayor of Utqiagvik

apparatus: lifestyle possibility - 1

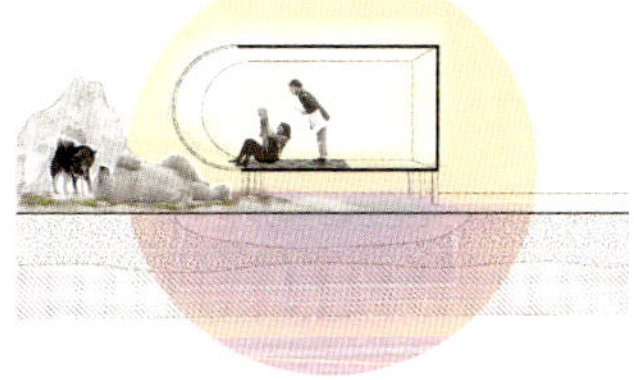

apparatus: lifestyle possibility - 2

apparatus: lifestyle possibility - 3

apparatus: lifestyle possibility - 4

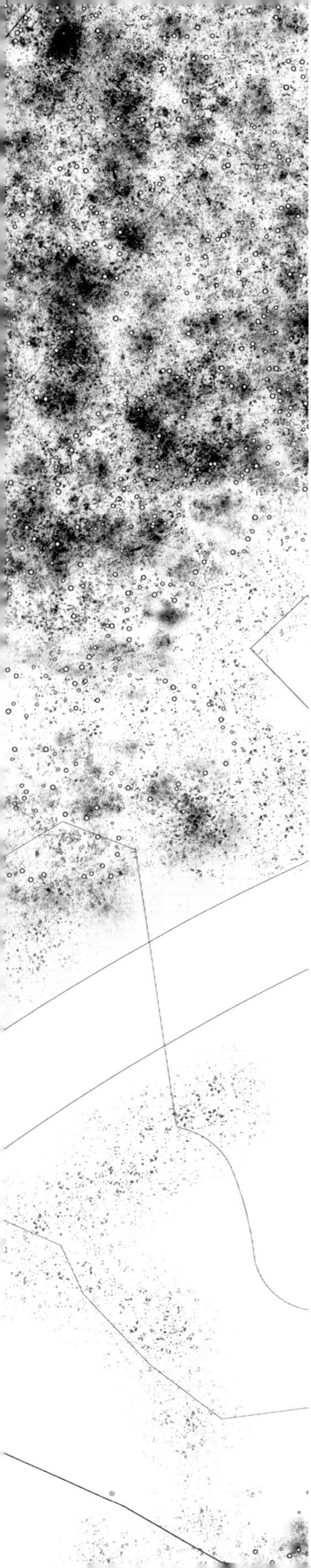

Program: School
Location: Minto, AK
Yin Yu Fong, Katie Kelly, Anna Morrison

THERMAL THRESHOLDS

"Thermal Thresholds: Education and Play in the Arctic" seeks to reconcile modern building techniques with native Athabaskan traditions and environment in Minto, Alaska by redefining the role of the village school as a primary public space and one of cultural reclamation. Formal and informal educational spaces are created within the landscape supporting a new experiential curriculum that is currently being implemented by the Yukon-Kuyokuk School District.

The school building prioritizes heat transfer in its design, mining thermodynamic principles for their spatial potentials. The primary indoor spaces are arranged around a central circulation and recreation space that is not heated mechanically. This "mudroom" acts as a thermal intermediary, mediating the cold outdoor air and the heated classrooms, as well as providing play spaces in the winter and much needed storage for the school. The programs are arranged vertically according to their activity level and required temperature, taking advantage of the natural rise of heat in the spatial organization of the building. Varying wall systems provide different insulating capacities based on the size of the room and desired connection to the outdoors. The gym, a large space difficult to heat efficiently but socially essential in Minto, is buried in a berm for insulating effect. The classrooms use a typical arctic wall section with sunken windows to provide light and views into the forest. Finally, the mudroom has a primarily glass wall with firewood shelving built in. In the winter, the wall is filled with firewood, providing fuel for the hearth within and extra insulation to the building. As the weather warms and the firewood is used up, the wall allows for more heat transfer and natural light to enter.

The design of the adjacent landscape creates microclimates to mediate the climate, protecting the indoor spaces and extending the usability of outdoor spaces. The school building is shielded from the harshest winds by positioning it at the edge of a black spruce forest and burying one side with a protective berm. These protective landscapes also generate an outdoor classroom in a forest clearing and a playful slope with pockets and mounds that intensifies with snowfall. To the south, the berm and building frame an outdoor playground and learning garden, bringing light into the classrooms and creating a protected and dynamic outdoor play space. Secondary berms buffer the playground from the street and slides are embedded for multiple play opportunities. Play structures constructed from traditional Athabaskan building techniques provide varying types of play, which can also extend beyond the confines of the playground out into the surrounding landscape. A network of trails connects the village to the southeast with the school and the spruce forest beyond. Native edible berries wrap along the classrooms on the south.

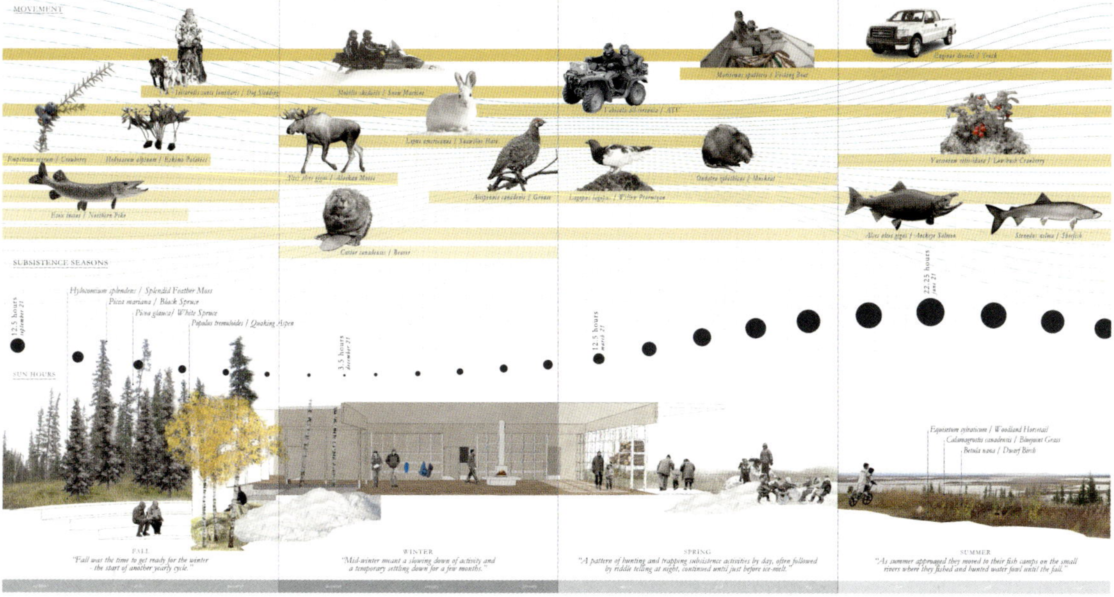
MOVEMENT
SUBSISTENCE SEASONS
SUN HOURS
12.5 hours
september 21
3.5 hours
december 21
12.5 hours
march 21
22.25 hours
june 21
Hylocomium splendens / Splendid Feather Moss
Picea mariana / Black Spruce
Picea glauca / White Spruce
Populus tremuloides / Quaking Aspen
Equisetum sylvaticum / Woodland Horsetail
Calamagrostis canadensis / Bluejoint Grass
Betula nana / Dwarf Birch
FALL
"Fall was the time to get ready for the winter - the start of another yearly cycle."
WINTER
"Mid-winter meant a slowing down of activity and a temporary settling down for a few months."
SPRING
"A pattern of hunting and trapping subsistence activities by day, often followed by riddle telling at night, continued until just before ice-melt."
SUMMER
"As summer approaged they moved to their fish camps on the small rivers where they fished and hunted water fowl until the fall."

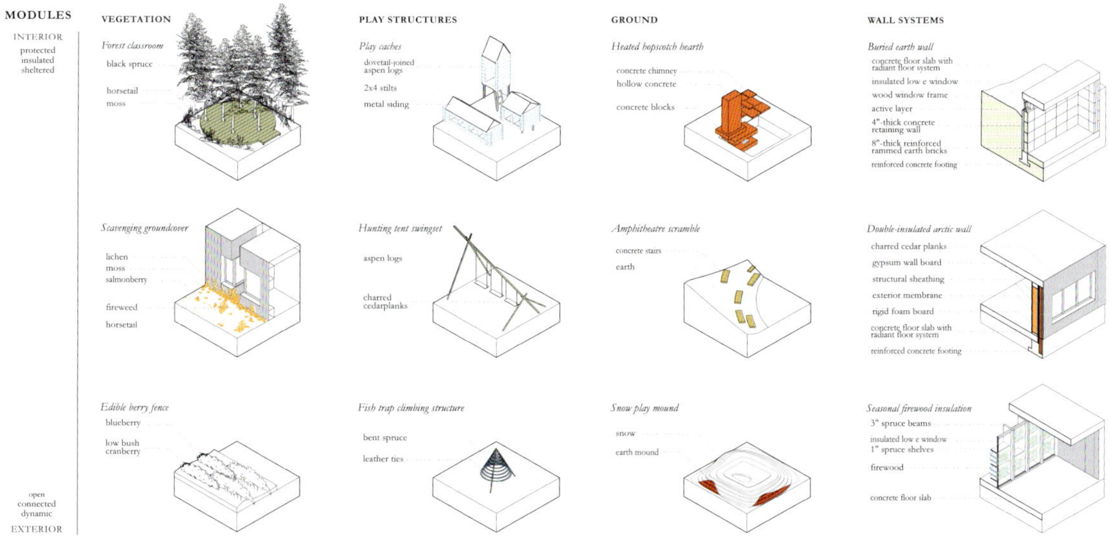
MODULES
INTERIOR
protected
insulated
sheltered
open
connected
dynamic
EXTERIOR
VEGETATION
Forest classroom
black spruce
horsetail
moss
Scavenging groundcover
lichen
moss
salmonberry
fireweed
horsetail
Edible berry fence
blueberry
low bush cranberry
PLAY STRUCTURES
Play caches
dovetail-joined aspen logs
2x4 stilts
metal siding
Hunting tent swingset
aspen logs
charred cedarplanks
Fish trap climbing structure
bent spruce
leather ties
GROUND
Heated hopscotch hearth
concrete chimney
hollow concrete
concrete blocks
Amphitheatre scramble
concrete stairs
earth
Snow play mound
snow
earth mound
WALL SYSTEMS
Buried earth wall
concrete floor slab with radiant floor system
insulated low e window
wood window frame
active layer
4"-thick concrete retaining wall
8"-thick reinforced rammed earth bricks
reinforced concrete footing
Double-insulated arctic wall
charred cedar planks
gypsum wall board
structural sheathing
exterior membrane
rigid foam board
concrete floor slab with radiant floor system
reinforced concrete footing
Seasonal firewood insulation
3" spruce beams
insulated low e window
1" spruce shelves
firewood
concrete floor slab

HOME
GUEST
PERIOD

WELCOME TO

"The new school and surrounding landscape provide a critical educational and recreational resource to the Minto community as it continues to hybridize its cultural practices. The project proposes a design strategy for extreme climates that explores alternative architectural potentials of engineered systems, thereby creating spaces with climate, not in opposition to it."

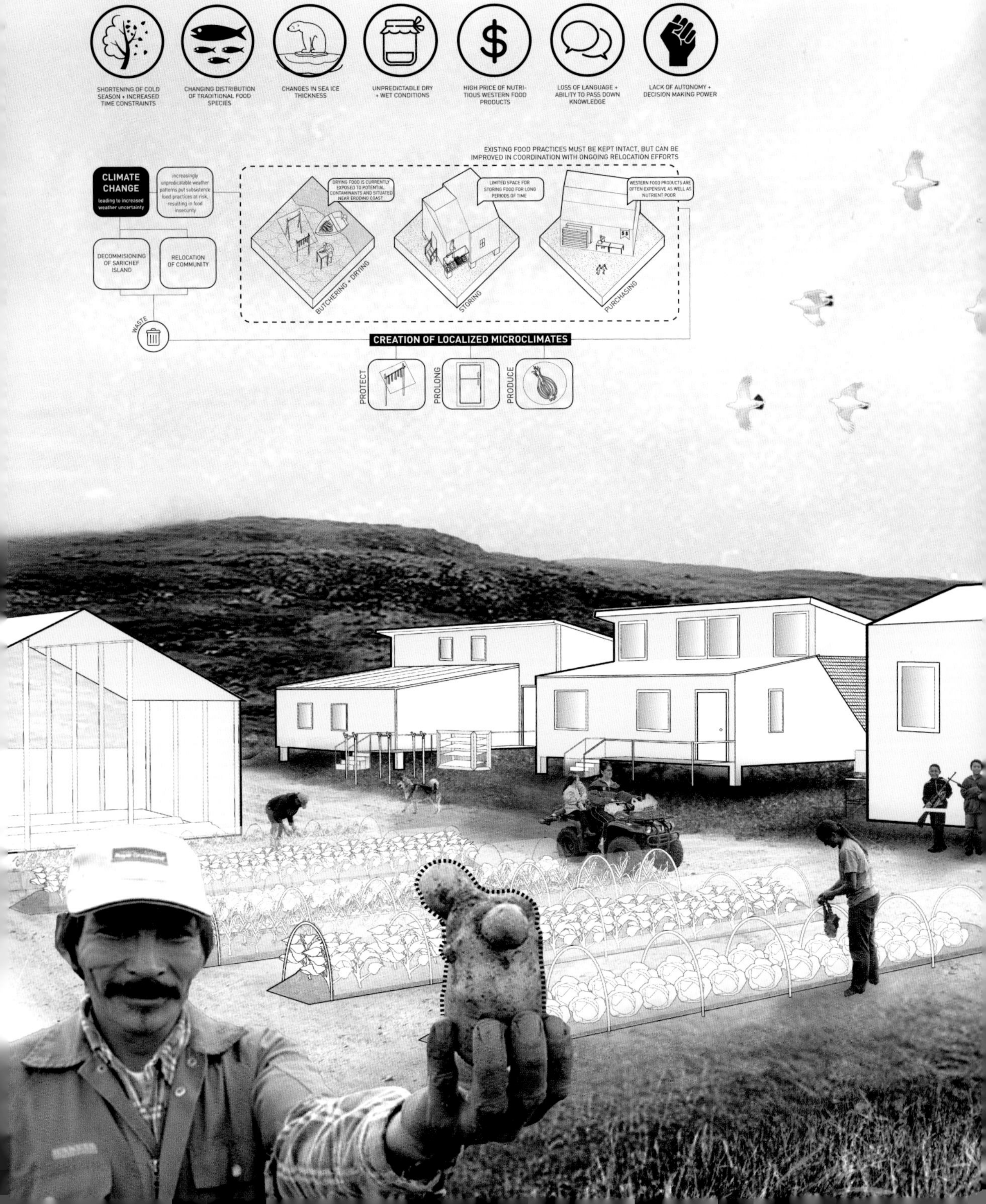

SHORTENING OF COLD SEASON + INCREASED TIME CONSTRAINTS
CHANGING DISTRIBUTION OF TRADITIONAL FOOD SPECIES
CHANGES IN SEA ICE THICKNESS
UNPREDICTABLE DRY + WET CONDITIONS
HIGH PRICE OF NUTRI-TIOUS WESTERN FOOD PRODUCTS
LOSS OF LANGUAGE + ABILITY TO PASS DOWN KNOWLEDGE
LACK OF AUTONOMY + DECISION MAKING POWER
EXISTING FOOD PRACTICES MUST BE KEPT INTACT, BUT CAN BE IMPROVED IN COORDINATION WITH ONGOING RELOCATION EFFORTS
CLIMATE CHANGE
leading to increased weather uncertainty
increasingly unpredicatable weather patterns put subsistence food practices at risk, resulting in food insecurity
DECOMMISIONING OF SARICHEF ISLAND
RELOCATION OF COMMUNITY
WASTE
DRYING FOOD IS CURRENTLY EXPOSED TO POTENTIAL CONTAMINANTS AND SITUATED NEAR ERODING COAST
BUTCHERING + DRYING
LIMITED SPACE FOR STORING FOOD FOR LONG PERIODS OF TIME
STORING
WESTERN FOOD PRODUCTS ARE OFTEN EXPENSIVE AS WELL AS NUTRIENT POOR
PURCHASING
CREATION OF LOCALIZED MICROCLIMATES
PROTECT
PROLONG
PRODUCE

Program: Relocation and New Village
Location: Shishmaref & West Tin Creek Hills, AK
Liz Camuti, Kun Liu, Hallie Miller, Pia von Barby

HACKING THE HOMESTEAD

This project recognizes the far-reaching implications relocation will have on the community's current way of life by prioritizing innovations in the mobility and flexibility of Inupiaq subsistence systems.

A series of climate amplifying components is developed through an in-depth study of the necessary microclimatic conditions for existing food practices, including butchering, drying, smoking, storing, and growing. The components are divided into four groups: collectors, directors, insulators, and conductors, and are easily constructed using existing materials and resources found in Shishmaref, such as netting, scrap metal, and snow. The components create hyper-localized microclimates that expedite and protect the processing and storing of food. These components can be constructed in isolation or systematized into various configurations, ranging in structural and material complexity, while remaining seasonally adaptable.

The components would be deployed on both Shishmaref and West Tin Creek Hills, the mainland relocation site. A portion of Sarichef Island is kept intact and used as a seasonal hunting ground, while the majority of the population resides in West Tin Creek Hills. This approach does not separate the two sites, but rather unifies them through food practice and embraces the Inupiat spatial conceptualization of the larger territory as their home. As Shishmaref will be utilized particularly for winter hunting, lighter and more flexible components specific to food practices for hunting, including butchering, drying, and storing, will be installed on the island. The island's infrastructure will be strategically decommissioned to create optimized microclimates for the components.

Rather than being constructed around government infrastructure, the layout of the new settlement in West Tin Creek Hills is predicated on subsistence practices central to the daily life and culture of Shishmaref. A cookbook created by the students of Shishmaref Day School is used to select types of vegetables widely used in Inupiat cooking and to calibrate microclimate strategies. The food hub on the mainland site doubles as a social and educational space, and is constructed through an aggregation of climate amplifying components. Not only does this space expedite and protect these food practices, it also supports the inherent sociality of these practices.

The design of the microclimate systems on both the mainland and the island recognizes an immediate need for improved food security, as well a need for a new settlement design that is focused on productive sustainment and evolution of traditional food practices. The project aspires to empower the community from within by returning agency to those who best understand how to adapt to and work within their own environments.

"Ensuring that the community retains control over its identity and lifestyle by way of a more robust food system, the project deploys microclimate-generating components enabling community members to opt into agriculture practices on the mainland."

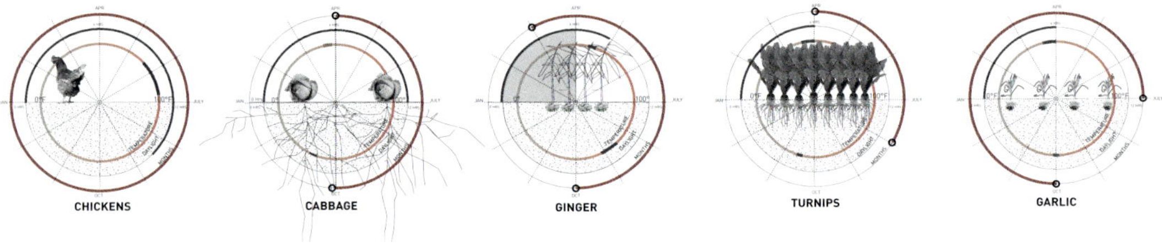

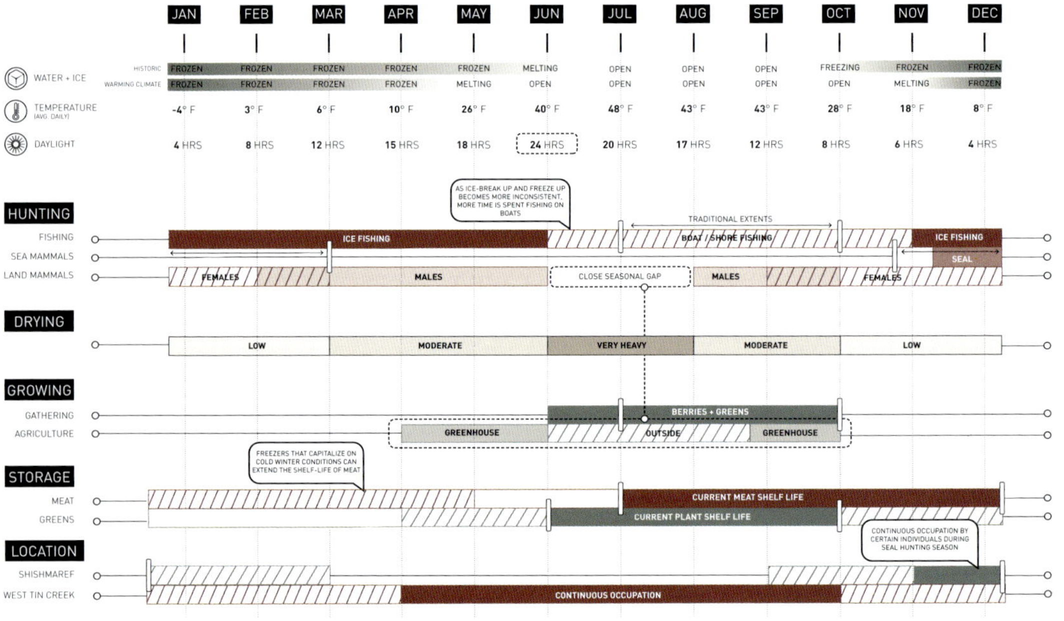

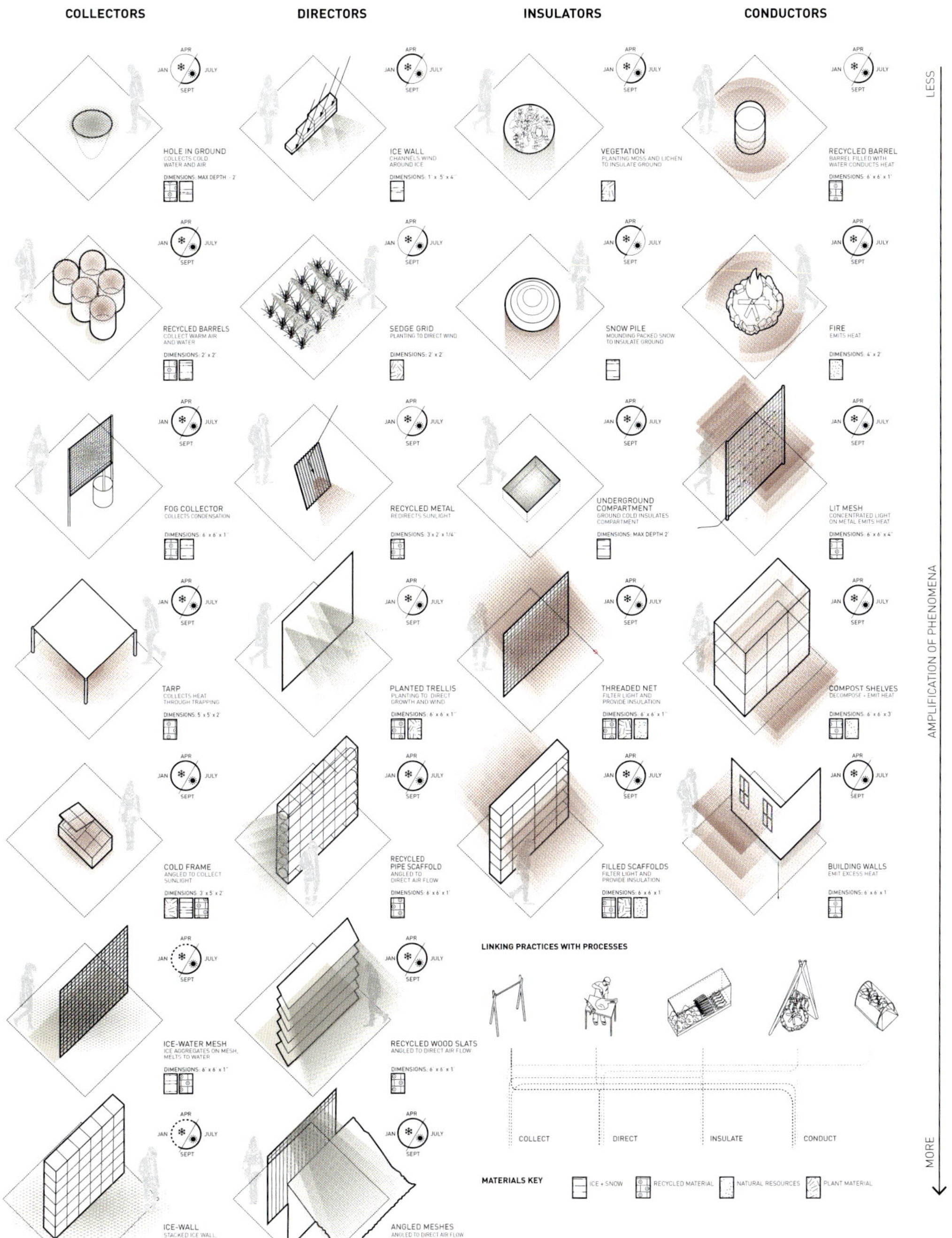

CLIMATE AMPLIFYING COMPONENTS
HARNESSESSING ON-SITE MATERIALS TO MANIPULATE CLIMATE

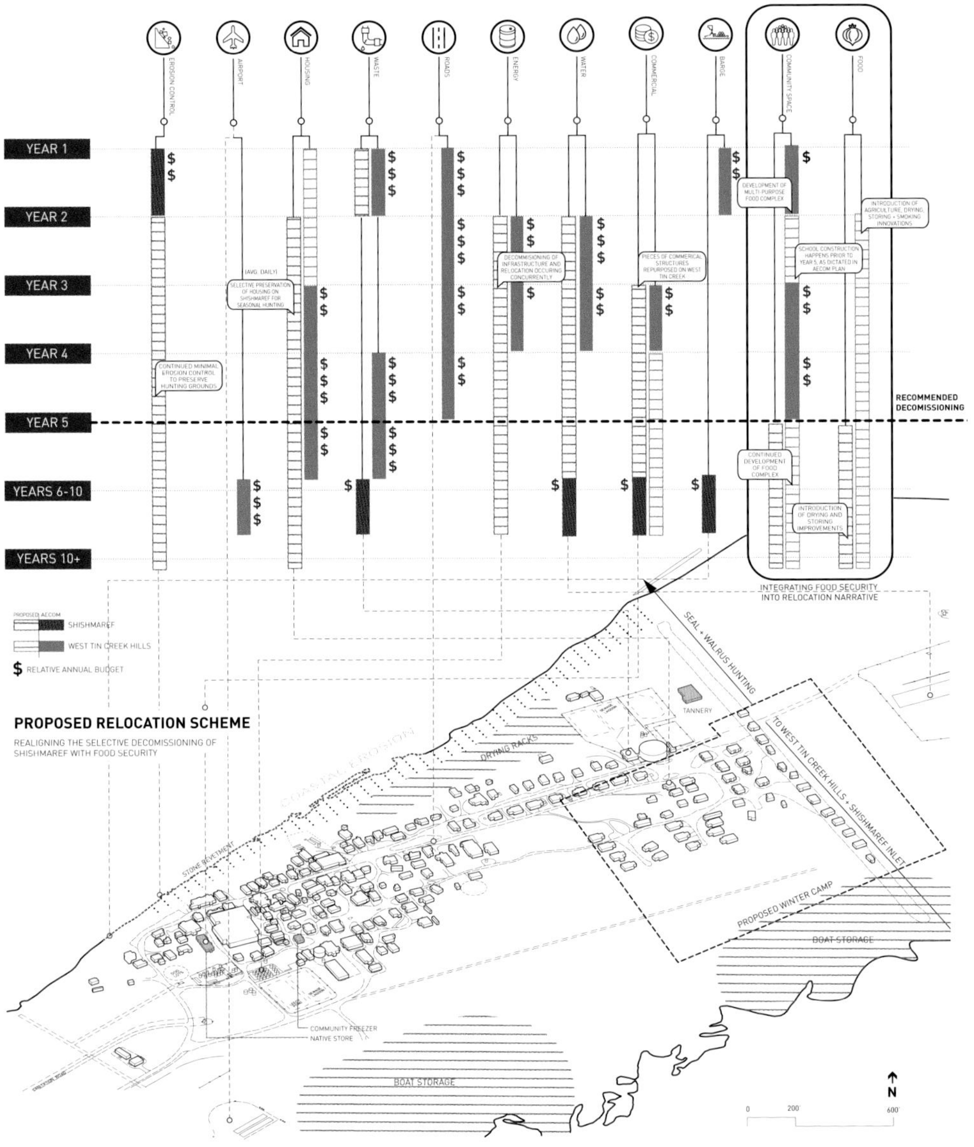

PROPOSED RELOCATION SCHEME

REALIGNING THE SELECTIVE DECOMISSIONING OF SHISHMAREF WITH FOOD SECURITY

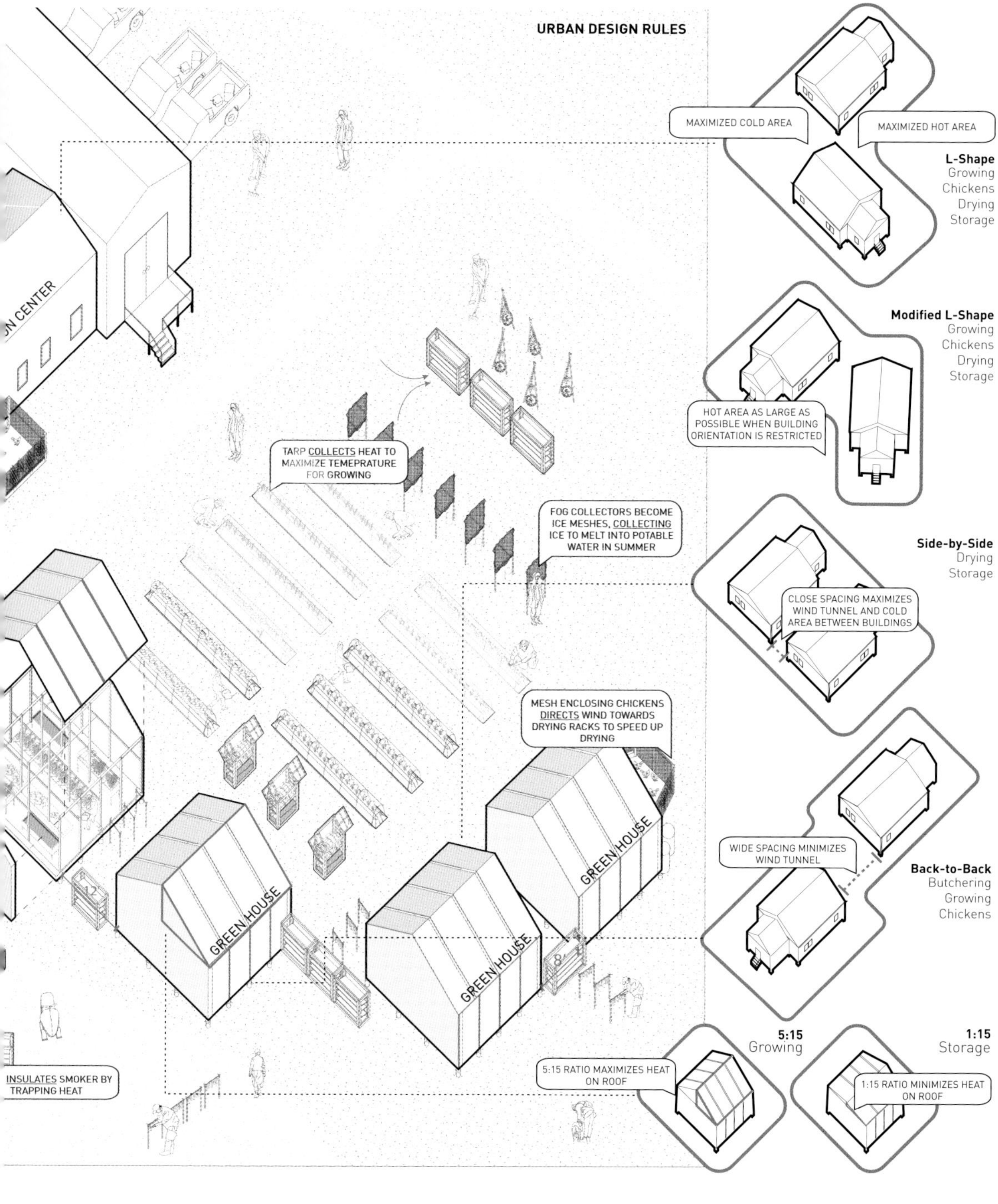
URBAN DESIGN RULES
MAXIMIZED COLD AREA
MAXIMIZED HOT AREA
L-Shape
Growing
Chickens
Drying
Storage
Modified L-Shape
Growing
Chickens
Drying
Storage
HOT AREA AS LARGE AS POSSIBLE WHEN BUILDING ORIENTATION IS RESTRICTED
Side-by-Side
Drying
Storage
CLOSE SPACING MAXIMIZES WIND TUNNEL AND COLD AREA BETWEEN BUILDINGS
Back-to-Back
Butchering
Growing
Chickens
WIDE SPACING MINIMIZES WIND TUNNEL
5:15
Growing
1:15
Storage
5:15 RATIO MAXIMIZES HEAT ON ROOF
1:15 RATIO MINIMIZES HEAT ON ROOF
ON CENTER
TARP COLLECTS HEAT TO MAXIMIZE TEMEPRATURE FOR GROWING
FOG COLLECTORS BECOME ICE MESHES, COLLECTING ICE TO MELT INTO POTABLE WATER IN SUMMER
MESH ENCLOSING CHICKENS DIRECTS WIND TOWARDS DRYING RACKS TO SPEED UP DRYING
GREEN HOUSE
GREEN HOUSE
GREEN HOUSE
INSULATES SMOKER BY TRAPPING HEAT

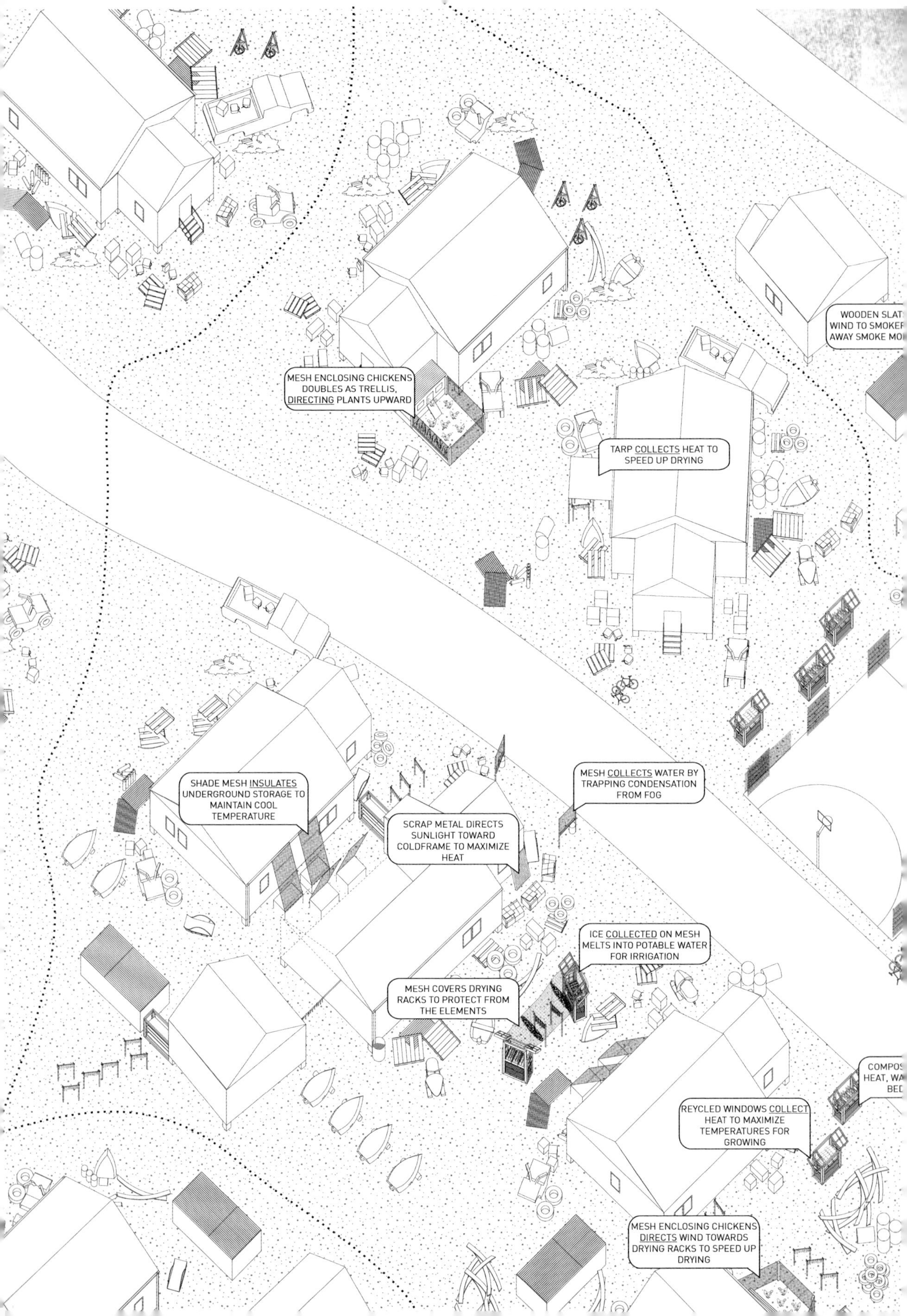
WOODEN SLAT
WIND TO SMOKER
AWAY SMOKE MO
MESH ENCLOSING CHICKENS DOUBLES AS TRELLIS, DIRECTING PLANTS UPWARD
TARP COLLECTS HEAT TO SPEED UP DRYING
SHADE MESH INSULATES UNDERGROUND STORAGE TO MAINTAIN COOL TEMPERATURE
MESH COLLECTS WATER BY TRAPPING CONDENSATION FROM FOG
SCRAP METAL DIRECTS SUNLIGHT TOWARD COLDFRAME TO MAXIMIZE HEAT
ICE COLLECTED ON MESH MELTS INTO POTABLE WATER FOR IRRIGATION
MESH COVERS DRYING RACKS TO PROTECT FROM THE ELEMENTS
COMPOS
HEAT, WA
BED
REYCLED WINDOWS COLLECT HEAT TO MAXIMIZE TEMPERATURES FOR GROWING
MESH ENCLOSING CHICKENS DIRECTS WIND TOWARDS DRYING RACKS TO SPEED UP DRYING

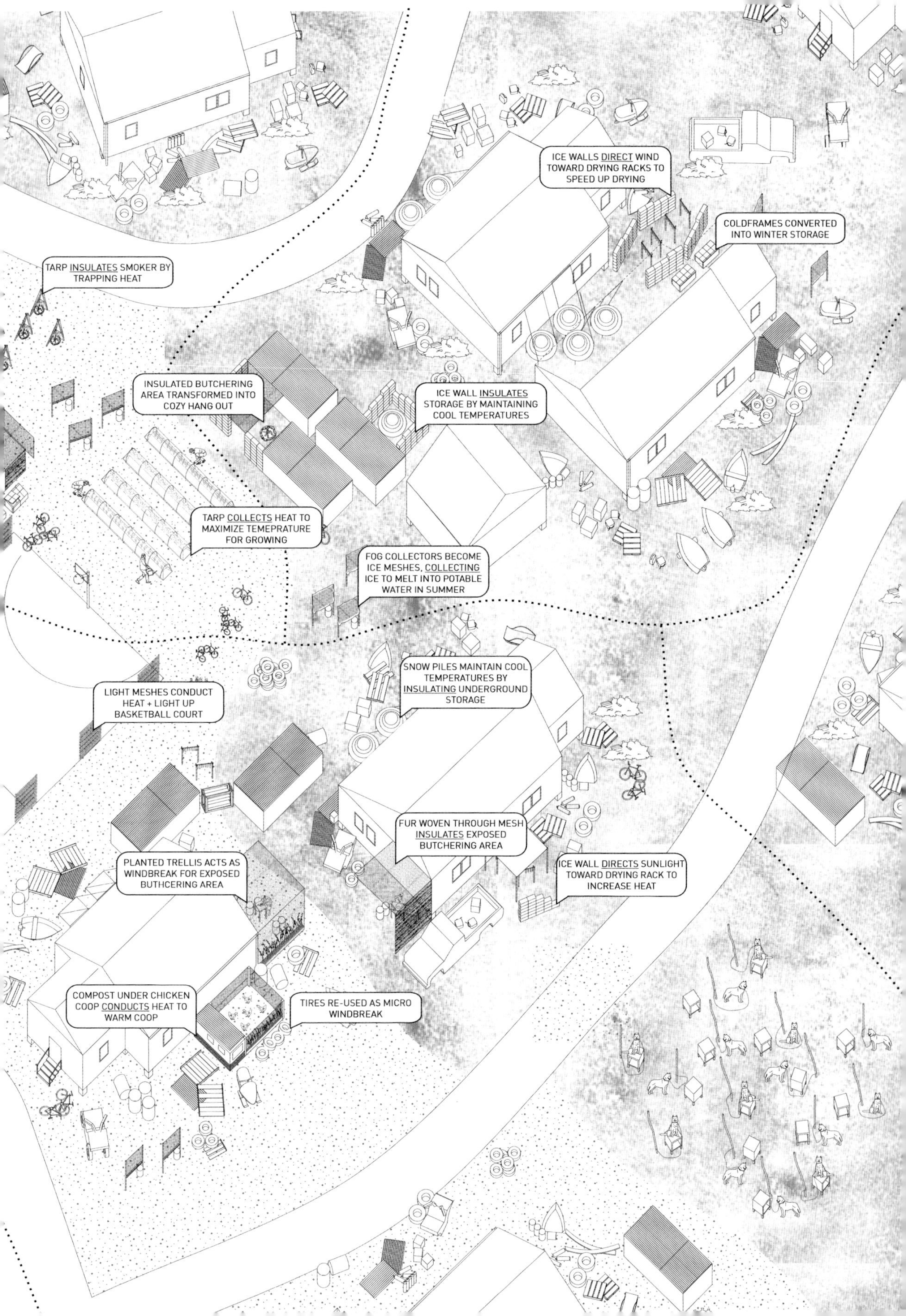
ICE WALLS DIRECT WIND TOWARD DRYING RACKS TO SPEED UP DRYING
COLDFRAMES CONVERTED INTO WINTER STORAGE
TARP INSULATES SMOKER BY TRAPPING HEAT
INSULATED BUTCHERING AREA TRANSFORMED INTO COZY HANG OUT
ICE WALL INSULATES STORAGE BY MAINTAINING COOL TEMPERATURES
TARP COLLECTS HEAT TO MAXIMIZE TEMEPRATURE FOR GROWING
FOG COLLECTORS BECOME ICE MESHES, COLLECTING ICE TO MELT INTO POTABLE WATER IN SUMMER
SNOW PILES MAINTAIN COOL TEMPERATURES BY INSULATING UNDERGROUND STORAGE
LIGHT MESHES CONDUCT HEAT + LIGHT UP BASKETBALL COURT
FUR WOVEN THROUGH MESH INSULATES EXPOSED BUTCHERING AREA
PLANTED TRELLIS ACTS AS WINDBREAK FOR EXPOSED BUTHCERING AREA
ICE WALL DIRECTS SUNLIGHT TOWARD DRYING RACK TO INCREASE HEAT
COMPOST UNDER CHICKEN COOP CONDUCTS HEAT TO WARM COOP
TIRES RE-USED AS MICRO WINDBREAK

BOATING LOOP
HORSESHOE DUNES
ESTUARY PADDLE
COASTAL TREK
ROUNDS

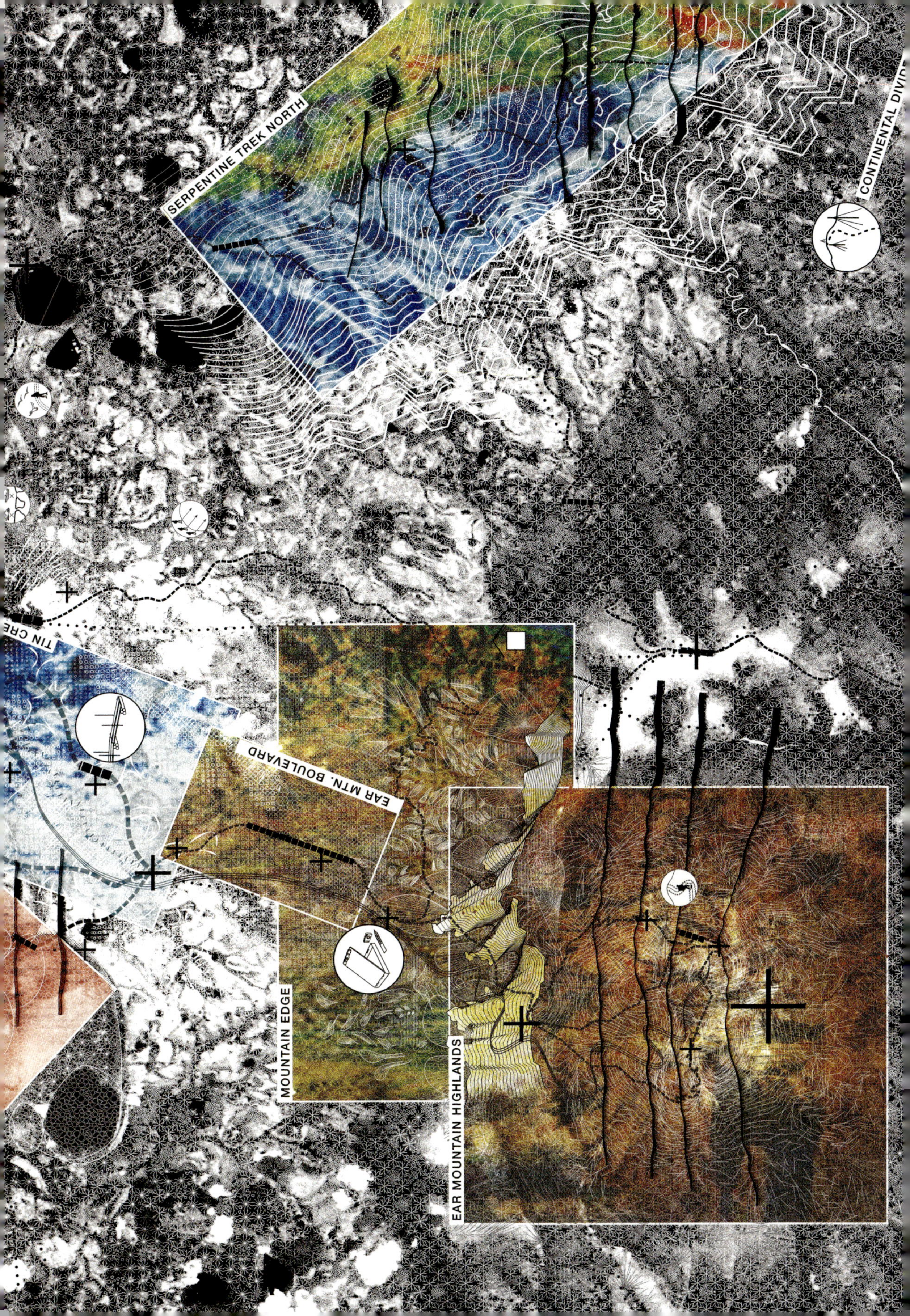
SERPENTINE TREK NORTH
CONTINENTAL DIVID
TIN CRE
EAR MTN. BOULEVARD
MOUNTAIN EDGE
EAR MOUNTAIN HIGHLANDS

Пирамида
GREENLAND

Arctic Desi
MASS MIGRA
NORTH POLE COURSE
CANADIAN OIL
ALASKAN OIL
china

Alex Wall

EXIT

Many Norths: The Making of an Arctic Vernacular

LOLA SHEPPARD & MASON WHITE

Associate Professor, University of Waterloo & Associate Professor, University of Toronto
Co-Founders, Lateral Office, Canada

Canada's northern regions vary widely from those of other circumpolar nations. Considerable differences exist with respect to geography, climate, national histories, aboriginal cultures, infrastructures, and connectivity among many other traits. Russia has several industrialized cities with populations of between 100,000 and 400,000, which is between two and four times the size of all the people living north of 60 degrees in Canada combined. Norway's northern fishing villages, while seemingly isolated, remain for the most part culturally and infrastructurally connected to the rest of their country. Alaska, which shares aspects of culture, climate, and geography with the western Arctic, tends to have a more developed infrastructure. However, the western region of Alaska shares similarities to Canada's eastern Arctic as it has smaller and discontinuously connected communities. Greenland arguably shares the most traits in common with Canada's eastern Arctic in its cultural and spatial realities, but its longstanding ties to Denmark, its greater year-round access by boat and its steady progress to devolution also produce marked contrast. So, to simply put it, the "Norths" of the circumpolar world are very different.

Figure 1: Newtown 1, Frobisher Bay Department of Public Works. This rendering places us in the conceptual design by The Canadian Architect, November 1958.

There are also vast differences within Canada, from east to west, from coast to inland, from territorial capital to remote hamlet. There are differences in terms of resource development approaches, infrastructure challenges, and urbanization. Most northern communities have emerged with little thought or planning beyond expediency and cost efficiency, although there is often a particular logic behind the planning, which I'll get to later. Transport via air, road, and water underlie strong disparities in terms of delivery of goods and services. For instance, in the eastern Arctic, there are no roads between communities, rendering the provision of housing, health, education and food much more complex and expensive. These factors result in political and economic imbalances across northern Canada that have yielded unique and very specific responses to the challenges of urban design, architecture, mobility, and monitoring.

For most people the Arctic region is characterized as an abstract territory, a sublime landscape of vast geography, a harsh climate, or an undeveloped tundra. And yet the Arctic is full of spatial contradictions and multiplicities with different meanings for different people. Instead of a singular, cohesive whole, a panoply of North appears. The Canadian Arctic becomes a kind

Figure 2: (Left) Truck Stop; (Right) View of Iqaluit with snow fence.

of mythic collective conscience, a terra incognita of extreme geography and climate. Even Canada's national anthem implies an identity enveloped in abstraction and heroism: "the True North strong and free!" And yet ultimately little is known of the region, particularly the daily realities of life for the 110,000 people living in the Canadian north. It is a region that has had modernity imposed, sometimes forced upon it, and its inhabitants have demonstrated a remarkable adaptability. Yet, the transition has been fraught and the consequences of that transformation are still palpably felt in the region culturally, socially, and ecologically.

Canada's North has the highest birth rate, per capita, of any region in the country, and in Nunavut, the largest northern territory, 50% of the population is under the age of twenty-five.[1] There is a hybrid culture emerging among Inuit youth who on the one hand are listening to contemporary music, using social media, and yet simultaneously are cultivating a strong connection to the past, going out hunting with elders, reviving language, renewing traditional crafts, among other practices. Similarly, there are emerging spatial practices: Inuit still go out on the land to hunt regularly, but have used snowmobiles and GPS for decades. And northern indigenous music, performing and visual arts speak to unique cultural cross-pollination. Architecture would do well to learn from such hybridizations of culture. How we learn from tradition and modernity at the same time is key.

There has been discussion during the Arctic States conference about the idea of the north as frontier; but it is only a frontier from a southern perspective. The question of viewpoint is very important in terms of how we look at and think about the north. Louis Edmond Hamelin,[2] the French-Canadian geographer famously wrote, "There are so many norths in this north." Similarly, in *Northern Realities*,[3] Jim Lotz notes the multiple northerners and their vastly different perspectives on the Yukon, one of Canada's three northern territories. This multiplicity of views underlies much of our work and research as we have tried to understand the role of architecture in the arctic, given its long history of colonialism in the North. Another point of note, Geoff Manaugh raised the question of vocabulary. Many polar anthropologists have dedicated their research to the rich spatial terminology employed by Inuit. In *Knowing Places: The Inuinnait, Landscapes, and The Environment*[4] Beatrice Collignon documents the language of navigation and place. In *The Meaning of Ice: People and Sea Ice in Three Arctic Communities* Gearheard et al.[5] equally examine multiple understandings, words, and roles of ice in the daily life and collective experience of Inuit. However, vocabulary is a central challenge with regard to urbanism and architecture in the Canadian North. We don't yet have the terms or concepts, as designers, or as users, to speak about urbanization, public space, the public realm, landscape, and so forth. To date, we've imported southern terms which often don't apply. As communities in the North continue to grow, and in effect begin to "urbanize" in some instances, we need an equally "developed," culturally relevant language to describe these new spatial phenomena. New vocabulary would imply new building and spatial typologies – a rethinking of the constituent components of Arctic urbanism.

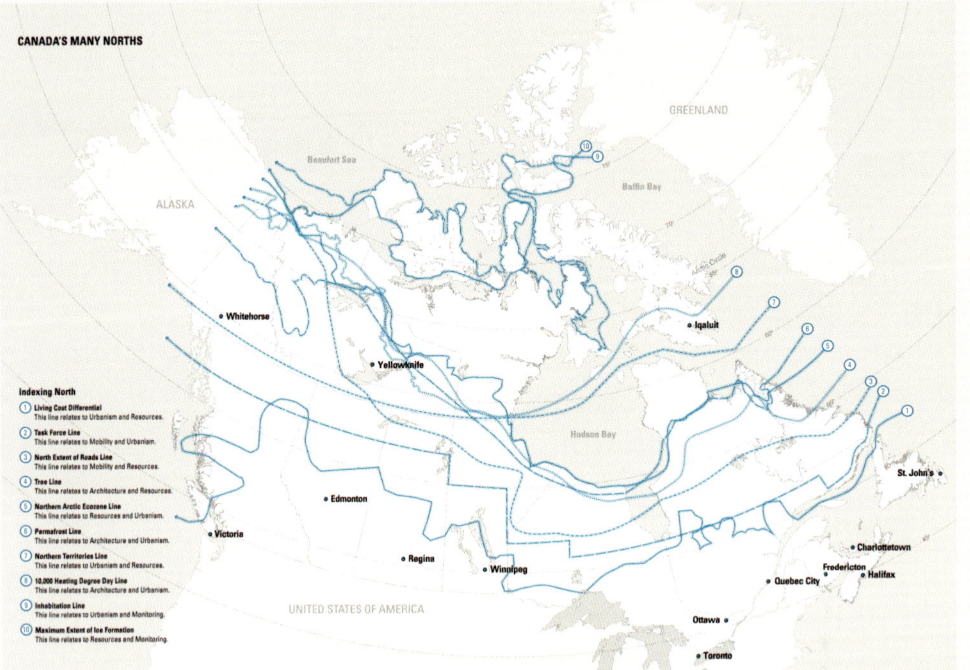

Figure 3: The map reveals some of the complexity of defining what is North. Many lines could be used to demarcate the North. The boundaries of permafrost and the tree line are just a few.

Many Norths: Spatial Practice in a Polar Territory argues that these spatial practices begin to form an expanded understanding of "vernacular" not simply defined by form, tectonics, or even urban patterns, but equally more ephemeral and distributed practices.[6] This interest in vernaculars shares some allegiance with the ideas of landscape theorist John Brinckerhoff Jackson, who was interested in American vernacular landscapes as reflections and materializations of cultural landscapes and values. In Jackson's writings, the rural, the vernacular, and the seemingly banal built environment were understood as worthy of investigation, and reflect a multiplicity of narratives about the people that inhabit them. *Many Norths* attempts to situate traditional, indigenous northern practices alongside the more recently arrived spatial disciplines of architecture, urban design, planning, and engineering. Contemporary practices continue to evolve, informed by new technologies, changing environmental conditions and evolving cultural traditions establishing—sometimes unintentionally—what we would call a "modern northern vernacular." If these spatial practices and vernaculars could be instrumentalized, they could shape a critical spatial practice for a modern north, one that eschews imported southern models, and reinforces local identity and culture without nostalgia. *Many Norths* documents modes of operating, whether in a tactical, everyday capacity or with a strategic interest. It is equally important to acknowledge that space here is not urban in the conventional sense.

The book also seeks to challenge what we understand as the "site" of architecture. In a context where culture, social infrastructure, and indeed, survival operate by occupying vast territories, understandings of site are constantly expanded and redefined, based on the questions being asked. This challenge to 'site' is exemplified in Hamelin's book, *Canadian Nordicity*.[7] The Canadian geographer spent much of his career looking at the idea of nordicity and developed gradients of nordic geographies. He divided Canada into five zones; base Canada, Near North, Middle North, Far North and Extreme North, and developed a classification of what he called polar values, ranging from 0 to 100 based on issues such as economies, infrastructural connection, climate, hot and cold days, and so forth. If an area obtained an overall value of greater than 200, it was considered to be in one of these gradients of the North. Hamelin also recognized that the north is the product of multiple perceptual understandings and that it's in continual transformation. He noted, for instance, that certain regions could be "de-nordified" as they developed economically and infrastructurally.

Indeed the question of how does one define north is fascinating. One could look to the "northern tax benefit line" which is the line beyond which you get certain tax credits to compensate for the cost of living; this would define one north. One could look at ethnographic regions where the Inuit live, and another north would appear. One could look at the tree line, which has implications for resources and building materials; or one could look at the line of permafrost, which also has impacts on how roads and buildings are built. One could look at the arctic eco-zone as a definer, or at the line of southern road access, the line beyond which there are no roads. Ones realize that defining what is north is complex.

The use of the term "spatial practice" in *Many Norths* is inspired by Henri Lefebvre's writings. In *The Production of Space*, Lefebvre writes, "the spatial practice of a society secretes that society's space.[8] It propounds and presupposes it. It produces it slowly." Both Michel de Certeau and Lefebvre used the notion of tactical practices in an opposition to the city; they understood spatial practice as resistance and subversion. In the context of the North, we look at spatial practices more broadly, whether bottom-up and subversive or top-down and engineered. The practice might leave no trace on the territory or it might leave very clear and permanent imprints on the land. This could range from the ability to detect ice thickness for safe passage, to knowing how and where to find food at certain times of the year, to large scale engineering innovations such as the seasonal construction of ice roads. The question of how to document these myriad spatial practices became a key preoccupation. Indeed, in the context of vast existing research in anthropology, sociology, history of the Canadian North, we often saw our contribution in visualizing and spatializing information previously only described in words. The research implicitly argues that if, as designers, we can expand the range of phenomena we document and innovate in the visual, spatial, temporal tools we use, we might expand the issues that architecture can incorporate into its design thinking.

Many Norths also intentionally expanded its research beyond merely architecture, as it became clear that one could not understand the history and legacy of architecture in the Canadian Arctic, without understanding the other forces shaping this built environment. There are thus five themes within the book: urbanism, architecture, mobility, monitoring, and resources. The book can be understood as a series of "stories" about spatial practice, through multiple modes of documentation. To this end, the book includes essays, interviews with a wide selection of people involved with and living in the North - from historians, to hunters to scientists; it includes time-lines which offer a broader documentation of the forces which shape each of the themes.

The case studies in the book served as a tool to examine specific phenomena in the North in relation to the five themes outlined earlier: architecture, urbanism, mobility, monitoring ad resources. Certain case studies seek to identify patterns, such as the relationship of urban form to land form, or the relationship of airport infrastructure to community form. Other case studies examine very unique phenomena – a bowhead whale hunt or the construction of diamond mines

Figure 4: Gordon Robertson Educational Centre, 1973, Iqaluit, Nunavut, Canada. Papineau Gerin-Lajoie LeBlanc Architects.

as radically different spatial practices pertaining to resources. The seasonal construction of ice road and the traditional Inuit trails and means of navigating on the land embody two different seasonal responses to northern mobility. DEW (Distance Early Warning) Line stations built all across the North American north, and traditional and scientific methods of measuring ice demonstrate different means and goals of monitoring the land. Above all, these case studies and stories seek to reveal our continued human relationship to land, to seasonality, to geography. In a highly infrastructuralized South, we forget this interdependency; in the North, the reminders are everywhere, and architecture becomes a key mediator and embodiment of culture, infrastructure, and environment.

It is common to think of the Arctic as remote, relatively untouched and hence more sublime and mythic. Equally understandable is a collective desire to preserve the ways and cultures of the many peoples who live there. But the Canadian Arctic is complex and rapidly changing; it embraces humans, ecologies, unique infrastructures and building types, research camps, and emerging cities. The fear (to some) and the promise (to others) of climate change is that the North will open up, and one of the last relatively untouched places on Earth may bear the irrefutable marks of development. For better or worse, if nothing else it is a shifting, multivalent territory. One could argue that these human transformations do not reduce the region's "Arctic-ness," but rather extend it. They challenge us to think with greater complexity and thoughtfulness about cultural, architectural, and infrastructural adaptability and responsiveness.

NOTES:

1. Statistics Canada. 2017. *Nunavut [Territory] and Canada [Country] (table). Census Profile.* 2016 Census. Statistics Canada Catalogue no. 98-316-X2016001. Ottawa. Released November 29, 2017.

2. Louis-Edmond Hamelin, *Canadian Nordicity: It's Your North, Too*, trans. William Barr (Montreal: Harvest House, 1979).

3. Jim Lotz, *Northern Realities: The future of northern development in Canada* (Toronto: New Press, 1970).

4. Béatrice Collignon, *Knowing Places: The Inuinnait, Landscapes, and the Environment* (Edmonton: Canadian Circumpolar Institute, University of Alberta, 2006).

5. Shari F. Gearheard, et al., eds., *The Meaning of Ice: People and Sea Ice in Three Arctic Communities* (Hanover: International Polar Institute, 2013).

6. Lola Sheppard and Mason White. *Many Norths: Spatial Practice in a Polar Territory* (Barcelona: Actar, 2017).

7. Hamelin, *Canadian Nordicity.*

8. Henri Lefebvre, *The Production of Space*, trans. Donald Nicholson-Smith (Oxford: Blackwell, 1991).

Looking at Future Norths

JANIKE KAMPEVOLD LARSEN

Associate Professor, Oslo School of Architecture and Design
Project Leader, Future North, Norway

Future North is funded by the Research Council Norway and has run for 3 ½ years. We are architects, literary scholars, landscape theorists, and media design researchers; in total eleven researchers counting guest researchers. We are looking at the formation and mediation of landscape and landscape changes in the Arctic. At this point in time, these changes are quite acute and immediate. The situation in parts of these territories may change over the course of a few months or even days based on political and corporate decisions. We study how landscape changes are met and dealt with by their inhabitants. We look at the contrasting ways in which landscapes are socially and materially produced simultaneously by external forces and by local responses, including forms of activism, art, and architecture. Most of all, we look at the relation between social agency and landscape change by studying local communities. We also work to re-conceptualize notions of landscape and territory. We study the landscapes of remote sensing, urbanism, ethnographies of the North, each researcher focusing on different aspects.

We are present day travelers in landscapes that have long since been discovered and developed; industrialized landscapes of the Kola Peninsula and Northern Quebec, the exposed fishing communities on the Barents Coast, and the part industrial, part research landscapes of Svalbard. Do these landscapes that we observe and work in have anything in common? They are quite rough in terms of climatic conditions, but not necessarily extreme. (Norway is pretty rough already.) They are large, so large that we cannot observe them from one place. One needs to travel around in them, to drive them, walk them, fly them. They are exposed to an increased, and in some cases rapid, industrialization. All of this implies that they do not fit the idea of landscapes that has been handed down to us by the European and North American landscape tradition. They are not easily comprehended. As attention increases they are, however, becoming more and more marketed as tourism landscapes.

Since the mid-sixteenth century, the landscapes of the North have been described and portrayed by explorers, painters, writers, and scientists. They have been portrayed as wild, terrifying, precious, and pristine. They have been portrayed as places of retreat, terror, and of bliss. The discourses on the Arctic have often rested upon what was not known. Imagination has played a large role in often fantastic discourses that also oftentimes are materialized in actual expeditions to the Arctic.

The new and massive interest in the Arctic rests upon what we do know. There are extractable resources. The Arctic holds about one-fourth of the world's remaining carbon reserves in addition to an abundance of rare-earth minerals. Assessing these resources and the changes that extraction might bring about for communities in the Arctic requires quite some imagination. Politicians imagine large national incomes from strategic positioning. For local politicians, it's about municipal prosperity. Yet, some of the imagination is about sustainable futures in an area under immense pressures – futures where societies thrive independently of the extraction industries.
During the last Ice Age, the median temperature was only five degrees Celsius lower than now in Norway. We know that the fjord landscapes in Svalbard are no longer "Arctic" because new species are moving in due to the temperature rise. We know that polar ice caps will probably be completely vanished as early as 2040. This opens new possibilities for transpolar sea routes, which will change coastal conditions for all bordering territories with an unimaginable potential for coastal communities to thrive on deep water harbors and transportation networks. We know that there are great land and sea-bottom mineral resources both on the Barents Sea and in Greenland; a mine in Kvanefjeld in the southern part of Greenland, due to open, holds large quantities of

uranium. The Norwegian government just officially decided that the ice flow can be moved farther north because that would make it easier to actually operate those northernmost oil fields. We also know that the Norwegian Johan Castberg oil field may be operated in a much lower break-even price than anticipated, as low as $38 per barrel. This field is the fifth largest oil field in Norway ever located. It's 200 square kilometers can be drilled for fifty years. This means that the potential for oil related industry in the North is still quite large, and it involves supply harbors, transshipment hubs, and extensive sea-bottom infrastructures. Despite the very radical re-structuring of the oil economy in Norway and due to plummeting oil prices, among other things, our northern landscapes will continue to be under pressure. The question is: can a prolific petroleum extraction development happen in a way that also allows local communities to maintain their culture and traditional means of sustenance, which is mostly fishing? Our concern, in relation to this question, is caused by the opportunistic spirit created by the petroleum industry in Norway and by the Norwegian ministry of foreign affairs. Finnmark, our northernmost community encompassing the Norwegian Barents Coast, was declared Europe's new oil province a few years back. Local governments in many of Finnmark's towns jumped at this first chance to profile their cities either as deep-water harbors, future supply harbors, or transshipment harbors.

Figure 1: Coal mining activity in Hotellneset, north-west of Longyearbyen, Svalbard.

The increased geopolitical interest in the Arctic has resulted in two things: extended possibilities for extraction industries and for tourism, particularly to the north of Norway and Svalbard. Hence, northern landscapes seem to be perceived in primarily two ways: as an above ground and a below ground landscape, one governed by the gaze and the other governed by the prices on raw materials; one a viewing landscape defined by tourism and the other defined by trade cycles and extractive industries such as oil production and mining [Figure 1]. They are based on desire for landscape beauty and revenue, respectively. And the landscapes that fall out of this simplified equation are the social landscapes of arctic settlements.

I will use one example: the arctic city of Vardø. This is an incredibly beautiful old fishing community situated in the extreme northeast of Norway. It has been a bustling and internationally connected city for hundreds of years. Its ups and downs have been intimately connected with events such as New York stock market crash of 1929, the Nigerian civil war in 1968-70, and variations in the fisheries. Italian fish buyers would come here for the sole purpose of buying the dried stock fish. The collapse in the cod populations at the end of the 1980s was the last of a series of blows, and its recent history is one of unemployment and depopulation. Vardø holds importance as a site of military presence and cultural heritage in the northeast of Norway. It makes a prime location for monitoring Russian military activities, transpolar ballistic missile trajectories between Asia and North America, as well as for supply service to the shipping and offshore installations in the Barents Sea. There is a NATO radar station on top of the island, a larger one is under construction. Unlike most other towns in northern Norway, Vardø was only partially destroyed in World War II and hence was left with a number of wooden buildings from the mid-19th and early 20th centuries. This is extremely rare for the northern parts of Norway where the German Nazis torched all of the communities as they were retreating. Its population, however, has declined by half, to 2,000 plus, and only two fishing factories are operating at this point in time. There are currently around twenty operating fishing boats compared to the hundreds only twenty years ago. Vardø has attempted to mobilize based on expectations of offshore activities on the Shtokman oil field, way up in the Barents Sea. A large industrial harbor on the mainland was upgraded [Figure 2], but since Shtokman was put on hold in 2012, it lies mainly vacant. The city thus shares destiny with the very small town of Teriberka on the Barents Coast of Russia, north of Murmansk. Vardø is still, however, the city that is located closest to the richest fishing in the Barents Sea. It could have been saved if a small amount of the NOK 1 billion spent to prep the industrial harbor for offshore petroleum operations had been spent on the old fishing harbor. Hence the city is still in despair.

Figure 2 (top): Vardø's industrial harbor.
Figure 3 (bottom): A dilapidated fish factory, Vardø.

In 1831, the Norwegian geologist, Baltazar Mathias Keilhau, described its landscape as barren and miserable, with only a few patches of green offering any solace for a traveling eye. What for us performs as an amazing geological scenery for him only served as proof of the area's godforsakenness. While being disappointed by the lack of scenic richness, Keilhau is concerned with the island as a hub to traders and fishermen. At this time the island experienced a dip in its economy. Still, 150 Russian trade ships visited the city every year, mainly for an exchange of flour and fish but also of peas, ropes, hemp, linen, tar, canvas, soap, pots and pans, leather, candles, etc. Migrating Scandinavians would travel either to America or to Vardø to seek fortune.

Michael Light, an aerial photographer who is extraordinarily reflective about his work, describes the American west as seen from the air: "In the arid west, both bones of the land and contours of the contemporary built world are strewn across space like writing of another world."[1] On the Varanger peninsula the bones of the land are visible, and the land actually appears as a kind of vertebra. Light describes the contours of the built world of the West as a human-made cultural skin that seems to be barely touching the ground on which it is spread. The Vardø island, often described as a desert island, has a cultural skin that is similarly thin, like an alien writing. The thinness of the built world on this bony land makes it easy to read, and the intimacy of the two is obvious. In fact, the shore geology is an active zone where much of the industry in Vardø has taken place. The thin strip of rocky coast in Vardø is exposed, and geology has had a strong local agency. It forms the grounds for several industries; it has been quarried, it has held stone quays, it has held fishing boats, still holds an abundance of herbs, and it has been used for the drying of fish and salting of seal meat brought in from the hunting in East Greenland. It was an active, dynamic zone where geology informed and defined human activity.

The people in Vardø do not consider their city beautiful. What they see is decay, empty houses, and board walks surrendered to entropic processes, and a lack of fishing boats [Figure 3]. All of this bears witness to the fact that the city has lost half of its population and several hundred work places since the 1990s. It bears witness to the lack of courage and ability of property owners to maintain their buildings. The inhabitants' sense of loss and hopelessness is very different from what we might experience as visitors. Where they see a hopeless ruin, we might see a potential restaurant, hotel, or science center. We know now that it is not that easy, but no matter how well we come to see the city, it is not our home.

Solastalgia is a recently developed concept that signifies people's stress in the face of climate change. It's connected with distress at seeing one's home-environment change. It describes a palpable sense of dislocation and loss that people feel when they perceive changes to their local environment as harmful. It was coined in 2003 by Glenn Albrecht, environmental philosopher at the University of Newcastle, School of Environmental and Life Sciences. Albrecht states that solastalgia's Latin roots combine three ideas, the solace from one's environment, the desolation caused by that environment's degradation, and the pain that occurs inside a person as a result. Effectively, it's used to signify changes that occur due to climate change such as drought and other natural disasters, but also due to external forces such as mining that cause a gradual and irreversible pollution of water and atmosphere. Vardø is an emblematic example of a solastalgic community. People have indeed been depressed to the extent of getting ill. The more people move away, the worse it gets for the remaining population. This is, however, turning around slowly, and much due to the work performed by local idealists, the Coastal Riot fighting to get the fishing quotas back, teachers, and Vardø Museum.

Figure 4: A dilapidated fish processing building in Vardø was decorated by street art during KOMA-fest in 2012. The festival was curated by Norwegian street artist Pøbel.

So, we approach the city in number of ways. We work with a local platform for innovation and place development called Vardø Restored[2]. They have been working ferociously over some years to secure cultural heritage funding to restore important buildings holding central services for the community; the pub, the hardware store, the café, the Grand Hotel, and many more. The hope is to make people move back, or to not move away, and ultimately to get the fishing industry back up again. This is something we are trying to help them do by sitting with owners and discussing potential programs for their, sometimes, very large structures. The work is about inspiration and empowerment [Figure 4]. We look at Vardø as a cultural landscape. And we look at Vardø as a vernacular landscape. Vernacular is a slippery word, and in our field it's used mostly for architecture. Vernacular architecture is usually owner and community-built buildings utilizing traditional technologies. Arnold R. Alanen effectively describes it as "built to meet specific needs, accommodating the values, economies, and ways of living of the cultures that produce them."[3] This pertains to pretty much all of Vardø – built to meet specific purposes and uses, especially fishing factories, fish oil distilleries, and dry lofts for cod. A vernacular landscape would be a human-made outdoor setting, not of a type usually attributed to design professionals, according to Alanen. Vernacular landscapes are marked by the capacity to embody and reflect their uses and expressions of a process. The vernacular landscapes and architectures of Vardø are intimately woven together. This is where the city landscape performs as a field where sets of actions, hopes, desires, and opportunities become manifest, all informed by the city's particular geographical and geological setting.

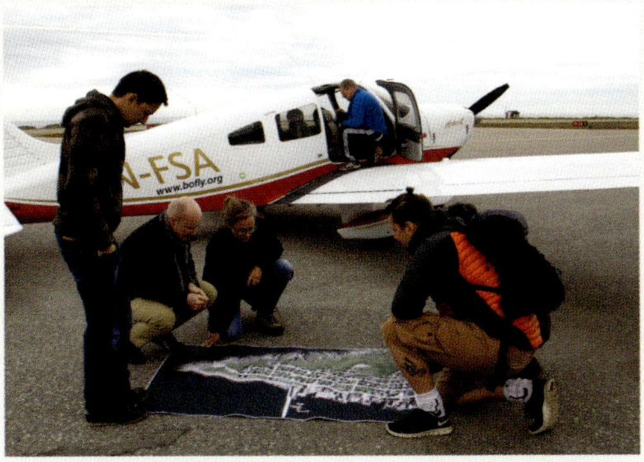

Figure 5: Future North and Vardø Restored work to map Vestervågen, the fishing quarter.

Working here, we realized that we need to let go of an idea of landscape that refers to the visible, but also to our idea of what a researcher is. We are working with Vardø Restored to map their four city parts. We have been doing this with and without students over the last few years. We are now producing a volume of the four city parts that maps the cultural heritage sites, both in the commons and within the building fabric. Mapping this, we focus very much on photography, even aerial photography [Figure 5], but also on in-depth interviews with, for instance, an eighty-eight-year-old fisherman who knows every detail about buildings and everybody who lived there in the city. By way of documenting stories, we are able to map both ephemeral and invisible heritage. With this work, Vardø has turned into a social landscape, a landscape where the rationale for change is driven by people, in a community always ready to battle on. It is a society run and built by individuals. They try to hold on to this slow process of community building, instead of surrendering to the rapid and high cost investments of oil and mining industries that would most certainly happen at the expense of local identity and resources.

NOTES:

1. Michael Light, *Some Dry Space: An Inhabited West* (Reno: Neveda Museum of Art, 2008), 9.

2. For more information on Vardø Restored, visit http://vardorestored.com

3. Arnold R. Alanen, "Considering the Ordinary: Vernacular Landscapes of Small Towns and Rural Areas," in *Preserving Cultural Landscapes in America*, eds. Arnold R. Alanen and Robert Z. Melnick, 112-142 (Baltimore: Johns Hopkins University Press, 2000), 113.

Polar Research Stations: Meeting the Challenge of Isolated Living

HUGH BROUGHTON
Principal, Hugh Broughton Architects, UK

Antarctica is the coldest, the windiest, and the driest continent on Earth. It's the sixth largest continent on our planet, apart from in the depths of winter when sea ice freezes to up to 600 miles out from the coast transferring it to the fourth largest continent. If all the ice were to melt on the continent of Antarctica, sea levels would rise around the world by up to 200 feet inundating many of the world's largest cities including New York, London, and Tokyo. The projects I'm going to talk about are geared towards understanding that phenomenon. They are science research stations, which focus on understanding the systems, which control the global warming of our planet.

The first station I'm going to look at is Halley Research Station. It sits at 75 degrees south on a floating ice shelf. The previous station was called Halley V. The station is located on the 475 feet thick Brunt Ice Shelf, which has flowed off the continent of Antarctica and is being supported by the Weddell Sea underneath. It's moving constantly out to sea at a rate of around 1,500 feet per annum. The original building, Halley V, constituted three different buildings. The main habitat had space for up to fifty people to live during the summer and fifteen during the winter. And the other two buildings are for different forms of science, one for ice science and the other for outer space science. Of course, one of the great challenges, whether you're working in the Arctic or the Antarctic, is the cold. At Halley, the temperature goes down to around minus seventy degrees Fahrenheit in the depths of winter. In addition to that, because it's close to the coast, it suffers from katabatic winds – where cold air drops off the main plateau of the Antarctic reaching speeds of up to 100 miles an hour at the coast. Through a combination of precipitation and drifting, the site receives around five feet of snow deposition every year. Anything that you leave on the surface will get buried whether that happens to be a small tool for construction or whole buildings. Leave it there long enough, and you will never find it again. As a consequence, Halley V was designed to be elevated up on 20 steel legs. But that in itself created some significant problems. Every summer season a crew of six steel workers was needed to realign distorted legs and help jack the building above the rising snow levels. They had to cut off the legs and straighten them up, weld in a special splice plate to connect the upper leg to the lower part which was buried in the ice. And then when all those legs were straightened up, everybody on the base had to help with the jacking of the building, working in suspended scaffold baskets with electric screw jacks to elevate the building up so that it sat four to five feet above the snow line ready for the next year's deposition. This was a highly labor-intensive process. Added to that, much like the north, Antarctica is subjected to three months of darkness. At Halley, there is 105 days of total darkness without the Sun rising above the horizon. Researchers live with just fifteen other people with their only neighbors being a colony of emperor penguins who live around fifteen miles away and which the crew are allowed to visit on an occasional basis.

Figure 1: Tractors pull one of the modules to its place on the Brunt Ice Shelf.

Figure 2: Broughton's Halley VI research station solves some of the problems of the five previous stations utilizing specialized cladding, hydraulic legs mounted on skis, and a communal space with an open plan.

Logistics also are complex. Everything has to be delivered by ship, using the British Antarctic Survey's logistics vessel, the *Ernest Shackleton*. This arrives around Christmas day when the sea ice has melted to within two to three miles of the edge of the ice shelf. It is important to be able to unload on to the sea ice because if you bring that ship up against the ice shelf, which is protruding around 30 to 40 feet above the sea level, you run the risk of shards of ice falling on to the deck causing severe damage. The sea ice is around six feet thick. Everything is unloaded on to it and then dragged carefully up to the edge of the ice shelf. At the junction between the sea ice and ice shelf, bulldozers are used to create a ramp so that supplies can be dragged up on to the shelf and then along to the station. It's a very precarious route and one, which determined the limits of prefabrication of the station. The sea ice has a bearing capacity of only nine tons. Therefore, every element that's needed to construct any new building has to be within that weight limit. So, one might ask oneself, why would anybody want to work in a place like Halley, that is so cold, so windy, so isolated, so dark? And the answer is really very simple, because the science research that is conducted there is of truly global significance. It was in 1985 that three British scientists working at Halley first discovered the hole in the ozone layer, a piece of research which led to the Montreal Protocol banning the use of carbo-fluorocarbons and to this day still one of the most important pieces of environmental legislation enacted on the planet. The station is also perfectly located for investigating the interaction between solar particles and the earth's outer atmosphere helping us to understand the concept of things like space weather, which has such a significant effect on the operation of satellites.

But a big problem was brewing. In around 2000, British scientists first observed that cracks were beginning to appear in the Brunt Ice Shelf. And the likelihood was that those cracks would start spreading towards each other and a large chunk of ice, the size of say New England in the States, might break off leaving Halley V on the wrong side of the crack. As Halley V had its legs frozen into the ice, the decision was therefore made to decommission the station and construct a new one on the right side of the crack line. Up until this point, the British Antarctic Survey had only ever used engineering companies in the designs of their stations. And while that had produced technically sensible and sophisticated solutions, it had not always answered all the requirements of science or of social well-being of the crew. They therefore held an international design competition to come up with new ideas, which would challenge the previous engineering-based solutions to living in Antarctica. At the point that we won the competition, the largest building that my office had designed was a 1,500 square foot building for

Girl Guides in the center of London. But we won this project because our submission combined an enthusiastic and imaginative approach to living in isolation with the engineering experience of AECOM, one of the largest global engineering companies, who had previous experience working on projects at McMurdo and South Pole for the National Science Foundation. Our design responded absolutely to the environment, in particular the requirement for a station which could be relocatable so that it wouldn't be lost on an iceberg should cracks appear on the Brunt Ice Shelf in the future, and which could respond to the rising snow levels experienced every year. The design also proposed a solution that could maximize the potential for prefabrication to ensure that it could be constructed in the very short Antarctic summer season which runs from the end of December through to the end of February.

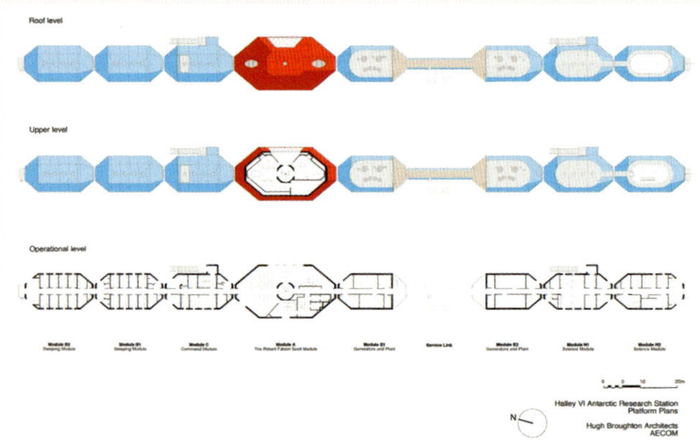

Figure 3: Roof, upper, and operational level plans show a modular design scheme.

We proposed a station made of very simple modular buildings, raised up on hydraulic legs supported on very large skis [Figure 1]. The hydraulics allowed each leg to be lifted up in turn, so that snow could be pushed underneath to form a pad to support the leg for the following year. When this had been done to all the legs, the hydraulics could be used to jack the station up so that it was four to five feet above the snow line ready for the deposition of the following year. Each one of the modules is around 1,600 square foot, and can be used for berthing, for offices, for science laboratories, and as the energy centers; containing generators, water treatment, sewage treatment, fire suppression systems, fuel storage, and the like. There are two energy centers so that if one fails, you can rely upon the other to keep you going through the winter months. So almost every requirement of the station could be housed within these1,600 square foot standard blue modules – apart from one key aspect, the main communal spaces for dining, drinking, bar games, and for just generally surviving together as a crew of fifteen people through a long, hard winter [Figures 2, 3]. For that we needed a much bigger building so we developed the central module, a two-story module containing open plan living space on the lower level and cellular spaces for watching TV, for a gym, for meetings, and Internet access on the upper level.

The open plan area on the ground level is a very important social device that was derived out of surveys we conducted with previous residents, whereby they revealed to us that when you have cellular space for living, for dining, for drinking, you tend to develop cliques in the community: one group who are really into playing cards, another group who are really into drinking beer and the two never cross because one shuts the door to the exclusion of the other. So, as a result we focused on the design of spaces that would allow all sectors of the community to live in harmony with each other much more like your home than previous incarnations of research facilities in the Antarctic. But how do you construct a building like this in a hostile environment like Antarctic?

Well, the key to the successful construction of any building in a cold climate is testing, testing, and testing again. So, at Halley, what we first did was we built test sledges to decide where we should put the ski on the bottom of the leg. Should it be central under the leg, should it be eccentric? What coating should we put underneath the ski and what was the maximum load that we could pull? When we determined those features, we then made mock up modules using the actual components that we would use for the station at a full construction in South Africa where we built most of the buildings. We used these mock-up modules for testing air permeability, for the operation of the hydraulics, to make sure that we would not get cracks in things like the cladding system. We tested all those elements and then when we were sure that the whole system would work, we began shipping out to the Antarctic. We used a very large Russian ice-strengthened cargo vessel to transport all the components of construction. The largest component of the construction was the space frame substructure of one of the models weighing just under nine tons and supported on smaller transit skis, allowing it to be dragged gently across the sea ice until it could then be pulled up on to the ice shelf.

In the first step of the construction process, the space frame sub-structure of a module was lifted up on to two shipping containers so that the hydraulic legs and the final skis could be added. Prefabricated timber floor cassettes were then added on to the top of the space frame to provide a working platform from which to construct the rest of the station. Prefabricated drainage systems, power lines, and air ducts were then installed within the space frame. The energy modules, generators, switching gear, fuel tanks, and other systems were installed on the floors and then the steel super structure was erected around them. Prefabrication was the key to successful construction, so, for example, prefabricated bathrooms, service rooms, and bedrooms were supplied, complete with all their furniture, and were loaded on to the platform before the super structure was installed around them like a cage, which minimized the time of construction. This allowed the construction crew to achieve key targets within the project schedule and for the station to be left at the ends of the summer seasons in a safe state ready for the next year's construction. Cladding was formed in large glass reinforced plastic panels. This material allowed us to make larger panels. It also has a very low coefficient of thermal transmission so that you get very little heat loss. The whole way the building was constructed was learned from the car industry, using a production line. One team was working on the blue modules, one team was dedicated to the big red central module, and a third team was installing mechanical and electrical systems. The whole of the station was erected next to the previous base so that the older buildings could be used for the temporary accommodation for the construction crew.

Figure 4: Researchers play pool in the open plan communal space.

And then when they were finished on the outside and more than half finished on the inside, the buildings were dragged ten miles from the site of Halley V to the site of Halley VI. The key to the success of the relocation was to drive along the ice road a number of times to make sure that it was very hard and compact so the skis didn't grind down into soft snow. The modules were towed by big tractors at a rate of around eight miles per hour. It took about an hour and half to move each module from the site of Halley V to the site of Halley VI. On arrival at the site of Halley VI all the modules were connected together and raised up on their legs, to create the new station. The weather isn't always fine. Unfortunately, your average walk to work can be a bit harsher on occasion. At the north end of the station is where the main science modules are. They include an upper level observatory where scientists continue to take ozone measurements using a Dobson spectrophotometer, and maintain data sets, which have been gathered at Halley now for over sixty years.

The main social module incorporates a very large window glazed with double glazed panels, some of which are filled with aerogel, which has a very good level of thermal resistance. It has a pool table that is central to the space [Figures 4, 5]. There's an open planned bar area, a staircase going up to the upper level, and even a photograph of our Queen. The upper level incorporates two big bubble roof lights so that people can watch the southern lights, which are spectacular over Halley, within the warmth of the building. The station is entirely self-sufficient and infrastructure free. It includes a doctor's OR, an air traffic control and communications center, and even a small hair dressing salon. In the design development stages, we worked very closely with a color-psychologist to come up with a palate to help the winter crew overcome seasonal affected disorder. We reduced water usage significantly at the station from 120 liters per person a day at Halley V, down to 25 liters per person a day at Halley VI. That was achieved by having a vacuum drainage system and far more efficient water supply taps and so on. Each crew member gets their own bedroom during the winter and then shares for three months during the summer. Within the bedrooms, the color psychologist was again at work. So, if you're wondering what the best color is to get you to sleep at night, it is the peachy pink. We also developed a special lamp with Philips, which has daylight simulation bulbs and an alarm clock feature to help crew members wake up with a false dawn at the start of each day to help maximize your serotonin and reduce melatonin. At the end of the summer season the station is left on level snow, raised up with a fifteen-foot gap to the underside of the modules. During the winter, the wind blows perpendicular to the line of modules and it scours underneath the station keeping the skis free of snow, with drifts forming on the leeward side.

Figure 5: Researchers socialize in the open plan communal space, designed to encourage community among the researchers.

The station is now used by the British government as a demonstration of innovation around the world. I believe it is the first British building ever to appear on a coin, but a coin which can only actually be used in the Antarctic territory. And then there is the greatest accolade of all. A man unknown to me has had the station tattooed on his arm and then posted that on to the Internet. The best benefit of course to us is the ability to work on other research stations. The Spanish station is a summer only base which gets around ten feet of snow accumulation in the winter. But then in the summer the snow all melts. It's a site with an extremely fragile ecology. One of the great things I've learned about working in the Antarctic—and it's even more true for the Arctic—is no particular location is the same. You may think that because you're working in a cold and icy location that one solution fits all. But nothing could be further from the truth. And this was particularly demonstrated here where all the parameters, apart from the fact that it was in the deep south, are entirely different to Halley. So, the solution we came up with was a fixed station, but still using modular components of construction. The design created three wings of accommodation with a central node that forces everybody to have occasional social interaction with each other to maintain a sense of community. A separate science building is included for safety if anything should happen in terms of fire in the main habitat. Big windows were designed for the ends of the buildings because everybody who works in the Antarctic loves to look out on the landscape. It's a passion born within them all. The station has recently been completed and is now fully operational. And from there, we've been able to work with the Koreans. Again, a very different set of parameters that we had to work with when we were working with Samsung on a design for a Korean station where a representation of Korean culture such as a 'gateway' became a key determinant of the design.

More recently we have worked with the National Science Foundation designing an atmospheric watch observatory at Summit Station at the top of the Greenland ice cap. It is a single module that will be used to benchmark levels of pollution by taking readings in one of the purest environments within the northern hemisphere. This building will be entirely prefabricated, delivered to Thule and then dragged up to Summit Station, which is a journey of around 700 to 800 miles. There will be much greater use of solar energy because any form of pollution around this building will impact the levels and the quality of the readings being taken by NOAA (National Oceanographic and Atmospheric Administration), who will run many of the experiments planned for the module.

This kind of work has great value because, although it's working at a very expensive high end of the cold region market, the lessons learned from these kinds of installations actually can have wide reaching impact on many other projects. For example, we designed a project for economic prototype housing in Cherepovets in the north of Russia. Learning from our experience in the Antarctic, we proposed using monocoque-structures, which are very quick and easy to assemble, raised up on screw piles to minimize impact on the permafrost. And then at the other end of the scale, the lessons we have learned designing for people in isolation can also have a bearing on designs for future space missions. Recently we enjoyed a short collaboration with the Human Factors team at NASA's base in Houston looking at what would be the minimum volume that astronauts need for satisfactory living on a eighteen-month long duration mission to Mars without all going completely stir crazy. And the answer, if you're looking for it, is around eighteen cubic meters.

Bibliography

Addington, Michelle. "Contingent Behaviours." *Architectural Design* 79, no. 3 (May/June 2009): 12-17.

Alanen, Arnold R., and Robert Z. Melnick, eds. *Preserving Cultural Landscapes in America*. Baltimore: Johns Hopkins University Press, 2000.

Alaska Department of Commerce, Community and Economic Development. *Shishmaref Relocation Site Selection Feasibility Study*, by AECOM. Anchorage, AK: 2016.

Banham, Reyner. *Architecture of the Well-tempered Environment*. 2nd ed. Chicago: University of Chicago Press, 1984.

Barnhardt, Carol. "A History of Schooling for Alaska Native People." *Journal of American Indian Education* 40, no. 1 (January 2001): 1-30.

Barozzi, Marta, Julian Lienhard, Alessandra Zanelli, and Carol Monticelli. "The sustainability of adaptive envelopes: developments of kinetic architecture." *Procedia Engineering* 155 (2016): 275-284. doi:10.1016/j.proeng.2016.08.029

Cold Climate Housing Research Center. *2018 Alaska Housing Assessment: Statewide Housing Summary*. Anchorage: Alaska Housing Finance Corporation, 2018. Accessed March 7, 2018.

Collignon, Béatrice. *Knowing Places: The Inuinnait, Landscapes, and the Environment*. Edmonton: Canadian Circumpolar Institute, University of Alberta, 2006.

Easterling, Keller. *Extrastatecraft: The Power of Infrastructure Space*. London; New York: Verso, 2014.

Fitch, J.M., and William Bobenhausen. *American Building: The Environmental Forces That Shape It*. New York: Oxford University Press, 1999.

Gearheard, Shari F., Lene K. Holm, Henry Huntington, Joe M. Leavitt, Andrew R. Mahoney, and Margaret Opie, eds. *The Meaning of Ice: People and Sea Ice in Three Arctic Communities*. Hanover: International Polar Institute, 2013.

Gropius, Walter. *Scope of Total Architecture*. New York: Collier Books, 1962.

Hamelin, Louis-Edmond. *Canadian Nordicity: It's Your North, Too*. Translated by William Barr. Montreal: Harvest House, 1979.

Herrmann, Victoria. "Investing in community: conceptualizing inclusive school design for America's Arctic." *Polar Geography* 39, no. 4 (November 2016). doi: 10.1080/1088937X.2016.1239280.

Hirst, Paul. *Space and Power: Politics, War, and Architecture*. Cambridge; Malden, MA: Polity, 2005.

Jull, Matthew. "South Camp Inn." *The Site Magazine*, November 2017.

Jull, Matthew. "Toward a Northern Architecture: The Microrayon as Arctic Urban Prototype." *Journal of Architectural Education* 70, no. 2 (September 2016): 214-222. doi: 10.1080/10464883.2016.1197672

Kolarevic, Branko, and Vera Parlac. *Building Dynamics: Exploring Architecture of Change*. London; New York: Routledge, 2015.

Kronenburg, Robert. *Flexible: Architecture that Responds to Change*. London: Laurence King, 2007.

Larsen, Janike K., and Peter Hemmersam, eds. *Future North: The Changing Arctic Landscapes*. London; New York: Routledge, 2018.

Lefebvre, Henri. *The Production of Space*. Translated by Donald Nicholson-Smith. Oxford: Blackwell, 1991.

Light, Michael. *Some Dry Space: An Inhabited West.* Reno: Nevada Museum of Art, 2008.

Loonen, R.C.G.M., M. Tr ka, D. Cóstola, and J.L.M. Hensen. "Climate adaptive building shells: State-of-the-art and future challenges." *Renewable and Sustainable Energy Reviews* 25 (Sept. 2013): 483-493. doi:10.1016/j.rser.2013.04.016.

Lotz, Jim. *Northern Realities: The future of northern development in Canada*. Toronto: New Press, 1970.

Marino, Elizabeth K. *Fierce climate, sacred ground: An ethnography of climate change in Shishmaref, Alaska*. Fairbanks: University of Alaska Press, 2015.

Menges, Achim. "Performative Wood: Integral Computational Design for Timber Constructions." In *reForm( ) – Building a Better Tomorrow: Proceedings of the 29th Annual Conference of the Association for Computer Aided Design in Architecture (ACADIA)*, edited by Tristan de Estree Sterk, Russell Loveridge, and Douglas Pancoast, 66-74. Chicago, IL: The School of the Art Institute of Chicago, 2009.

Moberg, Fredrik, and Sturle H. Simonsen. *What is resilience? An introduction to social-ecological research*. Stockholm: Stockholm Resilience Centre, 2014. http://www.stockholmresilience.org/download/18.10119fc11455d3c557d6d21/1459560242299/SU_SRC_whatisresilience_sidaApril2014.pdf

Peters, K, Phillip Steinberg, and Elaine Stratford, eds. *Territory Beyond Terra*. London: Rowman & Littlefield International, 2018.

Poppick, Laura. "Engineering new foundations for a thawing Arctic." *Eos, Trans, American Geophysical Union*, no. 98 (August 22, 2017). https://doi.org/10.1029/2017EO080435

Rice, Eb F. *Building in the North*. Fairbanks: Geophysical Institute of the University of Alaska, 1975.

Sheppard, Lola, and Mason White. *Many Norths: Spatial Practice in a Polar Territory*. Barcelona: Actar, 2017.

Skrimshire, Stefan. *Future Ethics: Climate Change and Apocalyptic Imagination*. London; New York: Continuum International, 2010.

Statistics Canada. 2017. *Nunavut [Territory] and Canada [Country] (table). Census Profile.* 2016 Census. Statistics Canada Catalogue no. 98-316-X2016001. Ottawa. Released November 29, 2017.

Strub, Harold. *Bare Poles: Building Design for High Latitudes*. Ottawa: Carleton University Press, 1996.

U.S. Department of Housing and Urban Development. *Housing Needs of American Indians and Alaska Natives in Tribal Areas: A Report From the Assessment of American Indian, Alaska Native, and Native Hawaiian Housing Needs: Executive Summary*, by Nancy Pindus, G. Thomas Kingsley, Jennifer Biess, Diane Levy, Jasmine Simington, Christopher Hayes, and Urban Institute. Washington, DC, 2017.

U.S. Government Accountability Office. *Alaska Native Villages: Limited Progress Has Been Made on Relocating Villages Threatened by Flooding and Erosion*. GAO-09-551. Washington, DC, 2009.

Image List

Cover: Arctic atlas, Arctic Design Group, 2018
P 1: West Tin Creek Hills ground study, Ben DiNapoli, 2016
P 4-7: First sunrise, Utqiagvik, AK, Arctic Design Group, 2008
P 9: Utqiagvik, AK, Arctic Design Group, 2008
P 12: Utqiagvik, AK, Yin-Yu Fong, 2017
P 20-21: Utqiagvik, AK, Andrew Shea, 2017
P 22-23: Utqiagvik, AK, Arctic Design Group, 2008
P 24: Houses mounted on stilts, Utqiagvik, AK, Dave Cohoe, 2007
P 25: City population comparison, Arctic Design Group, 2018; View of Norilsk, Russia, Gelio Vostok
P 26: Utqiagvik, AK, Arctic Design Group, 2008
P 27: Pictorial history of Resolute Bay, Canada, Matthew Jull, 2014
P 28-45: Arctic atlases, Arctic Design Group, 2018
P 46-51: Shapes of climate, Arctic Design Group, 2018
P 52: The T-3 camp, Fletcher's Ice Island, John Hall
P 53: Drift track, Fletcher's Ice Island, John Hall / *Hydro Magazine*, 2008
P 57: Norbert Schoenauer Housing Archive, McGill University
P 58: BFR spaceships on the surface of Mars, SpaceX
P 60-61: Nakasuk School, Iqaluit, Canada, Matthew Jull, 2014
P 65: Norilsk urban blocks, Russia, Google Earth image modified by Jackson Bewley, 2013
P 66-67: Fairbanks, Minto & Utqiagvik, AK, Jing Huang, Sam Kokenge, Sihan Lai, Andrew Shea, 2017
P 70-71: Raised building foundation, Utqiagvik, AK, Andrew Shea, 2017
P 72: Insulation detail from Cold Climate Housing Research Center, Yin-Yu Fong, 2017
P 73-75: Arctic house typology study, Ziggy Chen, Ben DiNapoli, Austin Edwards, Tyler Mauri, 2016
P 76-77: Resolute Bay, Canada, Nahanni Construction Ltd, 2014
P 79: Mediating Phenomena concept models, Arctic Design Group Alaska studio, 2017
P 80-81: Construction material study, Yin-Yu Fong, Katie Kelly, Anna Morrison, 2017
P 82-83: Drawing Bare Poles, Arctic Design Group studio, 2014 & 2018
P 84-85: Microclimate simulation of urban form, Hallie Miller, 2016
P 86: Heat studies, Ziggy Chen, 2016
P 87: Light studies, Dimitra Grigoriou, 2016 & Arctic Design Group, 2018
P 88-89: Heat studies, Yin-Yu Fong, Katie Kelly, Anna Morrison, 2017
P 90-91: Light studies, Tyler Mauri, 2016
P 92-93: Light studies, Jing Huang, Sihan Lai, Mengzhe Ye, 2017
P 94: Wind studies, Valerie Rottink, 2017 & Arctic Design Group, 2018
P 95: Water studies, Andisheh Ghofranitabari, 2017 & Arctic Design Group, 2018
P 96-97: Wind simulations of planting strategies, Pia von Barby, 2016
P 98: Air flow simulations, Erica Mutschler-Nielsen, 2016
P 99: Freezing phenomena study model, Scott Getz, 2016
P 100: Airflow study, Matt Johnson, 2015
P 101: Interior light study for a house, Shishmaref, AK, Brandon Adams, 2017
P 102: Permafrost ground studies, Liz Camuti, 2016
P 103: Tundra plants dynamic studies, Pia von Barby, 2016

P 104-105: Permafrost layer study, Taylor Hewett & Seth Salcedo, 2014
P 106-107: Freeze-thaw experiment model, Sam Kokenge, Andrew Shea, Michael Tucker, 2017
P 110-111: Design concept studies, Arctic Design Group studio, 2014 & Kazufumi Shimomura, 2018
P 112-115: Freeze-thaw experiments, Sam Kokenge, Andrew Shea, Michael Tucker, 2017
P 116-117: Sea ice, Northwest Passage, Canada, Arctic Design Group, 2014
P 118: Soil Conservation Service of Iceland
P 119-120: Marius Costan & Ivo Tedbury; Julian Nolan, Stine Bundgaard, Anders Nottveit & Sara Gøtze
P 121: David Garcia
P 122: Anaktuvuk Pass, AMRC. Ward Wells Collection, Alaska's Digital Archive, 1962
P 123: Aerial view of Point Lay, Google Earth; Separett toilet system, Separett
P 124: Houses in Newtok, AK, Cold Climate Housing Research Center
P 125: Integrated truss house with spray foam insulation, Cold Climate Housing Research Center
P 126: Arctic wall, Reina Properties
P 127: Construction of a truss house, Cold Climate Housing Research Center
P 128: Sentinel-1 radar image of Alert, Ellesmere Island, Canada, European Space Agency, 2017
P 133: Utqiagvik, AK, Andrew Shea, 2017
P 134: House interior, Utqiagvik, AK, Jing Huang, 2017
P 135: Chukchi coast, AK, Sihan Lai, 2017
P 136-137: Utqiagvik, AK, Andrew Shea, 2017
P 138-139: Utqiagvik, AK, Andrew Shea, 2017
P 142-143: Alaska atlases, Arctic Design Group, 2018
P 144: Typical house interior, Minto, AK, Claire Casstevens, 2017
P 146: Ground detail, Utqiagvik, AK, Andrew Shea, 2017
P 148: School gym, Minto, AK, Xinxin Huang, 2017
P 150: Utqiagvik, AK, Andrew Shea, 2017
P 152-153: Whale hunting, Utqiagvik, AK, Andrew Shea, 2017
P 154-155: Study model, Scott Getz, Andisheh Ghofranitabari, Erica Mutschler-Nielsen, Cara Turett, 2016
P 156-157: Model detail, Jing Huang, Xinxin Huang, Sihan Lai, 2017
P 158-159: House studies, Shishmaref, AK, Brandon Adams, Andrew Ashcraft, Melissa Brand, 2016
P 160-161: Minto, AK, Arctic Design Group, 2017
P 162-169: Framing Logics, Ziggy Chen, Ben DiNapoli, Austin Edwards, Tyler Mauri, 2016
P 168: Framing Logics model photo, Scott Smith, 2016
P 170-177: Full Spectrum Symbiosis, Yue Han, Xinxin Huang, Han Yu, 2017
P 178-185: Thermal Threshold, Yin-Yu Fong, Katie Kelly, Anna Morrison, 2017
P 186-193: Hacking the Homestead, Liz Camuti, Kun Liu, Hallie Miller, Pia von Barby, 2016
P 194-195: Beyond the Move, Liza Court, Dimitra Grigoriou, Bryce Vogel, Arctic Design Group, 2016/8
P 196-199: ADG exhibition & Arctic States symposium, Jake Fox and Arctic Design Group 2013/5
P 200: The Canadian Architect magazine
P 201: Justin Pineau, Ed Maruyama
P 202: Lateral Office, Northern Boundaries, 2016
P 203: Papineau Gerin-Lajoie LeBlanc Architects
P 204: Dew Line facility, Tuktoyaktuk, NWT, Canada, Harry Palmer, 1982
P 206: Arctic States Symposium, Arctic Design Group, 2015
P 208-211: Janike Kampevold Larsen
P 212-216: Halle VI, James Morris
P 218-221: Utqiagvik, AK, Arctic Design Group, 2008
P 222-223: Utqiagvik, AK, Andrew Shea, 2017
P 224-225: Near Minto, AK, Andrew Shea, 2017
P 234: West Tin Creek Hills ground study, Ben DiNapoli, 2016

Contributors

Hugh Broughton trained at The University of Edinburgh and set up his architectural practice in 1995. Hugh Broughton Architects' projects have won awards from numerous organizations including the RIBA, American Institute of Architects, Civic Trust, the *Architects' Journal*, the British Construction Industry and Architizer among many others. The practice has won a string of design competitions, including for a new gallery for The Portland Collection, for Maidstone Museum's new East Wing and most notably for a series of remote projects including Halley VI Antarctic Research Station, Juan Carlos 1 Spanish Antarctic Base, the Atmospheric Watch Observatory in Greenland for the US National Science Foundation and a new health facility on Tristan da Cunha, the world's most remote inhabited island. Hugh Broughton Architects has also been invited to prepare designs for polar bases for India, Korea and Brazil, and is now engaged as part of a team with Jasmax to design New Zealand's Antarctic station Scott Base. As a result Hugh is now considered the world's leading designer of research facilities in the polar regions. Projects in sensitive locations have been the mainstay of Hugh's career, in which field the practice has successfully completed projects for many high profile clients including English Heritage, and the Henry Moore Foundation, with projects in development for the Greenwich Foundation, Sheerness Dockyard Preservation Trust, and the Honourable Society of the Inner Temple.

David A. Garcia is a founder of MAP Architects and associate professor at the Royal Danish Academy of Fine Arts' School of Architecture in Copenhagen, Denmark where he also directs the Masters course "Architecture and Extreme Environments". Garcia's work often focuses on extreme environments at various scales, from the Arctic to deserts, from flood zones to highly polluted areas, aiming to challenge the architectural status quo through inventiveness and a constant collaboration with local knowledge, the arts, and pure and applied sciences. He graduated from the Bartlett School of Architecture, London in 2002. He has worked at Foster and Partners, London and was an associate partner at Henning Larsen Architects until 2011. He has been an active docent since 2002, being program director in Lund, Sweden, and at The Bartlett, UK, before joining the Royal Danish Academy. In 2007 he was awarded a prestigious three-year bursary grant from the Danish Art Council, his work was selected for the Danish pavilion at the 13th and for the 15th Venice Biennale of Architecture, and has been nominated for the Mies van der Rohe Architecture Prize. He is presently designing works in Greenland and researching in the Arctic context.

Judith Grunau's career has focused on humanitarian relief, green building, and sustainable community design. For the past decade, Judith has worked as a Project Manager at the Cold Climate Housing Research Center, an industry-based nonprofit in Fairbanks, Alaska whose mission is to promote and advance the development, use, and testing of energy-efficient, durable, healthy, and cost-effective building technologies for people in circumpolar regions around the globe. This team takes an interdisciplinary approach with programs focusing on building science research, sustainable design and construction, policy research, and education. After earning her Bachelor of Architecture at Virginia Tech University, Judith built her green building knowledge through design projects in India, Virginia, and Alaska. She is a LEED AP BD+C, a former board member of the Cascadia Green Building Council, and co-leader of the Living North Congress of the International Living Future Institute. Judith's professional goal is to create holistic designs that provide healthy, affordable, culturally appropriate, and environmentally sustainable housing for rural Alaskans and people of the circumpolar north.

Janike Kampevold Larsen is associate professor at the Institute of Urbanism and Landscape at the Oslo School of Architecture and Design. She is project leader for Future North, a research project observing and mapping changes in settlements and territories in subarctic regions. She was project leader of the newly established Tromsø Academy of Landscape and Territorial Studies. Recent research includes work on the Norwegian Tourist Routes as part of the research project *Routes, Roads and Landscapes: aesthetic practices en route 1750-2015*. The 2012 research project *Landscape Journeys* invited an interdisciplinary group of researchers to perform collaborative and investigative travels to Iceland and the Kola Peninsula, investigating the journey as a method for observation of landscapes of energy and entropy. Recent publications include: *Future North, The Changing Arctic Landscape*, Larsen, Janike Kampevold and Hemmersam, Peter (eds.), (London: Routledge, 2018), "Imagining the Geologic" in *Making a Geologic Now*, Ellsworth/Kruse (eds.), (New York: Punctum Book, 2013), and "Geologic Presence in the 21-centry wilderness garden" in *Studies in the History of Gardens and Designed Landscapes*, John D Hunt (ed.), 2014. She is currently working on a book on Arctic Landscapes.

Geoff Manaugh is a Los Angeles-based freelance writer and the author of BLDGBLOG (bldgblog.com), a long-running exploration of "architectural conjecture, urban speculation, and landscape futures." His 2016 book, *A Burglar's Guide to the City*, on the relationship between crime and architecture, was a *New York Times* bestseller and was optioned for television by CBS Studios. Manaugh is former co-director of Studio-X NYC, an off-campus event space and urban futures think tank at Columbia University. He has taught at Columbia, UC Berkeley, USC, and SCI-Arc, as well as lectured at venues around the world, including the Australian National Architecture Conference, the Bartlett School of Architecture, Bauhaus Universität, and Harvard GSD. Manaugh's design collaborations with the London-based architectural practice Smout Allen have been exhibited at the 2014 Venice Biennale of Architecture, the 2015 Chicago Architecture Biennial, and the University of Southern California. Manaugh regularly covers issues related to cities, design, crime, infrastructure, and technology for the *New York Times Magazine*, the *Atlantic*, and many other publications. His short story "Ernest," published by *VICE* in October 2017, is being adapted for film by Legendary Entertainment.

Lola Sheppard & **Mason White** are co-founders of Lateral Office (2003), a design and research firm which operates at the intersection of architecture, landscape, and urbanism. The studio describes its practice process as a commitment to design as a research vehicle to pose and respond to complex, urgent questions in the built environment, engaging in the wider context and climate of a project. Lateral Office has been pursuing research and design work on the role of architecture in the circumpolar and remote island regions, for the past eight years. Their work in the North examines the potential for architecture and infrastructure to be culturally responsive, geographically scalable, environmentally adaptable, and multi-purpose in its programmability. Sheppard and White are the authors of the book *Many Norths: Spatial Practice in a Polar Territory* (Actar, 2017) which examines the role of architecture, urbanism, mobility, resources and monitoring as spatial practices shaping the physical and cultural landscape of the Canadian North. Lateral Office represented Canada in the 2014 Venice Architecture Biennale with the exhibition "Arctic Adaptations: Nunavut at 15," for which they received an honorable mention. They received a PA award in 2013 and the 2012 Holcim Gold for Sustainable Construction for North America for their project "Arctic Food Network." Sheppard and White's work has been exhibited extensively and they have lectured across the USA, Canada and Europe. Sheppard and White are co-authors of *Pamphlet Architecture 30 - Coupling: Strategies for Infrastructural Opportunism* (Princeton Architectural Press, 2011) and they are co-editors of the journal *Bracket.* Sheppard is associate professor at the University of Waterloo; she received her B.Arch from McGill University and her M.Arch from Harvard University. She is a registered architect in Ontario and Quebec. White is associate professor at the University of Toronto; he received his B.Arch from Virginia Tech University and his M.Arch from Harvard University.

Philip Steinberg is professor of political geography at Durham University where he is director of IBRU: Durham University's Centre for Borders Research and also coordinates the Project on Indeterminate and Changing Environments: Law, the Anthropocene, and the World (the ICE LAW Project) and the Durham Arctic Research Centre for Training and Interdisciplinary Collaboration (DurhamARCTIC). Phil's research focuses on the projection of social power onto spaces whose geophysical and geographic characteristics make them resistant to state territorialization – spaces that include the world-ocean, the universe of electronic communication, and the Arctic. His publications include *The Social Construction of the Ocean* (Cambridge, 2001), *Managing the Infosphere: Governance, Technology, and Cultural Practice in Motion* (Temple, 2008), *What Is a City? Rethinking the Urban after Hurricane Katrina* (Georgia, 2008), *Contesting the Arctic: Politics and Imaginaries in the Circumpolar North* (I.B. Tauris, 2015), and *Territory beyond Terra* (Rowman & Littlefield, 2018), as well as recent articles in journals including *Annals of the Association of American Geographers, Transactions of the Institute of British Geographers, Environment and Planning D: Society & Space, Ocean Development & International Law, Antipode, Polar Geography, Polar Record,* and *Atlantic Studies.* He is also editor-in-chief of the journal *Political Geography.*

5	5	5	5	5	5	5	6	6	6	5	5	5	4	4	3	2	2	1	1	0	0	0
3	3	3	4	4	5	5	5	6	6	6	6	6	5	4	3	3	2	2	1	1	0	0
2	2	2	3	4	4	5	5	6	6	6	6	6	5	5	4	3	3	2	1	1	0	0
1	1	2	2	3	4	5	5	6	6	6	7	7	7	6	5	4	3	2	2	1	1	0
0	0	1	2	2	3	4	5	6	6	7	7	7	7	6	5	4	3	3	2	1	1	0
0	0	1	1	2	3	4	5	6	6	7	7	8	8	7	6	5	4	3	2	2	1	1
0	0	0	1	2	3	4	4	5	6	7	8	8	8	7	6	5	4	4	3	2	2	1
0	0	1	1	2	3	3	4	5	6	7	8	8	8	8	7	6	5	4	4	3	2	2
0	0	1	1	2	3	3	4	5	6	6	7	7	8	8	8	7	6	5	4	3	3	2
1	1	1	1	2	3	3	4	4	5	6	6	7	7	7	7	7	7	6	5	4	4	3
1	1	1	2	2	2	3	3	3	4	5	5	6	7	7	7	7	7	7	6	5	4	4
1	1	1	1	1	2	2	2	3	3	4	4	5	6	7	7	7	7	8	7	6	5	5
1	1	1	1	1	1	1	1	2	2	3	3	4	5	6	7	7	7	8	8	7	6	5
1	1	0	0	0	0	1	1	1	2	2	3	3	4	5	6	7	8	8	8	8	6	5
0	0	0	0	0	0	0	0	1	1	1	2	3	4	5	6	6	8	8	8	8	7	6
0	0	0	0	0	0	0	0	0	1	1	2	2	3	4	5	6	7	8	8	8	8	6
0	0	0	0	0	0	0	0	0	0	1	1	2	3	4	4	5	6	7	8	8	8	7
0	0	0	0	0	0	0	0	0	0	0	1	2	2	3	4	5	6	7	8	9	9	8
0	0	0	0	0	0	0	0	0	0	0	1	1	2	3	4	4	6	7	8	9	9	8
0	0	0	0	0	0	0	0	0	0	0	1	1	2	3	3	4	5	6	7	9	9	9
0	0	0	0	0	0	0	0	0	0	0	0	1	2	2	3	4	5	6	7	8	10	10
0	0	0	0	0	0	0	0	0	0	0	1	1	2	2	3	4	5	6	7	8	9	10
0	0	0	0	0	0	0	0	0	0	0	1	1	2	2	3	4	4	5	6	7	8	9
0	0	0	0	0	0	0	0	0	0	0	1	1	2	2	3	3	4	4	5	6	7	8
0	0	0	0	0	0	0	0	0	0	0	0	1	1	2	2	3	3	4	5	5	6	6
0	0	0	0	0	0	0	0	0	0	0	0	0	1	1	2	2	3	3	4	4	5	5
0	0	0	0	0	0	0	0	0	0	0	0	0	0	1	1	2	2	3	3	3	4	5
1	1	1	1	0	0	0	0	0	0	0	0	0	0	0	1	1	1	2	2	2	3	4
1	1	1	1	1	0	0	0	0	0	0	0	0	0	0	0	1	1	1	1	2	2	3
2	2	2	1	1	0	0	0	0	0	0	0	0	0	0	0	0	1	1	1	1	1	2
3	2	2	1	1	0	0	0	0	0	0	0	0	0	0	0	0	0	0	0	1	1	2
3	3	2	1	1	0	0	0	0	0	0	0	0	0	0	0	0	0	0	0	0	1	1
3	3	2	2	1	0	0	0	0	0	0	0	0	0	0	0	0	0	0	0	0	0	1
3	3	2	2	1	0	0	0	0	0	0	0	0	0	0	0	0	0	0	0	0	0	0
2	2	2	2	1	1	0	0	0	0	0	0	0	0	0	0	0	0	0	0	0	0	0
2	2	2	2	2	1	1	0	0	0	0	0	0	0	0	0	0	0	0	0	0	0	0
1	1	1	1	2	2	1	1	1	0	0	0	0	0	0	0	0	0	0	0	0	0	0
1	1	1	1	1	2	2	1	1	1	0	0	0	0	0	0	0	0	0	0	0	0	0
0	0	0	1	1	2	2	2	2	1	0	0	0	0	0	0	0	0	0	0	0	0	0
0	0	0	1	1	2	2	3	2	1	1	0	0	0	0	0	0	0	0	0	0	0	0
0	0	0	1	1	2	2	3	3	2	1	1	0	0	0	0	0	0	0	0	0	0	0
0	0	1	1	2	2	3	3	3	2	2	1	1	1	0	0	0	0	0	0	0	0	0
0	1	1	2	2	3	3	4	4	3	2	2	1	1	1	1	0	0	0	0	0	0	0
1	2	2	3	3	3	4	4	5	4	3	3	2	2	2	1	1	1	1	0	0	0	0
2	2	3	4	4	4	5	5	5	4	4	3	3	3	2	2	2	2	1	1	0	0	0

Credits

Authors & Editors: Leena Cho & Matthew Jull

Next Cities Series Editor: Ila Berman

Copy Editors: Jake Anderson & Sneha Patel

Publication Team: Kathleen Adams, Claire Casstevens, Zhenfang Chen, Liwei Liu, Kazufumi Shimomura, Michael Tucker, Cara Turett, Pia von Barby

The publication of *Mediating Environments* is facilitated by the Next Cities Institute at the University of Virginia School of Architecture. We would like to extend our sincerest gratitude to Dean Ila Berman, Sneha Patel, Hugh Broughton, David Garcia, Judith Grunau, Janike Kampevold Larsen, Geoff Manaugh, Lola Sheppard, Philip Steinberg, Mason White, and our publication team of students. The research, teaching, and events sampled in the book are results of collaborative works that took place between 2013-2018, many of which were made possible and were sponsored by the following organizations: the Anchorage Museum, the Graham Foundation, the National Science Foundation, the Rotch Foundation, UVa Center for Global Inquiry and Innovation, UVa Environmental Resilience Institute, and the Jefferson Trust. We would also like to thank Charlotte and Eugene Brower, Julie Decker, Bruno Grunau, Jonny Hayes, Jack Hébert, Kamu Kakizaki, Mara Kimmel, Andrew Kroll, Chris Rose, Jackie Qatalina Schaeffer and Bryan Thomas for warmly welcoming us to Alaska.

ADG

UVA SCHOOL OF ARCHITECTURE

Arctic Design Group | www.arcticdesigngroup.org

Directors: Matthew Jull & Leena Cho

Research Associate: Claire Casstevens

Research Assistants: Jackson Bewley, Henry Brazer, Arisa Chentaphun, Artem Demchenko, Darcy Engle, Yin-Yu Fong, Adriana Giorgis, Madelyn Hoagland-Hanson, Karilyn Johanensen, Kaitlynn Long, Tyler Mauri, Cong Nie, Benjamin Scott, Michael Tucker, Cara Turett, Christopher Weimann, Han Yu

Students (2013-2018): Jenny Adair, Brandon Adams, Kathleen Adams, Isabel Argoti, Andrew Ashcraft, Jackson Bewley, Melissa Brand, Henry Brazer, Liz Camuti, Oscar Castro-Villacorta, David Calvillo, Michelle Chen, Ziqi Chen, Arisa Chentaphun, Chris Cortner, Liza Court, Emilio Craddock, Artem Demchenko, Aleksander DeMott, Ben DiNapoli, Brianne Doak, Brandon Eck, Austin Edwards, Yin-Yu Fong, Cameron Fullmer, Katie Gallagher, Scott Getz, Andisheh Ghofranitabari, Christina Griggs, Dimitra Grigoriou, Biyuan Gu, Yue Han, Fatin Hameed, Calvin Heimberg, Jennifer Hsiaw, Jing Huang, Xinxin Huang, Jared Huggins, Katie Jenkins, Matt Johnson, Katie Kelly, Sam Kokenge, Sihan Lai, Ben Lawson, Yijun Li, Kun Liu, Shaocong Liu, Jennifer Livingston, Athena Loi, Kaitlynn Long, Boning Luo, Tyler Mauri, Anna McMillen, Hallie Miller, Lemara Miftakhova, Emmitt Moore, Anna Morrison, Erica Mutschler-Nielsen, Christine Nguyen, Sangyoon Park, Michael Peterson, Bella Purdy, Valerie Rottink, Kari Roynesdal, Peter Russell, Rebeca Sanchez, Benjamin Scott, Suzanne Sharp, Scott Shinton, Arshaya Sood, Parker Sutton, Rachelle Trahan, Bryce Vogel, Yan Wang, Dirk Wilkins, Dixi Wu, Chunyao Xu, Mengzhe Ye, Han Yu